THE
ULTIMATE
GUITAR
SOURCEBOOK

THE ULTIMATE GUITAR
SOURCEBOOK

Race Point
PUBLISHING

Tony Bacon

A division of Book Sales, Inc.
276 Fifth Avenue Suite 206
New York, New York 10001

RACE POINT PUBLISHING and the distinctive
Race Point Publishing logo are trademarks
of Book Sales, Inc.

This 2012 edition published by Race Point Publishing
by arrangement with
Outline Press Limited
2A Union Court, 20-22 Union Road,
London SW4 6JP, England
www.jawbonepress.com.

EDITOR Owen Bailey
DESIGN Paul Cooper

ISBN-13: 978-1-937994-04-4

Printed in China

2 4 6 8 10 9 7 5 3 1

www.racepointpub.com

CONTENTS

CHAPTER FOUR
HOLLOW & SEMI-SOLID ELECTRIC GUITARS

CHAPTER FIVE
ELECTRIC BASS GUITARS

CHAPTER SIX
BEYOND GUITAR

INTRODUCTION

This book tells the story of the guitar through one of the best collections of guitars ever brought together in one book. Dig deep and you'll see guitars from the late 16th century to the early 21st century, with everything from the cheapest beginner's acoustics to expensive instruments designed to appeal to the most demanding players and collectors.

The book shows hollowbody, semi-solid, and solidbody guitars and basses: acoustics, electrics, and hybrids of the two. Laid out before you are great guitars, silly guitars, guitars to make you catch your breath, and guitars to make you smile. Here are famous guitars, everyday guitars, valuable guitars, battered guitars, guitars from museums and guitars from the stage, pointy guitars that fuel the mosh pits, and gentle guitars that soothe the ear.

Simplicity

The guitar's essential simplicity has always offered a challenge to anyone who chooses to make one guitar, one thousand guitars, or one hell of a guitar. How do you improve on such a straightforward, practical object?

People from many different backgrounds have risen to the challenge, building instruments that they hope will bring guitarists nearer to their ultimate guitar. Some of these designers have been musicians, like the inventive and influential Les Paul, bringing a player's mind to bear directly on the nuts and bolts of the guitar. Other makers have been engineers, keen to apply their natural skills with raw materials or with electronics to an object that links craftsmanship, science, and art—just as radio-repairman Leo Fender did in the 1950s when he showed how to take the guitar into the age of mass production.

This book shows how hundreds of makers, from one-man workshops to vast corporate factories, have put their own improvements into practice. It demonstrates how each of them has taken the basic designs that have inspired all who build guitars. Some ideas have succeeded, many more have failed. This book is intended to show the successes and the failures, as well as plentiful examples of the countless guitars that fall somewhere between the two.

Technique

The guitar is an attractive musical instrument, and most who pick it up for the first time find it a simple matter to achieve a relatively successful sound from some rudimentary notes and chords. In this respect, it is an easy instrument for the beginner. But as with all musical instruments, there are very few players who can be said to have mastered the guitar. This opposition of simplicity and difficulty is at the root of the guitar's popularity.

Another reason for the guitar's great popularity is its almost universal musical adaptability. Probably no other instrument has been used regularly in such a wide variety of music, with the possible catch-all exception of percussion. Try to imagine an absence of guitars in rock, flamenco, blues, metal, rhythm 'n' blues, country, punk, bluegrass, jazz, folk, rock 'n' roll, pop, reggae, grunge, indie, thrash, or even (if you can remember it) rockabilly.

And in its "classical" form, the guitar, a largely non-orchestral instrument, has its own solo repertoire. It has occasionally been placed in ensemble and orchestral settings, as in the works of the 20th-century Spanish composer Joaquín Rodrigo. Even the piano, the only other serious contender for the title of the world's most popular musical instrument, does not feature in quite so diverse a range of styles and forms.

Given this universality, one might imagine that the guitar would help establish common ground between the various musical styles. But the interchange between players involved in the broadly defined "classical" and "popular" areas is limited. This isn't down to any limitations imposed by the instrument, however: the neo-classical shred guitarists of the 1980s, exemplified by Sweden's Yngwie J. Malmsteen, proved that in the right hands the electric guitar could be every bit as fluidly expressive as Niccolò Paganini's violin had been.

Young musicians learning the guitar have traditionally been encouraged to amass knowledge on the technical aspects of playing, to fill their heads with scales, arpeggios, and impressive licks. The negative side of this admirable diversity comes when new players begin to wonder about taking their playing beyond the merely technical. Technique is, of course, essential, but not if it is at the expense of the most valuable quality a guitarist can posses—what some call feel, or soul, or spirit.

The balance between technique and feel on any guitar is a constant negotiation, and guitarists usually fall into one camp or the other. Very few players have ever been celebrated as equally adept at both aspects of guitar playing.

Versatility

The guitar is a unique musical instrument: nothing else combines in such a portable package so much harmonic, melodic, and rhythmic potential. Even played on its own, the guitar offers a remarkable range of harmony to the player, who has continuous access to over three octaves (four on many modern electrics), with polyphony limited only by the guitarist's dexterity and the musical context. The guitar's ability to sustain notes or chords is also of great importance.

The overall musical potential of the guitar is kept in a continual state of development by pioneering players. Just one example from many will suffice: during the 1980s, a two-handed "tapping" style was extended and updated by some fusion and metal guitarists. It gave them the ability to play with rapid violin-like leaps, impossible with normal playing techniques. This is a good demonstration of the constant interplay between guitarists and those who design and make guitars. Tapping benefits from a long fingerboard: suddenly, guitars were regularly seen with 24 frets (and more in some cases).

But what comes first? The player's need, or a new kind of guitar? Often it's hard to work out the source of such developments. Is it the new type of instrument that inspires a style of playing, or do guitarists' new methods provoke new kinds of guitars and hardware? Did Floyd Rose and Dave Storey's locking vibrato systems encourage the new breed of tapping guitarists to start using extreme vibrato techniques? Or were these designers trying to provide a device that could do things that players were trying unsuccessfully to achieve with existing systems?

Did dance-band musicians lead the way to electric guitars in the 1930s and 1940s, or was it the guitar companies looking to expand their market? At the end of the 18th century, was it players or guitar-makers who decided that a six-string instrument should supersede the contemporary guitars with five or six doubled courses?

It has always been a mixture of both, and as long as this dialogue between guitarists and guitar-makers continues—and each side listens to what the other is saying—then the future of the instrument should be a healthy one.

The guitar has been fashionable on and off since the 1660s, but during the 20th century it became one of the most popular of all musical instruments. Its popularity has experienced various peaks, particularly in the early 1970s, the mid 1980s, and at various times in the decades that followed. And it has regularly outsold other instruments since its rise to prominence.

Despite the trends of popular music, there has been no shortage of newcomers to the instrument. Most major manufacturers provide a steady stream of quality beginners' instruments, and a shift by big American brands to offshore production in the Far East, especially since the early 1980s, has made it possible for them to maintain profit margins, even during leaner times. One often-lamented development has been the decline of the music store as the place where these beginners make their first purchases. The digital age has seen the rise of the online store, with its lower overheads, increasing success, and distinct lack of community.

Collectables

Many guitars have become collectable: as musical instruments, certainly—but also as historic objects, maybe even as pieces of industrial art, or cultural icons. We have tried to make sure that the guitars in this book are genuine and—a great worry to collectors—that wherever possible they are in original condition, without major modifications or restoration.

To the musician, this obsession with originality is absurd, as the very modification that might make a guitar more playable instantly devalues it in the eyes of the collector. To the collector, any alteration is, at the extreme, an irreversible molestation of the past. It depends on what the guitar has been bought for. Is it to play, or is it to hang on the wall? Ideally, both should be possible.

Collectors and musicians were among the many observers who drew a deep breath in 2004 when Eric Clapton's "Blackie" Stratocaster was sold at auction for a record-breaking $959,500 (plus buyer's premium) to benefit the guitarist's Crossroads drug-rehabilitation charity. In 2011, actor and guitarist Richard Gere sold by auction his collection of more than 100 vintage guitars and amplifiers, raising $936,000 for humanitarian causes. Among them were guitars once owned by Albert King and Peter Tosh.

Many collectors reject these value-by-association sales and argue that a guitar is made valuable by its inherent quality as an instrument, its condition, its desirability among other collectors, its age, its rarity, and, probably last, who owned it. Musicians are often left in the cold when guitars become fashionable among collectors, who can push up prices up to a level where players cannot hope to afford them. The choicest examples of the original Gibson Les Paul sunburst-finish Standard model have commanded five- and six-figure sums, so an example is unlikely to turn up on stage at the average concert. Some of these guitars have inevitably attracted the professional investor, who considers them merely as commodities with a certain market value. Far from reaching the stage, some rare instruments are more likely to be found locked in a climate-controlled bank vault, an environment not usually noted for its musical stimulation.

There is sometimes snobbery attached to the use of old guitars. "They don't make them like they used to" is a commonly heard defense. This value attached to the mojo of vintage instruments has led companies to create brand new artificially-aged instruments for a willing clientele eager to buy fresh vintage. Fender's Time Machine series of so-called "relic'd" Stratocasters, Telecasters, and Precision and Jazz Basses come with various levels of ageing. Even up close, the effect can be convincing. Today, in Fender's Custom Shop, it seems as if they really do make them like they used to—down to the last ding, scratch, and pickup-wind.

When it comes to guitars, however, age is no guarantee of quality. Makers will tell you that two guitars built in exactly the same way from exactly the same piece of timber can sound very different from one another. Move up a step or two to mass production and, despite the consistencies of such a process, there are still the vagaries of timber and the Friday-afternoon guitar to deal with. Each batch of guitars has potentially good and bad instruments. Some say that an old worn guitar is the best bet, the theory being that it has been played because it is a good one. But then it could just as easily be a bad one that has been abused by careless owners.

Materials

Science can tell us a little about the way a guitar behaves as a physical object, but it begins to flounder when it tries to advise guitar-makers about their craft. Of course, some makers do analyze in a scientific manner the nature of the instruments they are building and react to that information in their production methods. Many firms use such techno-inspired facilities as computer-controlled routing on their production lines. While you are unlikely to see a craftsman tuning and carving an individual guitar top in a modern mass-production guitar factory, science has at least brought a greater degree of consistency to the still essentially human process of mass-production.

The American success story that is Taylor Guitars is an example of how a company can cleverly refine its mass-production process by continually incorporating new technology. However, to emphasize the predominance of know-how over materials, in 1995 Taylor created a guitar from oak pallets that demonstrated the importance of construction over expensive exotic woods, later adorning a small run of the guitars with a fingerboard-inlay showing a forklift truck. The message was simple: materials are only part of the story.

Despite that and the continuing importance of the luthier's craft, materials are of prime concern to today's manufacturers. Environmental responsibility and the scarcity of traditional tonewoods has led guitar-makers of all stripes to experiment with new types of wood and even, in some cases, new materials altogether. As you'll see in these pages, guitar makers have messed with carbon-fiber, plastic, and other synthetic materials in attempts at new designs and new processes. Ecological concerns and the emergence of more sustainable guitar woods mean we will probably see more experiments with alternative materials and construction methods in the future.

Great guitar designs are not quantifiable, and that in itself is part of their greatness. The ultimate guitar has yet to be produced, but this sourcebook will acquaint you with many of the others.

EARLY GUITARS
16th & 17th CENTURIES

To appreciate more fully the modern guitars dealt with in the main body of this book it is useful first to consider the early history of the guitar. To begin, a simple definition: the guitar is a plucked, stringed instrument that has a "waisted" body with incurved sides. There is, according to experts on its history, little evidence of such an instrument existing before the 15th century. That is not to say that broadly similar stringed instruments did not exist long before that time. But a barrage of confusing instrument names and hazy historical data cloud the issue, and even the experts disagree.

In this book we are concerned with surviving guitars, and the late-16th-century instrument shown below is among the earliest that are still in existence. The earliest guitars had four "courses" (a single, double, or even triple string): the four-course "treble" instrument, despite being surpassed by the five-course guitar, lasted until at least the 17th century. Some early guitars feature superb decoration, exemplified by the ornate soundhole on the 17th-century Italian example on the facing page. These guitars, which were probably owned by the wealthy, may well have survived more for their charm as objects than their utility as instruments. The guitar was a great popular success at this time, yet peasants' guitars have rarely survived.

Italian music book, c.1620

c.1590 five-course guitar

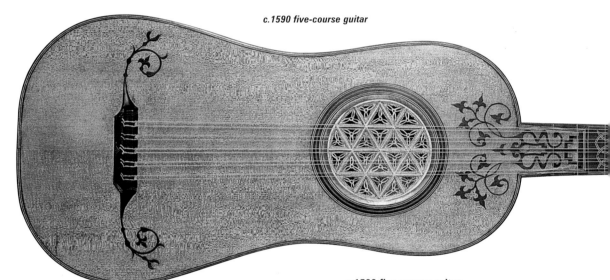

c.1590 five-course guitar
This may be the oldest surviving "full size" guitar, according to its former owner, Robert Spencer. Construction and decoration are similar to a small guitar dated 1581 by Portuguese maker Belchior Dias that is in the Royal College of Music collection, London.

Music book, c1620

1836 Panormo

EARLY GUITARS

c.1760 Salomon modified five-course guitar

c.1760 Salomon modified five-course guitar

The guitar was made in Paris by Jean-Baptiste Dehaye Salomon. It has been modified with two added tuners and an extra bridge channel, designed to accommodate a sixth course. There is no room on the neck for more strings, so the sixth course probably ran free of the neck on the bass side, over an extended nut.

1832 Fernando Sor Method

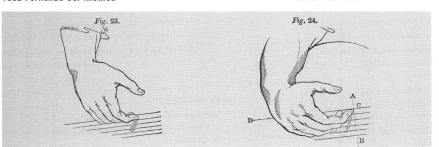

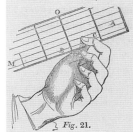

1832 Fernando Sor Method

The book of music on the facing page is a collection of Italian songs from about 1620, handwritten with tablature and rhythmic symbols for a strummed guitar accompaniment. The three hand illustrations (above) are from Fernando Sor's 1832 book, *Method For The Spanish Guitar*; the two on the right are "to be avoided".

c.1804 Pagés six-course guitar

This instrument was made in Cadiz, south-western Spain, by Joséf Pagés. He was among the first in Spain to use a fan-strutting system, later developed by Antonio de Torres (see pages 18–19).

c.1804 Pagés six-course guitar

17th-century decorated soundhole detail

1836 Panormo

The son of an Italian violin-maker, Louis Panormo ran a prolific workshop in London. This 1836 specimen shows how Panormo often included elements from the best contemporary instruments (compare its shape to that of the Pagés, pictured right, for example). Panormo regularly fitted superior machine heads rather than pegs, and was one of the few makers outside Spain using fan-strutting.

13

LYRE, CITTERNS, HARPS
EARLY ODDITIES

The instruments shown on this page are not mainstream guitars, but they do highlight an interesting tributary of European design.

Principally in France and as a result of the so-called "classical revival," the lyre guitar (below left) rather fancifully adopted the shape of the ancient Greek lyre—an outline often used in the West as a symbol of music. It has been suggested that its great popularity around the early 19th century, mainly with amateur players, influenced the move at this time by many makers of conventional guitars to six single strings.

The "English guitar" with six metal-strung courses and a small, rounded body shape was very popular in Britain from the middle of the 18th century to the early 1800s, when it was ousted by the conventional Spanish-style guitar. As we have seen, guitar

makers had begun by the mid-16th century to adopt five courses and a generally larger instrument than the early "treble" four-course guitar. Tunings of the "baroque" five-course guitar varied widely, but by the middle of the 18th century had started to become standardized toward A/D/G/B/E—in other words, as the top five strings of the modern guitar.

At about the same time as a vogue (primarily in France and Britain) for some unusual instruments related to the guitar, conventional makers started around the late 18th century to move from five to six courses on their guitars, with the extra course tuned to a low E. From there a simple refinement was made, at first in Italy and France, to six single strings: the result, adopted widely elsewhere, was an instrument looking and sounding a little closer to the modern guitar.

c.1810 Wornum lyre guitar
Lyre guitars were made around 1800 when a classical revival made fashionable such combinations as guitar and lyre or guitar and harp. This Wornum lyre guitar (below) was made in London around 1810. Note the complement of six single strings, by-then becoming predominant. A similar example is seen in the print on the facing page, from around the same period.

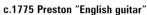
c.1775 Preston "English guitar"

c.1810 Wornum lyre guitar

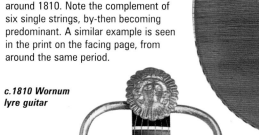

c.1775 Preston "English guitar"
The above instrument was not a guitar at all, but a type of cittern. John Preston worked in London around the 1750s and made many "English guitars," which were more popular in Britain at this time than the conventionally shaped guitar.

c.1920 Larson harp guitar
Brothers Carl and August Larson of Chicago crafted many fretted innovations between the mid-1890s and the early 1940s, including these two contrasting harp guitar designs.

Painting of Wornum lyre guitar player, c.1810

*1910 Bohmann
harp guitar*

1910 Bohmann harp guitar
Joseph Bohmann was born in Neumarkt, Bohemia (now the Czech Republic) and settled in Chicago in 1878, where he supplied guitars to Sears. Harp guitars were a specialty, and this example features 12 sub-bass strings and seven "sympathetic strings" inside.

c.1920 Larson harp guitar

1920 Dyer Symphony Harp Guitar Style 8

1920 Dyer Symphony Harp Guitar Style 8
William John Dyer was an instrument dealer in Minnesota. His Symphony series of harp guitars were built by the Larson Brothers, the Chicago-based maker. This Style 8 specimen has six sub-bass strings and ornate inlays.

CHAPTER ONE
ACOUSTIC GUITARS

There are principally two kinds of acoustic guitar: the flat-top and the archtop. The general description of a flat-top with a round soundhole covers classical nylon-strung instruments as well as steel-strung "folk" guitars. The archtop acoustic was a later development, designed to increase the volume of the basic instrument.

Volume has driven many subsequent innovations in the acoustic guitar's history. The resonator tradition that began in the late 1920s, with spun metal cones inside the body to amplify the sound, was one such solution. Meanwhile, ever-larger bodies and refinements to the construction and internal bracing of purely acoustic instruments led to increased projection of the instrument's voice.

Companies such as Martin progressively evolved the steel-string instrument, and in doing so came to dominate the market and define what we think of as an acoustic guitar in our mind's eye. Meanwhile, the parallel traditions of the classical and the flamenco guitar thrive to this day.

The opportunities afforded by mass production, particularly in the Far East, have placed affordable and often quality acoustic instruments in the hands of many more aspiring players in recent times. As we approach the present day, larger US firms such as Taylor and Japanese manufacturers such as Yamaha peacefully coexist alongside a procession of specialist "boutique" makers around the globe.

High-end hand-made creations from artisan luthiers such as Lowden, Collings, and others offer a variety of woods, shapes, and sizes, with modern cutaway and pickup options, alongside classic traditional designs. Meanwhile, the abiding popularity of acoustic music and the enduring romantic ideal of the lone troubadour strumming away into the night guarantee a healthy future for the acoustic guitar.

CLASSICAL GUITARS
ANTONIO DE TORRES

During the 19th century the guitar began to develop into the instrument generally referred to now as the "classical" guitar. The maker most responsible for this development was Antonio de Torres of Spain.

Around 1800, the European guitar had moved away from five courses to six single strings. Many of the early six-string instruments had relatively small bodies with transverse strutting inside the top, such as those made in the 1830s by the Frenchman René Lacôte. Torres, however, introduced a bigger but not heavier body with wider bouts, and established the fan-strutting pattern inside the top of the body as the most effective for the Spanish guitar.

Torres's methods produced a tonally more wide-ranging instrument, particularly in the bass, and his ideas for an integrated guitar were widely adopted in Spain, and also in other guitar-making centers far beyond.

Torres was born near Almeria, and worked in Seville (1852–69) and Almeria (1875–92). His designs developed his theory that the guitar's top was the key to its sound. Torres's fan-strutting pattern for the top's underside, his characteristic "doming" of the lower bout, his shifting of the bridge proportionally further up the body, and his uses of relatively thin woods all combined to produce strong but not heavy guitars with a responsive, rounded sound and an elegant plainness.

The best known contemporary guitarist to use Torres instruments was Francisco Tárrega (1852–1909), who was among the first to establish the guitar as a "serious" musical instrument. The maker José Romanillos, in his book *Antonio de Torres—Guitar Maker*, estimated that Torres made some 320 guitars during his two active periods, of which 66 had been traced.

1860 Torres first epoch (I)

1860 Torres first epoch (I)
This early example of Torres's influential handiwork has a spruce top, a four-piece cypress back, and cypress sides.

1888 Torres second epoch
Torres left Seville and gave up guitar-making for a time in 1870, but returned to the craft five years later in Almeria, beginning his "second epoch." This 1888 instrument was one of 320 he built up until his death in 1892, at the age of 75.

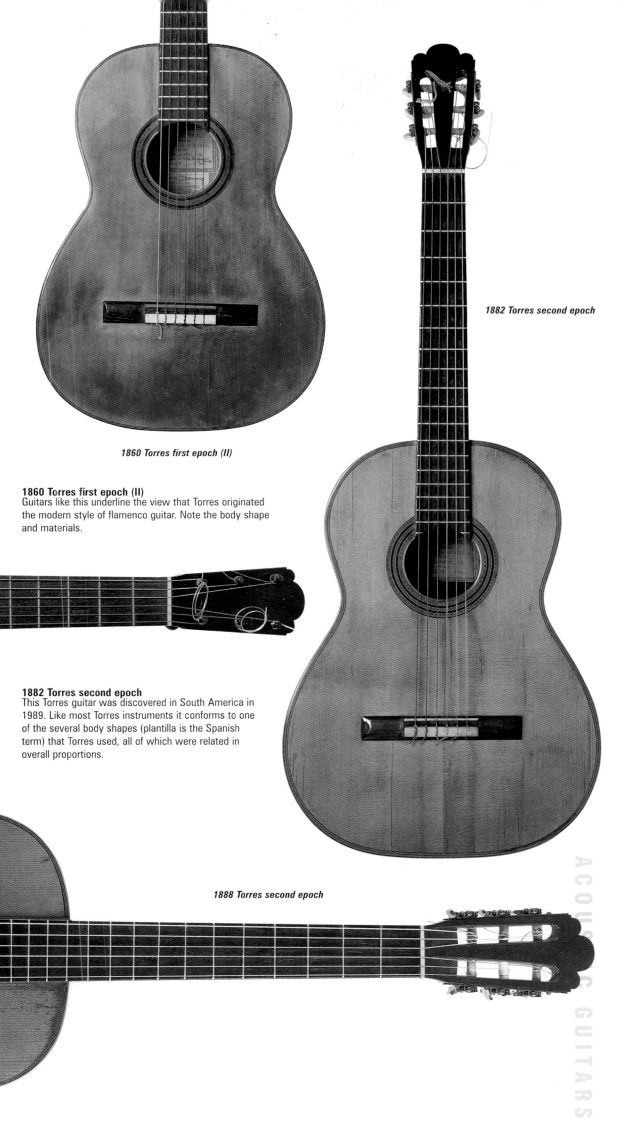

1882 Torres second epoch

1860 Torres first epoch (II)

1860 Torres first epoch (II)
Guitars like this underline the view that Torres originated
the modern style of flamenco guitar. Note the body shape
and materials.

1882 Torres second epoch
This Torres guitar was discovered in South America in
1989. Like most Torres instruments it conforms to one
of the several body shapes (plantilla is the Spanish
term) that Torres used, all of which were related in
overall proportions.

1888 Torres second epoch

CLASSICAL GUITARS
EUROPE

Visually, most modern "classical" guitars bear the shape and general characteristics of Torres's 19th-century designs, though some makers now use bigger bodies. Efforts for change have also taken place inside the guitar, principally in the layout of strutting under the guitar's top, crucial to its overall tone and volume. It is the production of the latter quality, while retaining or even improving upon the former, that has exercised many maker's minds, as the legendary Segovia pointed out in Christopher Nupen's 1969 film about the great guitarist: "When I arrived in the musical world I began to play in very big halls, and from that moment all the makers tried to do a guitar that sounds better and stronger. To have this instrument with the strong sounds, and mellow, it is really a great achievement of the guitar makers."

Born near Granada in southern Spain, Andrés Segovia (1893–1987) did more than any other player to popularize the "classical" guitar on the concert stage. In 1912 Segovia replaced his first guitar (by Benito Ferrer) with a Manuel Ramírez (probably made in the Ramirez workshop by Santos Hernández). He changed in the late 1930s to a Hermann Hauser, which he used until about 1970, when he moved to new guitars by Fleta and José Ramírez.

1935 Hermann Hauser 1

1985 Romanillos "La Buho"
José Romanillos was born in Madrid in 1932 and has lived in Britain since 1959. He set up a workshop near Julian Bream's home in England in 1970. Romanillos's son Liam has made guitars since 1991. Bream played Romanillos guitars, among others, from 1973 and used the guitar shown until 1990.

1935 Hermann Hauser I
Based in Munich, Hermann Hauser (1882–1952) made a variety of stringed instruments. Some earlier guitars were in an older, non-Spanish style, but he soon adopted the Torres style. His son and grandson were both also named Hermann Hauser: Hermann II continued to make guitars until his death in 1988, and Hermann III is still active.

1985 Romanillos "La Buho"

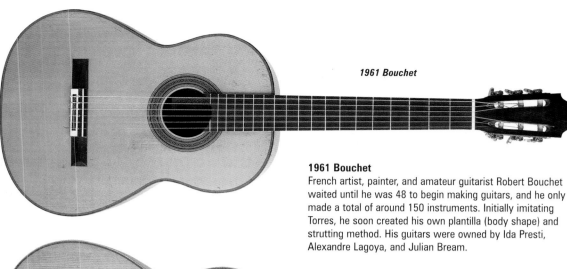

1961 Bouchet

1961 Bouchet

French artist, painter, and amateur guitarist Robert Bouchet waited until he was 48 to begin making guitars, and he only made a total of around 150 instruments. Initially imitating Torres, he soon created his own plantilla (body shape) and strutting method. His guitars were owned by Ida Presti, Alexandre Lagoya, and Julian Bream.

1906 Arias

1906 Arias

No photos or documents of Madrid-based maker Vicente Arias survive, and he left no heirs or apprentices. But his legacy is one of the finest of the early classical period, and the quality of his guitars bears comparison to those of Torres. Smaller and lighter than those of the master, they employed different body shapes and between four and eleven internal struts.

Hofner press ad from 2003

1988 Hauser III

This instrument has three generations of German guitar-building expertise resonating through its body. Herman Hauser I began in 1905, and eventually created instruments in the Spanish style that Segovia declared "the greatest guitar of our epoch." Herman Hauser III continues the family tradition to this day from his Reisbach workshop, as does his daughter Kathrin Hauser.

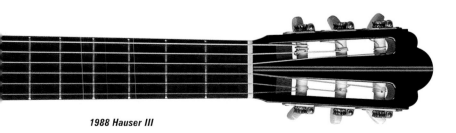

1988 Hauser III

CLASSICAL GUITARS
REST OF THE WORLD

Credit for the classical guitar's development is primarily associated with European makers. But like language, its appearance in cultures outside Europe can be traced along ancient colonial and trade lines—ever since Spanish colonizers brought their protean vihuelas to the Americas in the 16th century. Later, its popularity exploded as a consequence of industrialization, when transport advances brought increased exposure for touring classical musicians such as Segovia. The migration of skilled guitar makers to countries such as the USA paved the way for the instrument's ineluctable rise.

Today's classical guitar landscape has been enriched by the various traditions and innovations of guitar makers from outside of Spain—although that country still plays a leading role. Against an industrial backdrop on a scale that Torres and Hauser could not have imagined, makers in the United States, Japan, and Australia have continuously refined the design of the soundboard and explored new materials in the pursuit of the perfect classical musical instrument. Torres and his contemporary makers would undoubtedly have been shocked to see what the guitar has become, but they would be fascinated by the way their ideas have been adapted by makers such as Greg Smallman in Australia. They probably would have been gratified to observe that handmade guitars and keen craftsmanship are still prized above all, wherever you are in the world.

Guild press ad from the 1960s

1998 Nuñez

1965 Oribe

1998 Nuñez
Francisco Nuñez (1841–1919) was a Spanish immigrant to Argentina who opened a workshop and store in Buenos Aires in 1840. His workshop used European machinery to mass-produce classical instruments, and Nuñez continued to hand-build guitars. The store, Antigua Casa Nuñez, still trades today.

1965 Oribe
José Oribe from Pennsylvania left his job as a machinist in the aerospace industry and began building guitars a few years later, in 1962. Barely three years on, he'd progressed to building outstanding instruments like this wide-bout concert guitar with its spruce top and Brazilian rosewood back and sides.

c.1983 Contreras Carlevaro

1972 Alvarez Yairi 5011

Kazuo Yairi is a Japanese acoustic maker whose output includes handmade flat-top acoustic and classical models. Sold in the States under the name of their importer, Alvarez, the Yairi family has been making guitars for over seven decades. This cedar-top classical is typical of Alvarez's value-for-money offerings of the early 1970s.

1972 Alavarez Yairi 5011

1992 Smallman

1992 Smallman

Australian luthier Greg Smallman's revolutionary designs employ a thin soundboard supported by a lattice of carbon-fiber and balsa, which produces a bright and loud projection. Classical player John Williams is the brand's highest-profile ambassador and has done much to popularize Smallman internationally. This example has a western red cedar top.

1980 Ruck

1980 Ruck

Milwaukee-born guitar maker Robert Ruck is a classical and flamenco player and celebrated builder. He has built a wide range of stringed instruments, and until he stopped taking commissions, his specialty was designing and building custom orders.

1966 Yamaha Model 150c

One of the earliest guitars the Yamaha behemoth ever produced, the 150c was built at the company's subsidiary in Los Angeles. Yamaha continued to refine its classical line's features and introduce models in rosewood, mahogany, or maple alongside its first steel-string guitars.

1966 Yamaha Model 150c

Sada-Yairi press ad 1975

c.1983 Contreras Carlevaro

This Spanish classical maker's conversation with Uruguayan guitarist Abel Carlevaro led to this eyecatching model. Featuring a one-sided waist, a slotted outline in place of a soundhole, and double sides and back, it continued the experimentation of Carlevaro's 1974 "double-top" guitars, where two tops resonate together in sympathy.

ACOUSTIC GUITARS

FLAMENCO GUITARS
TRADITIONAL & MODERN

The influence of Torres spread throughout Spain and into the rest of Europe. Madrid became the center of guitar-making expertise, and instruments from some of the most famous of these guitarreros (the Spanish word for guitar-makers) are shown on these pages. For some time into the early 20th century the flamenco guitar was the most popular kind of Spanish guitar. It was not until the great Andrés Segovia began to perform widely during the 1920s and 1930s that the idea of the serious "classical" guitar took root, since when this instrument has become the dominant type of Spanish guitar. There have also been important makers outside Spain: for example, in Germany and France.

"Flamenco" is the word generally applied to the folk music of the gypsies of Andalusia, southern Spain. The form combines song (cante), dance (baile), and guitar playing (toque).

The percussive guitar style includes rhythmic tapping of the guitar's top (often protected by a plastic golpeador, or tap plate) and requires an attacking sound with little sustain. Differences from the "classical" guitar include the extreme lightness of the flamenco guitar and the low action of the strings to aid percussion and speed. Recent performers tend to use instruments combining design elements of flamenco and "classical" guitars.

1934 Esteso flamenco

1954 Barbero

1936 Julián Gómez Ramírez
Julián Gómez Ramírez (1879–1943) was a student of either José Ramírez I or Manuel Ramírez before he moved to Paris, and influenced French makers to follow the Spanish tradition. This concert guitar, with its understated rosette and bridge, has been opened up for repairs but still plays beautifully.

1936 Julián Gómez Ramírez

1913 Manuel Ramírez

Manuel Ramírez (1864–1916) is highly regarded, for both "classical" and flamenco guitars. His workshop spawned many later great makers. Early guitars were in the style of his brother, Jose Ramírez 1, but Manuel soon defined his own style.

1990 José Ramírez 1A

1913 Manuel Ramírez

1934 Esteso flamenco

Domingo Esteso (1882–1937) trained at Manuel Ramírez's workshop in Madrid, later setting up in that town in his own right to wide praise.

1954 Barbero

Marcelo Barbero (1904–1956) worked for Ramírez II, and in the latter stages of his career, when this instrument was made, he had moved toward a more solo-performer suited tone. This was in contrast to the bright sound of traditional flamenco instruments, which are designed for accompaniment.

1990 José Ramírez 1A

The Ramírez dynasty began with brothers Jose I (1858–1923) and Manuel. The business passed to José II (1885–1923), José III (1922–95), who headed the workshop that produced the guitar shown, José IV (1953–2000), and today a team led by Amalia Ramírez (born 1955).

1897 José Ramírez I

1897 José Ramírez I

This guitar's cypress back and sides and spruce top are more typical of flamenco instruments. The Ramírez catalogue described smaller guitars of this type as "suitable for senoritas". The rosewood fingerboard and bridge and its mother-of-pearl and coloured mastic-and-wood rosette would have made it an expensive model for a cypress guitar.

MARTIN
EARLY GUITARS

For more than 150 years, the Martin company has been producing some of the finest acoustic flat-top guitars in the world. Martin's designs for the shape of the guitar's body, its internal bracing, and its decorative inlay work have influenced virtually every maker of acoustic guitars, both directly and indirectly. The company has been in the hands of the Martin family since the beginning, when Christian Frederick Martin emigrated from Germany to set up a music store in New York City in 1833. He soon moved to Nazareth, Pennsylvania, where Martin is still based today.

Arguably, Martin's real success started in the 1930s and was consolidated following World War II, but many of Martin's classic designs were formulated well before that

time, and a number of fine guitars were made by the company before the start of the 20th century. Christian Frederick Martin was born in 1796 in Germany, the son of a guitar-maker. He worked for his father and other makers, including Stauffer in Austria, but emigrated to the United States in 1833. The business was moved from New York to Pennsylvania, a factory established, and Christian Frederick Martin's grandson, Frank Henry Martin, took over the running of the company in 1888. Since then successive generations of Martins have headed the company; the most recent is C. F. Martin IV, who became Chairman of the Board in 1986.

c.1820s Stauffer (attributed)
C. F. Martin Sr. (1796–1873) worked for guitar-maker Johann Stauffer of Vienna—and, not surprisingly, this Stauffer guitar from the 1820s looks very much like the early Martins, with its scroll headstock, six-on-a-side tuner unit, "moustache" bridge ends, and relatively large upper bout.

c.1839 Martin & Bruno
Charles Bruno was a New York-based distributor of musical instruments, and C.F. Martin Sr. had a partnership with him for just seven months.

c.1820s Stauffer (attributed)

c.1839 Martin & Bruno

c.1840 Martin & Coupa

1830s Martin Stauffer-style

c.1840 Martin & Coupa
C.F. Martin Sr.'s partnership with John Coupa,
who was a guitarist and teacher based in
New York City, continued until 1850.

1830s Martin Stauffer-style
The Johann Stauffer-esque
appointments, including the
extended treble-side on this
1830s model, gave way to a
plainer and more austere design.

1830s Martin Stauffer-style

MARTIN

X-bracing is used by almost all acoustic makers today, and its introduction was a fundamental design innovation for which we owe our thanks to Martin. In the period up to the end of the 19th century, Martin's guitars started to shed obvious European influences such as the Stauffer-style headstock. The company began to formulate its own designs and schemes, including the famous X-bracing. This refers to the pattern of wooden strips inside the top of the body, which contributes to the particular quality of tone produced by an acoustic guitar. Martin developed its X-shaped pattern in the 1850s and has used it ever since. Most other acoustic makers followed suit.

The Nazareth stamp was another landmark change for the company. At the end of the 19th century, Frank Henry Martin, who had taken charge in 1888, decided no longer to use Martin's New York distributor, Zoebisch. Frank began to sell guitars direct to dealers in 1898, giving Martin more control over their own business. So it was at this time that the brand stamp changed from "C F Martin & Co, New York" to "C F Martin & Co., Nazareth PA." Zoebisch had insisted on retaining the "New York," despite Martin's move to Nazareth some 40 years before.

Late-1830s Martin

c.1830s Martin & Schatz

c.1860s Martin 1-28
The Martin "style number" classification system (see pages 30–31) was well under way by 1860, having been introduced in 1856. The "1" denotes Martin's largest body shape of the time, Size 1, and the "28" denotes mid-level ornamentation, already featuring herringbone in the trim, and with an unusual pearl soundhole ring.

c.1860s Martin 1-28

c.1883 Martin 2-27

c.1883 Martin 2-27
This later, smaller Size 2-bodied example shows the Style 27 ornamentation. The abalone soundhole ring is seemingly out-of-sequence—it was considered a more luxurious appointment and was usually only found on 30-series Martins. The small pickguard is not original.

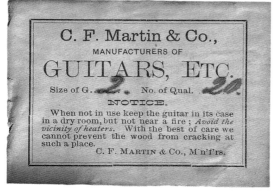

Martin case label

Late-1830s Martin
This model has a straight-sided peghead, three-ring soundhole rosette, and displays an early use of herringbone in the binding. It shows how Martin was progressively evolving beyond European design principles at this time, although this body shape had been used in Spain since the early 1800s.

c.1860s Martin

c.1860s Martin
From the 1850s and through the next few decades that followed, Martin's guitar designs were refined rather than revolutionized. C.F. Martin took on his son, C.F. Martin Jr, in 1867, but both had died by 1888, which is when 22-year-old Frank Henry Martin took over and steered the traditional German company into the 20th century.

c.1830s Martin & Schatz
Martin & Schatz guitars were either made with or marketed by Martin's friend from Markneukirchen, Heinrich Schatz. Martin followed Schatz to the US in 1833 and it's believed Schatz may have had an influence in the development of X-pattern bracing. Martin again followed Schatz in 1835, buying a home that still stands today in Cherry Hill, just outside Nazareth, eastern Pennsylvania.

c.1874 Martin 1-40
Along with the 1-42, the 1-40 was the most ornately decorated model in the range at the time, with its liberal use of abalone around the soundhole and the edge borders. The bridge is of the firmly established "pyramid" type, introduced in the 1840s and so-called because of the shape of its carvings.

c.1874 Martin 1-40

MARTIN
STYLES & SIZES

Two significant changes came to Martin guitars in the 1920s and 1930s. First, the guitars were adapted to use steel strings rather than the previous gut types. To take the greater strain, during the 1920s Martin's guitars were braced more strongly, the tougher "belly" bridge was added around 1930, and necks were strengthened in the mid 1930s. Second, the neck was moved further out of the body to make the playing of higher frets easier. The more playable design with a 14th-fret body join first appeared on the OM models (1929) and was quickly adopted for other Martins. It became a standard for acoustic guitar design.

Model codes
Martin's simple model-number system has a number or letter code before the hyphen that gives the size of the body. The number following the hyphen refers to Martin's body "Style"; generally, a higher number means fancier finishing.

1930 Martin OM-45
The OM, new in 1929 and standing for Orchestra Model, was Martin's first guitar with a neck joining the body at the 14th fret. Such guitars, referred to as "14-fret" models, give better access to higher frets than "12-fret" types. The OM had a body like that of Size 000, but with a longer scale length, and was first made until 1933.

1974 Martin press ad

1931 Martin 000-45

1930 Martin 2-17
This guitar illustrates how the depression of the 1930s in the USA hit some Martin models. This plain and spartan instrument was made from mahogany, with simple bridge and minimal inlay. It sold for $25, compared to $80 for a 000-28.

1930 Martin 2-17

1973 Martin press ad

Martin body sizes

The measurements given for the body shapes (right) are approximate. The first figure is for the body height; the second is across the widest part of the body. There are some differences in size between 12- and 14-fret versions.

1930 Martin OM-45

1931 Martin 000-45

The size 000 is favored by players who want a guitar without the bass-heavy sound of the Dreadnought size, but with a larger body than the 0 and 00 sizes. The ebony bridge was added to Style 45 in 1919, and this guitar's bracing for steel strings was an option, not becoming standard until 1928. This particular one is believed by its owner to be the only left-handed model Martin made before World War II, and it was converted from a seven-string set-up.

Size 2: c.1886 Martin 2-40
12 fret, 46.4×30cm, (18¼×12in)

Size 1: c.1874 Martin 1-40
12 fret, 48×34.4cm, (18⅞×12¾in)

Size 0: 1923 Martin 0-28K
12 fret, 48.5×34.3cm, (19⅛×13½in)

Size 00: 1904 Martin 00-21
14 fret, 48×36cm, (18⅞×14⁵⁄₁₆in)

Size 000: 2002 Martin 000-28LD
14 fret, 49×38cm, (19⅜×15in)

Size D: 1939 Martin D-18
14 fret, 51×39.5cm, (20×15⅝in)

MARTIN
DREADNOUGHTS

The Dreadnought acoustic guitar is among the most famous of Martin's models, and like many innovations from the company has been of great influence on other makers. It has a distinctive square-shouldered, wide-waisted look. The bass-heavy tone designed for vocal accompaniment has been widely adopted by country and bluegrass players.

The Dreadnought, named after the British battleship of the time, was designed in 1916 by Frank Henry Martin and Harry Hunt, who was at the time manager of the Ditson music store in New York City. Originally, Martin made the first dreadnought models for Ditson, who sold the early Dreadnoughts exclusively. When the store went out of business in the late 1920s, the Martin company went on to experiment with the basic design. The archetypal Martin Dreadnoughts, the D-18 and D-28 models, came into general production in 1935, while the classic D-45 was made in limited numbers at this time.

The models became the go-to guitars for a new generation of musicians. Elvis—who was a fantastic rhythm guitarist as well as being able to sing a little—owned both a D-18 and D-28 in the early stages of his career. He used either one of these guitars in the rock'n'roll power trio set-up to lay down his classic Sun sessions.

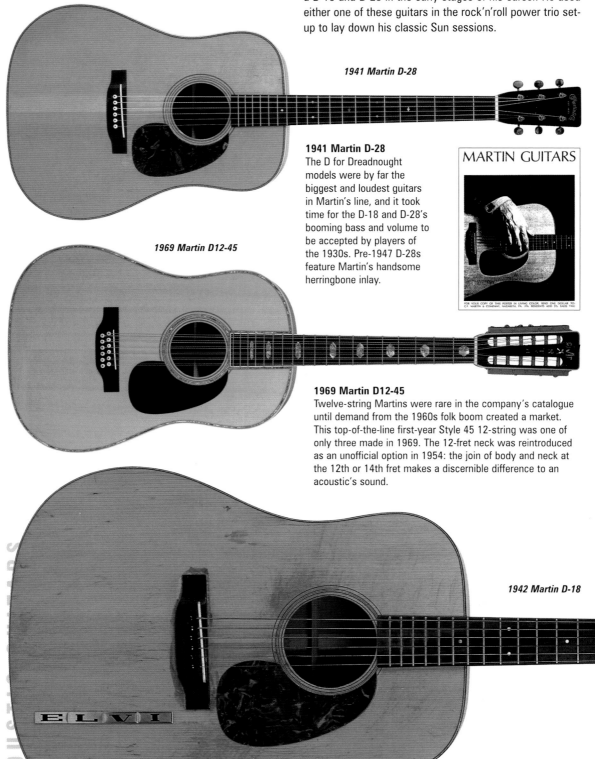

1941 Martin D-28

1969 Martin D12-45

1942 Martin D-18

1941 Martin D-28
The D for Dreadnought models were by far the biggest and loudest guitars in Martin's line, and it took time for the D-18 and D-28's booming bass and volume to be accepted by players of the 1930s. Pre-1947 D-28s feature Martin's handsome herringbone inlay.

MARTIN GUITARS

FOR YOUR COPY OF THIS POSTER IN LIVING COLOR, SEND ONE DOLLAR TO:
C.F. MARTIN & COMPANY, NAZARETH, PA. (PA. RESIDENTS ADD 5% SALES TAX)

1969 Martin D12-45
Twelve-string Martins were rare in the company's catalogue until demand from the 1960s folk boom created a market. This top-of-the-line first-year Style 45 12-string was one of only three made in 1969. The 12-fret neck was reintroduced as an unofficial option in 1954: the join of body and neck at the 12th or 14th fret makes a discernible difference to an acoustic's sound.

ACOUSTIC GUITARS

1940 D-45

1940 Martin D-45

The first D-45 was made in 1933 for singing cowboy star Gene Autry. An early D-45 is among the rarest of Martin's guitars: only 91 were built until the model was stopped in 1942. Demand led to its reintroduction in 1968, and the guitar remains in production today. It combines Martin's biggest body size with the best, most ornate style. The list price of a new D-45 in 1938 was $200; in 2011, $9,999.

Martin
Dreadnought
Model D-45

A superior instrument constructed in the finest Martin tradition by our skilled craftsmen. Intricate details and appointments similar to the first D-45 introduced in 1937.

Beautiful mother-of-pearl inlay on all borders, sound hole rosette and bridge pins makes this Dreadnought an outstanding and unique example of design and craftsmanship. Gold-plated Grover tuning machines, white binding, C.F. Martin mother-of-pearl headstock inlay, and large pearl fingerboard position marks accentuate the neck.

Select rosewood and spruce give the D-45 the superior tone that the professional expects. Easy fingering is assured by the thin hand-shaped mahogany neck and oval ebony fingerboard.

Available once again in limited production on a special order basis. Case included.

C.F. MARTIN & CO., Nazareth, Pa.

1968 Press advertisement

DATING GUITARS

Labels
The earliest Martins have paper labels, sometimes mentioning associates such as Schatz, Coupa, and Bruno.

Stamps
The C.F. Martin stamps are found in one or more places: on the center strip inside the back, visible through the soundhole; on the neck block further inside the body (sometimes upside down); and on the back of the headstock (or on the outside back near the neck/body join). The center-strip stamp gives the approximate date of manufacture, as shown in the lists here.

C.F. Martin New York 1833–1867
C.F. Martin & Co, New York 1867–1898
C.F. Martin & Co, Nazareth PA since 1898. "Made in USA" was added from the 1960s.

Serial numbers
Usually found on the neck block inside body.
Up to 11,018: 1898–1909
Up to 14,512: 1910–1919
Up to 40,843: 1920–1929;
Up to 74,061: 1930–1939
Up to 112,961 1940–1949
Up to 171,047 1950–1959
Up to 256,003 1960–1969
Up to 419,900 1970–1979
Up to 493,279: 1980–1989
Up to 724,077: 1990–1999
Up to 1,406,715: 2000–2009

1994 Martin CHD-28

1942 Martin D-18

This Martin was used by Elvis Presley during the early part of his career, probably around 1954 and 1955 when he was recording for Sun Records of Memphis, Tennessee. From the date of the instrument's manufacture, it is clear that Elvis bought the D-18 used, and later he traded it in for another guitar (at O.K. Houck's music store in Memphis). The guitar, used by Elvis at a time when his music still had strong country influences, was donated in 1974 to the Country Music Hall of Fame in Nashville.

1994 Martin CHD-28

Cedar is used on this HD-28 model instead of the more conventional spruce top. During the 1990s, Martin introduced walnut, maple, and koa woods, and reintroduced all-mahogany construction. Shortages of traditional tonewoods have driven up prices, leading makers to experiment with alternative timbers and materials in the modern era.

MARTIN
NEW GENERATION

In 2008, Martin celebrated its 175th anniversary, making the company the oldest-surviving guitar manufacturer in the world. It had sold its millionth instrument in 2004 (an exquisitely inlaid Dreadnought covered in precious metals and gemstones worth an estimated $1,000,000), and reached the 1.5 million milestone in 2011.

Despite energetic and largely successful attempts to diversify its product line and appeal to a wider range of players, the Martin company of today still focuses attention on the core of its business—selling classic flat-top steel-strings such as the HD-28 and D-35.

Recent developments at both ends of the product line have helped to enhance the reputation for quality while extending the reach of the brand. Signature models and the active courting of star endorsements had been a relatively unknown phenomenon for Martin: that all changed in 1994, when all 66 of the company's first "Signature Edition" model—a replica of Gene Autrey's D-45—sold at $22,000 each. A series of signature models followed, with 1995's 000-42EC Eric Clapton model a huge success, and an impressive roll call of artists ranging from Paul Simon to John Mayer has featured since.

The 1996 Vintage Series line capitalized on the guitar industry's seemingly unquenchable thirst for nostalgia, but

2006 Martin 000X1

2006 Martin 000X1
The X1 Series had a solid spruce top, an HPL body, and an unbound top, and it offered a relatively inexpensive way in to the Martin line-up that has proved popular with players.

2002 Martin JML
The "Road Series" was another less expensive and popular range in recent Martin catalogues. This left-handed model has a mortise-and-tenon neck joint, laminated back and sides, and a morado fingerboard, and there was a range of wood options and body shapes on offer.

2002 Martin JML

2000 Martin Backpacker

Martin has continued to integrate new technological advances and keep pace with the advances of its rivals, especially fellow US builder, Taylor. As of 2005, Martin had over 180 models on offer.

Martin used new materials (laminated Stratabond necks, ash and walnut bodies, Ebonite fingerboards), new construction technology (X-Series' High Pressure Laminate bracing, High Performance neck profiles), and moved some production to Mexico. All this enabled the company to maintain its environmental and sustainability commitments and offer guitars at lower prices.

2000 Martin 000-42 ECB Eric Clapton

2006 Martin FeLiX II Limited Edition

2000 Martin 000-42 ECB Eric Clapton
Clapton's career-rejuvenating *Eric Clapton Unplugged* concert of 1992 saw the legendary guitarist deliver a bluesy set on a Martin 000-42. Martin subsequently made 461 000-42ECB models, with Sitka spruce tops and rosewood back and sides, and followed it up with an ongoing series including 1998's 000-28EC that, a decade later, had sold 4,000 units.

2006 Martin FeLiX II Limited Edition
The HPL technique created a blank canvas for graphic artists. The three-quarter size FeLiX II was a limited run, with graphics from Don Oriolo, son of Felix The Cat's original co-creator, Joe Oriolo. The FeLiX II also has a cost-cutting Stratabond laminate neck and black Micarta fingerboard.

2000 Mini Martin Limited Edition

2000 Mini Martin Limited Edition
The Backpacker's success led to this diminutive "real" Martin. Based on Martin's "Size 5" body, the 295-piece Limited Edition model didn't want for luxury appointments, sporting herringbone and abalone ornamentation. It's based on a terz design, and should be tuned to a pitch a minor-third higher than a normal guitar.

2000 Martin Backpacker
The Backpacker came into being in 1994, to give workers something to do in Martin's newly acquired Mexican factory. It was a hit, and it lived up to its monicker when astronaut Pierre Thuot took a customized version on a Columbia space shuttle mission in March 1994.

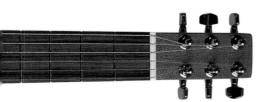

2012 press ad

ACOUSTIC GUITARS

ARCHTOPS
D'ANGELICO

New York archtop maker John D'Angelico (1905–1964) created instruments that are today considered synonymous with the classic era of the archtop guitar, and which remain highly prized. D'Angelico began his career by emulating the original archtop design, the Gibson L-5 (see page 46).

D'Angelico added his signature to the headstock in mother-of-pearl, and his own "stair-step"-adorned pickguards to the blueprint of Lloyd Loar's 1922 creation. But otherwise, D'Angelico was influenced by Gibson's aesthetics, copying Gibson's 17- and 18-inch updates to body dimensions, and, by 1947, copying Gibson's introduction of cutaway body styles.

D'Angelico's two later models, the Excel and the New Yorker, became his most celebrated. Jazz players loved the powerful tone of D'Angelico's guitars, and star endorsers included Oscar Moore, Johnny Smith, Benny Martell of the Buddy Rogers Orchestra (a favorite act of Al Capone), and country star Chet Atkins, who played an Excel cutaway between 1950 and 1954, when he famously became a Gretsch endorsee.

The instruments' ornate appointments and Deco-style details would vary from order to order, producing significant variations such as the Teardrop model below. D'Angelico hand-made all his guitars and was only ever assisted by two builders: Vincent "Jimmy" DiSerio, who left to work with Favilla; and James L. D'Aquisto, who went on to continue D'Angelico's legacy and become a legendary archtop maker in his own right. D'Angelico died in 1964 aged 59: he made a total of 1,164 guitars, with the last ten finished by D'Acquisto.

2003 press ad for modern, electric D'Angelico recreations, opposite.

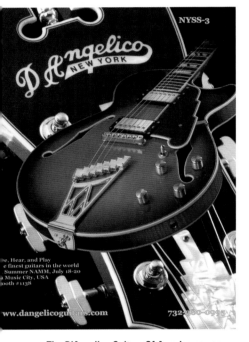

The D'Angelico Guitars Of America company of New Jersey makes re-creations of original models and new electric designs.

1949 D'Angelico Special

1955 D'Angelico Excel Cutaway

1955 D'Angelico Excel Cutaway

This mid-period cutaway Excel model has a characteristic "broken scroll pediment" flared headstock with an "ornamental cupola", reminiscent of Italian mandolin designs from the 19th century. The construction of D'Angelico's guitars matched their looks and sound, making them a popular choice for pro musicians.

1941 D'Angelico Special

1941 D'Angelico Special

This is thought to be the only guitar that John D'Angelico ever made in mahogany. As a result, it constitutes a distinct departure from the classic D'Angelico sound, and it is markedly different when compared to the regular maple-body D'Angelico guitars, sounding perhaps lighter and more "open." Many feel that maple produces a higher quality sound, and so it is perhaps understandable that D'Angelico made only this one mahogany example.

1950 D'Angelico Excel

1949 D'Angelico Special

This Special shows how willing D'Angelico was to vary his designs. Believed to be the largest guitar D'Angelico ever built, with a width close to 19 inches, the Special has a less refined sound than many of its siblings. The addition of a central oval soundhole, instead of the more orthodox f-holes, is another unusual touch. It's unlikely D'Angelico would make a guitar without f-holes unless the customer—in this case one F. Orlando—requested it.

1950 D'Angelico Excel

The Excel was an extension of John D'Angelico's interest in the Gibson L-5 guitar, but overlaid with his own character and his own ideas.

1957 D'Angelico New Yorker Cutaway Special "Teardrop"

1957 D'Angelico New Yorker Cutaway Special "Teardrop"

Known as the Teardrop, this specially commissioned New Yorker was created for club performer Peter Girardi. This unique guitar was at one time owned by collector Scott Chinery, who said it sounded unlike any other guitar, with immense power in the bass range. Its rarity and heritage have turned it into one of the world's most valuable musicial instruments.

ACOUSTIC GUITARS

37

ARCHTOPS
D'AQUISTO

James "Jimmy" L. D'Aquisto (1935–1995), a Brooklyn-born Italian-American, joined the workshop of his mentor John D'Angelico (see pages 36–37) in 1951, as a 17-year-old jazz guitarist. After John became ill in the early 1960s, Jimmy began to carry out most aspects of the guitar-building operation. When D'Angelico died in 1964, D'Aquisto bought the business, and although he lost the right to trade under the D'Angelico name, he continued where the famous maker left off.

D'Angelico left ten unfinished guitars behind when he died, which D'Aquisto completed work on, expediting his reputation as his master's successor in the process. D'Acquisto kept the Excel and New Yorker model names,

but quickly made changes to their aesthetics. He removed a notch from the f-holes to make them elliptical "S-holes", replaced the New Yorker's skyscraper motif with a large scroll, and replaced the "broken-scroll" headstock cutout to a circular shape. He also began using composite brass and ebony adjustable tailpieces, all of which amounted to breaks with the tradition set by his friend and former boss.

Jimmy also progressively modified the sonic characteristics of the D'Angelico designs to incorporate his ideas. Unlike his master, he was a guitar player, and the series of modifications he made to the construction of his archtops over the years that followed were fine-tuned with the benefit of a musician's ear.

1992 D'Aquisto Centura

1992 D'Aquisto Centura
The Centura belongs to what D'Aquisto called his "futuristic" group of instruments—probably his most significant guitars. They have a more open sound than traditional archtops, and while the old-style guitars were primarily designed for rhythm in a jazz band, these modern, versatile D'Aquistos seem destined for spacier soundscapes.

1968 D'Aquisto New Yorker

ACOUSTIC

1986 D'Aquisto New Yorker Classic

1973 D'Aquisto New Yorker Oval Hole

1973 D'Aquisto New Yorker Oval Hole
D'Aquisto explained his passion for oval soundholes by likening the effect to a squeezed garden hose; the sound, like the water in the hose, would come out more powerfully. The design here shows signs of D'Aquisto's own emerging identity.

1986 D'Aquisto New Yorker Classic
In the late 1980s D'Aquisto developed the elegant Classic, with minimal binding and decoration, and largely wooden fittings. This one was originally owned by cult cartoonist and D'Aquisto fan Gary Larson.

1968 D'Aquisto New Yorker
Jimmy D'Aquisto added his own touches to the D'Angelico style. This 1968 example has a small pickguard and smooth-sided f-holes.

ARCHTOPS
D'AQUISTO II

Jimmy D'Aquisto focused his evolution of the D'Angelico blueprints increasingly on the bridge, tailpieces and soundhole areas. Between 1967 and 1969, he altered the f-holes to "S-holes" and he changed the size and weight of the bridge and removed the inlay from it. He also reduced the length of the tailpiece, altering the tone in the process. Between 1970 and 1973, he used ebony tailpieces and pickguards and widened fingerboards, adding a flatter radius. Later, he reduced ornamentation still further.

He also created flat-top instruments in the early 1970s, and electric instruments in the style of Gibson's ES-175 and Les Paul. D'Aquisto told Paul William Schmidt, author of *Acquired Of The Angels*, a book about D'Angelico and D'Aquisto, how his work compared to his mentor's. He said: "I always tried to put all I believed in into my work. It can only work if one strives to better one's self. I never tried to be better than John. He was D'Angelico trying to make a D'Angelico guitar. I am D'Aquisto, and I'm making my guitar."

D'Aquisto's forward-thinking vision was exemplified by the Advance (see below), the model he created in the 1990s before his untimely death. It had elliptical soundholes and came with a set of inserts that could be placed in them to create 18 different tonal permutations. Recently, Aria has produced reissues of some of D'Aquisto's creations.

Catalogues for recently revived Centura (here) and New Yorker (opposite)

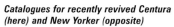

1992 D'Aquisto Solo Cutaway

1992 D'Aquisto Solo Cutaway
The Solo was the flagship design of his later career, yet D'Aquisto only made nine before his death. It had a hollow headstock, a radically reshaped, projection-amplifying ovoid soundhole design, a Tyrolean maple and spruce body, and a weighty ebony bridge.

1994 D'Aquisto Advance

New Yorker
DQ-NY (non-electric)
DQ-NYE (with pickup & controls)
COLOR: N or ALB

1998 D'Aquisto Avant-Garde

1998 D'Aquisto Avant-Garde
By this time, D'Aquisto had lost superfluous decoration to get closer to the true heart of the archtop instrument. An apt name, too: it means the leader in new or unconventional movements.

1996 Fender D'Aquisto Custom Ultra
D'Aquisto had designed models for Fender in the 1980s, but this one-off example was created by Stephen Stern at Fender's Custom Shop for collector Scott Chinery's Blue Guitar project.

1996 Fender D'Aquisto Custom Ultra

1994 D'Aquisto Advance
"Look into a crystal ball and show me what an archtop guitar is going to be like a hundred years from now," was collector Scott Chinery's brief to D'Aquisto: this unique guitar is what he came up with. The tailpiece adjusts to alter both the break-angle and length of the strings, and the soundholes have baffles that pop in and out to create tonal variations (it's shown here with the baffles in place).

1994 Fender ad featuring James D'Aquisto and Robben Ford

ARCHTOPS
EPIPHONE & STROMBERG

The Epiphone brand began in 1928, named after guitar-maker Epaminondas Stathopoulo—"Epi" for short. His Greek immigrant father, Anastasios, built flutes and violins and had founded the House of Stathopoulo in New York City. Epaminondas was president of the company when in 1928 it changed names from House Of Stathopoulo to the Epiphone Banjo Corporation. The principal products were guitars, mandolins, and banjos (in that order). The best of its archtop acoustic models established during the 1930s were quickly taken up by many leading jazz guitarists. These fine guitars have since become widely sought after.

As well as the superb Emperor shown here, and the Deluxe, Epiphone made a number of other significant archtop acoustics, some of more humble manufacture.

These included the Broadway, Triumph, Royal, Spartan, Blackstone, Devon, and Zenith models.

The magic did not last. Epi Stathopoulo died in the early 1940s, and Epiphone never really took off again after World War II. Business complications in the early 1950s led to changes, including a move out of New York to Philadelphia.

Although still in production, during this period Epiphone was reportedly making guitars from existing parts. In 1957 Epi's brother Orphie, who had taken over as president, sold Epiphone to Gibson.

The Stromberg business was based in Boston: Charles Stromberg, a Swedish immigrant, made banjos and drums, while his son Elmer made guitars. All Strombergs were built to order, but from the early 1930s to the mid 1950s, when they became popular with jazz players, Elmer offered seven basic models. In descending order, they were the enormous Master 400 (wider even than the Gibson Super 400), Master 300, Ultra-Deluxe, Deluxe, G-3, G-2, and G-1.

1952 Epiphone Emperor Regent

1952 Epiphone Emperor Regent
Epiphone launched this archtop acoustic around 1936 as a response to the huge new Super 400 produced by Gibson, Epiphone's chief competitor. The Emperor, too, was enormous and was apparently so named as Epiphone wanted a "royal" word to tie in with the news in 1936 of Edward VIII's abdication from the British throne. The example shown is a cutaway model, introduced in 1948.

1954 Epiphone Emperor Cutaway

*c.1951 Stromberg
Deluxe Cutaway*

c.1931 Stromberg

c.1951 Stromberg Deluxe Cutaway

Many collectors have in mind specific instruments
that they particularly want to track down, and high
on the list for some wealthy hunters are two mighty
Stromberg guitars: this blonde Deluxe cutaway; and
the blonde Master 400 cutaway. These are without
doubt the "blue chip" Strombergs, of which only a
tiny handful of examples exist.

c.1945 Stromberg G-1

c.1931 Stromberg

Here is an example of Stromberg's earliest style of guitar,
produced during the 1930s. The most distinctive visual
feature of the period is the "three-piece" f-hole—meaning a
type where the "serifs" at each end are separate from the
central element. Later, as seen in the other examples on this
spread, Stromberg used one-piece f-holes. At such an early
stage in the company's guitar development, when Elmer
Stromberg made guitars more or less as a sideline, this
instrument's label still only refers to Stromberg as a "maker
of banjos and drums."

c.1945 Stromberg G-1

Although each one was made to special order, Stromberg
guitars came in seven principal models. In descending order
these were the Master 400, Master 300, Ultra-Deluxe,
Deluxe, G-1 (sometimes called the G-100), G-2, and G-3.

*c.1948 Stromberg
Ultra-Deluxe*

1954 Epiphone Emperor Cutaway

Epiphone offered the Emperor in
cutaway versions from 1948. Natural
guitars, said Epiphone's advertising,
"had a hand-rubbed finish in which the
beautiful grain of the selected wood is
the decorative motif."

c.1948 Stromberg Ultra-Deluxe

This guitar was made in Stromberg's Boston workshop,
probably in the late 1940s, and was ranked third in the maker's
range. Note the beautiful checkered binding on the body, and
the decorated fingerboard inlays (including a personalized block
at the 17th fret).

ARCHTOPS
EARLY GIBSON

The earliest Gibson acoustic guitars were built around the turn of the 20th century by Orville H. Gibson (1856–1918). Born the son of an English immigrant in Chateaugay, NY, he combined his skills with woodworking and a keen interest in music when he bought a small workshop in Kalamazoo, Michigan, and began making professional-style mandolins, violins, and guitars. His designs contained many innovative features. Gibson was the first guitar maker to incorporate the construction ideas of European violin makers, "tuning" the guitar's arched tops by carving them from one piece of spruce, believing his method of using wood that remained neither stressed nor bent would produce superior tone.

His early guitar designs included such oddities as a large harp guitar, a ten-string guitar-mandolin (his earliest surviving instrument, dating from 1894), and a large zither.

Orville's "regular" guitars were noticeably bigger-bodied than those of contemporary makers, resulting in a fuller, richer sound. He also used unorthodox materials such as walnut for backs and sides instead of rosewood.

When demand increased beyond Orville's capacity to supply it, a consortium bought the rights to his company name and patents, in 1902. He remained as a consultant for only a few months before severing his ties, and he receiving a stipend until his death in 1918.

The revitalized company published a catalogue with two archtops—a Style O, with an oval soundhole, and a Style L, with a conventional soundhole. The catalogue also heavily promoted harp guitars, and Gibson made these well into the 1920s, despite the fact that their unwieldy design never really caught on.

c.1912 Gibson Style U harp guitar
This example of Gibson's Style U harp guitar shows the later changes made to bridge and tailpiece and to the arrangement of the sympathetic strings' tuners. It also has the standard fingerboard markers and bears the classic slanted "The Gibson" peghead logo, which appeared at various times on particular models between the early 1900s and the late 1920s.

c.1906 Gibson L-Artist
The new Gibson company was formed in 1902, and its earliest guitars generally divided into oval-soundhole models (O series) and round-soundhole models (L series). Early instruments sometimes don't exactly match catalogue descriptions; the guitar here is an example. "L-Artist" is a name adopted by collectors for instruments with features such as the fancy fingerboard markers seen here, which are more extravagant than the examples in period catalogues.

1908 Gibson L-1 catalogue

c.1906 Gibson L-Artist

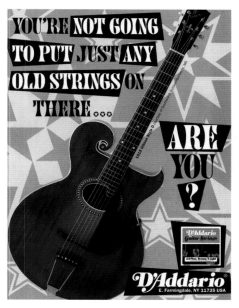

1993 D'Addario strings press ad

c.1906 Gibson Style O

c.1912 Gibson Style U harp guitar

c.1906 Gibson Style O
This Style O is from a brief period around 1906 when the model was produced with an extra-large 18-inch wide body. It has a slotted peghead, a transition from the "paddle" type to Gibson's later, more familiar solid design. From about 1907, the Style O gained a distinctive "flat" cutaway with a carved scroll.

1924 Gibson L-4
This early L-4 looks similar to the first "pre-scroll" Style Os. It was introduced in the early 1910s; the oval soundhole is an Orville Gibson trademark. Mid-1920s L-4s have this "snake-head" headstock.

1924 Gibson L-4

c.1916 Gibson Style O

c.1916 Gibson Style O
Introduced in 1903, this was Gibson's leading archtop until replaced by the L-5 around 1923. By about 1907, the unusual scroll decoration and flat cutaway had appeared. "The Gibson" was added to the headstock after 1916.

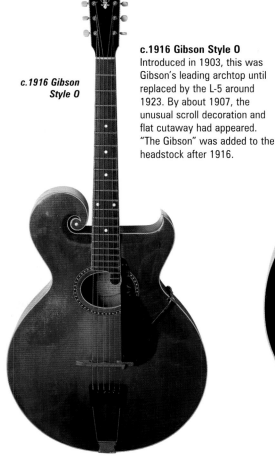

ACOUSTIC GUITARS

45

ARCHTOPS
EARLY GIBSON II

Orville Gibson's beautiful and elegantly thought-out early archtop creations cast long shadows over Gibson's later output and had a long-lasting effect on the company's product line. For decades, Gibson's archtop guitars led the way, and the success of these designs influenced the development of new models, particularly the emerging flat-top instruments of the 1920s (see pages 54–55).

The L-4, released in 1912, would become the standard-bearer for Gibson's guitars, seeing off the mandolin craze and the tenor banjos of the Jazz Age until the company ceased production in 1956. But it was its innovative successor in the range, the L-5, introduced in 1922, that would provide the benchmark for all subsequent archtop designs.

Gibson hired mandolin virtuoso and engineer Lloyd Loar (1886–1943) in 1919, and during his five-year stay as the company's chief instrument designer his L-5 would revolutionize guitar construction in two important areas. First, it had Gibson employee Ted McHugh's adjustable truss-rod, which improved strength and enabled necks to be slimmer. Second, it had a height-adjustable bridge. Combined with the violin-style f-holes replacing the soundholes, the L-5 was playable, powerful, reliable, and tonesome, and became a favorite of influential players of the day such as Eddie Lang.

After Loar left the company, Gibson introduced new L-series models in 1929 (the L-10) and 1930 (the L-7 and L-12), subsequently enlarged the body sizes from 16 inches to 17 inches, and debuted a flagship archtop model. The 18-inch Super 400 was named after its $400 price tag, and cost almost twice as much as the L-5. It featured gold-plated metalware and other elaborate appointments, and proved popular despite the historical timing of its release. In 1939, a rounded cutaway was introduced to these models, but the post-war development of the electric guitar spelled the end for the acoustic archtop.

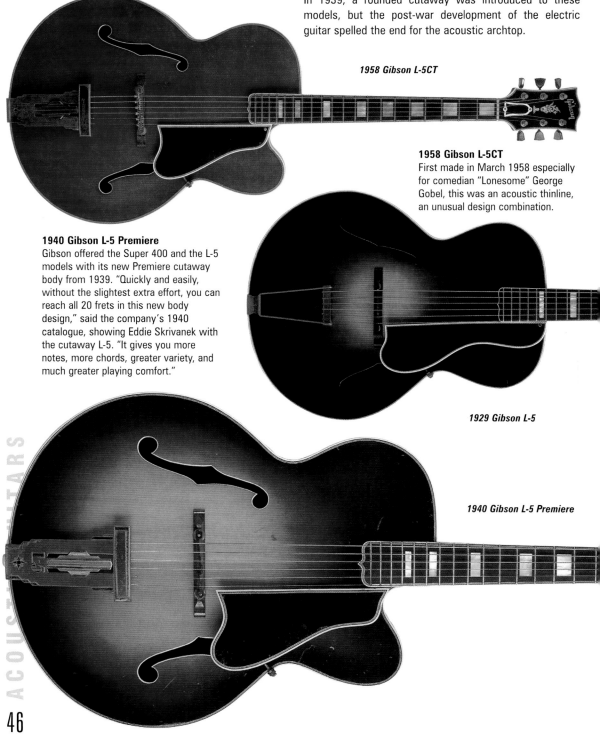

1958 Gibson L-5CT

1958 Gibson L-5CT
First made in March 1958 especially for comedian "Lonesome" George Gobel, this was an acoustic thinline, an unusual design combination.

1940 Gibson L-5 Premiere
Gibson offered the Super 400 and the L-5 models with its new Premiere cutaway body from 1939. "Quickly and easily, without the slightest extra effort, you can reach all 20 frets in this new body design," said the company's 1940 catalogue, showing Eddie Skrivanek with the cutaway L-5. "It gives you more notes, more chords, greater variety, and much greater playing comfort."

1929 Gibson L-5

1940 Gibson L-5 Premiere

ACOUSTIC GUITARS

c.1935 Gibson Super 400

1977 Gibson Super 400C-WR

c.1935 Gibson Super 400

Gibson introduced its finest archtop yet, the Super 400, in 1935. Two years later, the company widened the upper bout by almost an inch-and-a-quarter, and while at first it continued to apply X-bracing to the underside of the top, by 1940 Gibson had moved to parallel-bracing, which provided a rather more open sound that suited the archtop design. World War II halted production of most guitars, including the Super 400.

1977 Gibson Super 400C-WR

Normally, the Super 400 has been available only in sunburst or natural finishes, but in the late 1970s Gibson offered two further color options. These were the wine red of the example shown here, as well as ebony. These relatively solid colors were instituted to use up stocks of plainer wood that was less suitable for use with natural or sunburst where the grain and figure would be more evident.

1939 Gibson Super 400 Premiere N

1939 Gibson Super 400 Premiere N

This is a very important instrument: Gibson's Super 400 was its finest archtop, and this one was made in the first year it came with a cutaway. It is without question the rarest and most desirable Super 400 and is today an extremely valuable instrument. It represents Gibson's attempt at the time to make the best-ever guitar.

1929 Gibson L-5

The L-5 is where the f-hole archtop guitar began its life, in 1922. By 1929, Gibson had replaced the original model's dot fingerboard markers with these pearl (or pearloid) blocks.

1928 catalogue showing Gibson's logo style (top facing page)

1993 press ad for Gibson's Historic Collection (right)

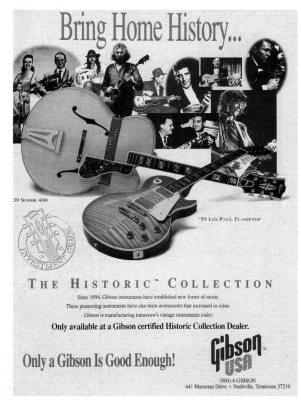

ACOUSTIC GUITARS

47

ARCHTOPS
AMERICAN-MADE

The Fred Gretsch Manufacturing Co. was established in 1883 when a German immigrant, Friedrich Gretsch, left the employ of a small New York City banjo and drum maker, Houdlett, to set up on his own. Soon Gretsch was producing a line of drums, banjos, tambourines, and novelty toy instruments from his new firm's humble premises in Brooklyn.

The stylish and distinctive Synchromatic archtop line appeared in 1939, apparently displayed for the first time at that year's New York World's Fair. With various changes of style and name, some of the Synchromatic models and designs would stay in the Gretsch line for ten or more years, into the mid 1950s.

Gretsch's 1939 catalogue extolled the new line's virtues with "seven points of supremacy": the new "non-pressure" asymmetrical neck; the "synchronized" bridge; "chromatic" tailpiece; large carved-top body; "streamlined" cat's eye soundholes; "perfect finish"; and an "ironclad guarantee." Popular guitarist Harry Volpe, Gretsch's leading endorser of the day, was quoted as saying: "My fingers seem to travel twice as fast on my new Synchromatic."

Harmony was another US company that made inroads

1939 Regal Prince 1170

Regal described the Prince as having an "ease of action that leaves you unwearied after hours of playing." The guitar's catalogue description also mentioned a spruce top and mahogany body. Later versions of the Prince were sold by the Montgomery Ward mail-order company as its top Recording King model, a brand recently revived.

Pages from a 1950s Harmony catalogue

1939 Regal Prince 1170

c.1945 Gretsch Synchromatic 400

c.1945 Gretsch Synchromatic 400

The 400 was top of the five Synchromatics introduced by Gretsch in 1939, alongside the 300, 200, and 160 models. The big 18-inch body of the 400 and the long 26-inch scale of all five original Synchromatic models shows they were designed to be powerful, gutsy instruments. The 400 was intended to compete with Gibson's Super 400 and D'Angelico's New Yorker.

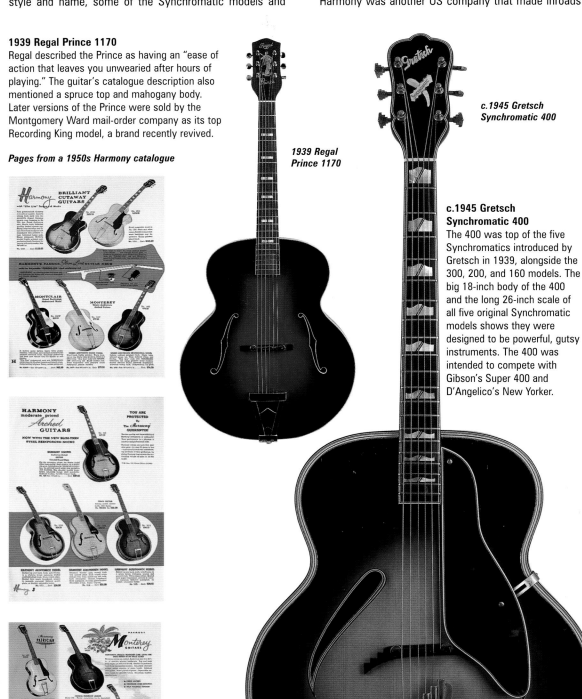

into the archtop market. The Chicago maker was bought by its initial customer, the Sears, Roebuck mail-order company, and during the 1930s released popular models such as the 14-fret neck Cremona in 1932, and continued producing archtop instruments after the war, with cutaway models debuting in 1952. The company was sold in 1976 to Global, and little else was heard until 2008, when new owner Charlie Subecz launched historical reissues including four archtop acoustics with pickups.

1957 Rickenbacker Model 390 and 1958 Model 385
Pioneering electric guitar company Rickenbacker produced just two examples of the 390 and 385. They were both displayed at American instrument trade-shows in 1957 and 1958 but didn't make it into production.

1957 Rickenbacker Model 390

1958 Rickenbacker Model 385

1966 Harmony Patrician No.1407
The Patrician was produced between 1932 and 1973 and was usually made with a mahogany body. The later models, such as this example, came with dot markers. Harmony also released the popular Cremona, and created carved-top versions for Sears.

1938 Martin F-7
Despite its reputation as the greatest flat-top guitar maker of the time, the Martin company made a number of archtop models during the 1930s, although none survived the war. The distinctive hexagonal fingerboard markers of the F series, seen on this F-7, were adopted for the D-45 when that guitar's original "snowflake" markers were dropped in 1939.

1966 Harmony Patrician No.1407

1938 Martin F-7

ARCHTOPS
AMERICAN CONTEMPORARY

Robert Benedetto emerged in the 1990s as the most successful of a new wave of independent makers, as evidenced by an artist-endorsement list including Jimmy Bruno, Andy Summers, and Earl Klugh.

Benedetto led a modern school of archtop design characterized by the use of wood instead of metal or plastic for tailpieces, pickguards, and bindings, along with a general tendency to simplify, if not minimalize, the ornate, traditional style of D'Angelico and D'Aquisto (see pages 36–39).

Benedetto began making guitars in 1968 in New Jersey. He went back to the original inspiration for the archtop design—violins—and has made over 50 violin-family instruments. His first guitar model, the Cremona, was introduced in 1972. Through the 1980s, Benedetto straddled tradition and modernism with the Cremona and Fratello.

In 1989, a new model, the Manhattan, still showed elements of both schools. In 1999, Benedetto was hired by the Fender company to consult on its Guild line of archtops (Fender acquired Guild in 1995), and Fender's Custom Shop in California offered a range of Guild Benedetto archtops. Today, Benedetto offers a full line of models.

Aside from Benedetto, other US craft makers of note include Rhode Island builder Mark Campellone, whose archtops are inspired by the 18-inch orchestra models of the 1930s and '40s; and Long Island luthier John Monteleone, regarded today as a leading builder of archtop designs. Monteleone's style is inspired by Gibson and D'Angelico, as well as a diverse range of Americana, evidenced by the Art Deco appointments of his Radio Flyer model (pictured below).

1995 Monteleone Radio Flyer

1995 Monteleone Radio Flyer
This spruce-topped jazzer is signed inside by its respected maker, John Monteleone, with the legend "Islip, New York, No 168."

1995 Campellone Special

2003 Benedetto La Venezia
Robert Benedetto based this guitar on one he built ten years earlier while working with jazz guitarist Chuck Wayne. The instrument took the all-wood/minimalist concept to a new level, with no inlay or binding.

2003 Benedetto La Venezia

1977 Koontz Custom

1977 Koontz Custom
New Jersey-based guitar-maker Sam Koontz was known for his unusual designs, and would even mount amplifiers and tape recorders into his instruments. Note the exaggerated scrolled upper horn on this imposing cutaway model.

1995 Campellone Special
This was made by Mark Campellone in Providence, Rhode Island, and it has strong ties to traditional archtop design. The sheer physical presence of this Campellone is notable: the abalone pickguard almost seems to jump off the instrument as you look at it.

ARCHTOPS
EUROPEAN

Starting out in 1887 as a violin maker, Germany's Hofner was by World War I the largest German guitar maker. It was one of the firms whose electric-guitar arm benefited directly from the UK's post-World War II import ban on US instruments. But the company's archtop acoustics were among its most celebrated products, and from 1953, the Committee, President, and Senator models built for Selmer UK appealed to many British players of the time, including a teenage George Harrison.

The 1950s saw Hofner elaborate on its archtop designs, adding inlays, binding, elaborate headstocks, and asymmetrical f-holes. In 1994, production was augmented by Chinese reissues of historical models, and the current German catalogues offer acoustic and electric models.

Dutch company Egmond, founded in 1934, was another guitar maker whose electric, acoustic, and archtop models ended up in the hands of European guitar players during the boom of the 1950s and '60s, among them Brian May and Paul McCartney. At the higher end of the quality spectrum, Spanish classical guitar artisan Ignacio Fleta and his sons created some archtop designs in the 1940s.

Guitarist and traditional guitar-builder Mario Maccaferri, who left Selmer in 1933, was an industrious entrepreneur who set up a successful plastics business and invented the plastic clothes-pin. He also produced a line of ukuleles and guitars made from Styron polystyrene resin: the G-30 flat-top and G-40 archtop of 1953 were endorsed by no less a light than classical guitar great, Segovia.

Framus catalogue from 1960

1945 Fleta jazz guitar
This unusual guitar was built in Barcelona by the renowned "classical" guitar-maker Ignacio Fleta. It is thought that Fleta experimented with the construction of a few archtop jazz guitars toward the end of World War II.

c.1956 Egmond
The Egmond company provided many aspiring European guitarists with their first plaything. For George Harrison and Brian May, it was a Toledo acoustic model; for Paul McCartney and countless others, it was a Solid 7 electric.

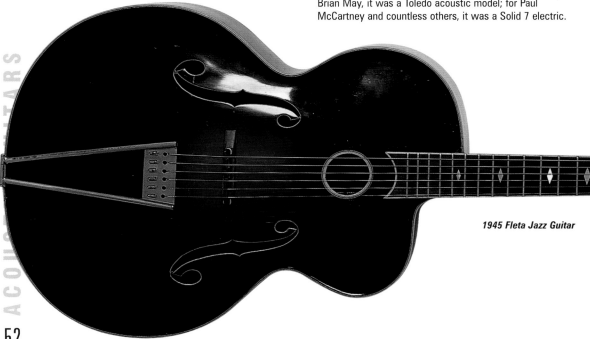

1945 Fleta Jazz Guitar

c.1958 Hofner 458/S
This cutaway archtop model has typically German full-width pearloid block position markers and matching headstock facings.

1996 Scharpach "Blue Vienna"
Austrian-born Theo Scharpach, designer of this one-off "Blue Vienna," works in Groessen, in The Netherlands, with classical guitar builder Menno Bos, making bespoke archtop and classical models.

c.1958 Hofner 458/S

1996 Scharpach "Blue Vienna"

c.1956 Egmond

c.1955 Maccaferri G-40

c.1955 Maccaferri G-40
Maccaferri's first plastic guitars were the flat-top G-30 ($29.95) and archtop G-40 ($39.95) of 1953, manufactured by his French American Reed company in New York City. The neck was bolted to the body, and, despite a plastic exterior, it had a central metal core that extended the length of the instrument. This was the "stay true neck" of Maccaferri's ads, which also boasted that the plastic guitars were "not affected by atmospheric conditions—will not crack or swell."

Maccaferri plastic-guitar press ad from 1958

ACOUSTIC GUITARS

FLAT-TOPS
GIBSON

Three main factors influenced the development of Gibson's flat-top guitars, both directly and indirectly: its main competitor, Martin; the US Depression of the 1930s that formed a backdrop to its early product line; and trends in popular music that necessitated a move in the post-World War II years toward bigger-bodied instruments designed for accompaniment.

Gibson's 1926 L-1 was its debut flat-top. It was only 13½ inches wide but became famous a half-century later as the guitar that blues legend Robert Johnson held in a studio photograph from the mid-1930s. It had the typical archtop-like circular lower body that would later be copied for Gibson's most famous flat-top, the J-200.

Nick Lucas, the man who had committed the first hot guitar solo to wax in 1922—"Pickin' The Guitar"—was another important Gibson endorsee with the arrival of 1928's official Nick Lucas model.

Hawaiian music was also still popular, and Gibson's 1929 trio of HG models (HG for Hawaiian Guitar) had thicker 16-inch waists. These guitars served as prototypes, in effect, for Gibson's classic "round-shouldered dreadnought" design.

In 1934, Gibson debuted the Jumbo, and used the term for all its 16-inch flat-tops. The rest of the world came to describe them as round-shouldered dreadnoughts (as distinct from Martin's square-shouldered shape). The Jumbo was succeeded in late 1936 by a pair of dreadnoughts, the J-35 and the Advanced Jumbo. In late 1937 the company made a 17-inch flat-top for singing-cowboy movie star Ray Whitley, which appeared a year later as the Super Jumbo—a large-bodied, highly ornamented flat-top—and then came the SJ-200.

1937 Gibson SJ-200 "Ray Whitley" Jumbo
This is the prototype of Gibson's top-of-the-line flat-top acoustic guitar. It was made specially for one of Hollywood's earliest singing cowboys, Ray Whitley. He suggested several ideas to Gibson to enhance the guitar's bass sound. The 200 went very quickly into general production.

1937 Gibson SJ-200 "Ray Whitley" Jumbo

1952 Gibson J-200
Called variously the Super Jumbo 200, the SJ-200, and the J-200, Gibson's "King of the Flat-top Guitars" is seen here in scarce blonde finish.

Gibson acoustic ad

1952 Gibson J-200

*2001 Gibson Western
Classic SJ-200*

John Lee Hooker and the Gibson Blues King Electro

1995 Gibson press ad featuring John Lee Hooker

2002 Gibson J-45
The worthy, workaday J-45 is perhaps *the* classic of
Gibson's standard-sized Jumbos (often known as
round-shouldered Dreadnoughts), and a worthy
Bozeman-built reissue.

c.1928 Gibson Nick Lucas "Florentine"
This custom-ordered example of the popular guitar
star's signature model features an intricately inlaid
fingerboard of the style more often seen on Gibson's
Florentine banjo.

2002 Gibson J-45

2001 Gibson Western Classic SJ-200
Gibson's Bozeman factory offered yet
another take on Gibson's self-proclaimed
"King of Country Rhythm" instrument, this
one based on Ray Whitley's guitar (the
original is pictured opposite).

*c.1928 Gibson Nick Lucas
"Florentine"*

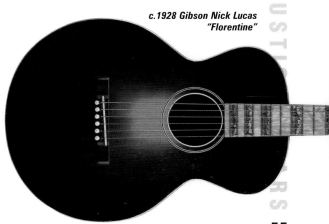

FLAT-TOPS
GIBSON II

After the war, Gibson's short supplies led it to abandon rosewood for mahogany backs and sides, and the SJ-200 (soon to be just J-200) went back into production with maple back and sides. A smaller J-200 variant, the J-185, appeared in 1951. The CF-100, a small-body flat-top, debuted the same year with a cutaway and pointed bout, and optional pickup. Three years later a dreadnought body was fitted with a pickup and introduced as the J-160.

Then came the 1960s folk boom. The Dove was a beautiful, stylishly adorned square-shouldered dreadnought with a maple body; the Everly Brothers model was similar to the J-180 "jumbo" (non-dreadnought) body with a black finish and a pinless bridge designed by the Everlys' father, Ike.

Alas, the combination of higher production, unwise changes in specifications, and increasing competition from cheap imports from Japan and elsewhere resulted in a slow deterioration of quality through the 1960s that picked up speed in the 1970s. One catalyst to Gibson's fall was the acquisition of its parent company by Norlin. The company's attempts to recreate the flat-top design with technology and scientific testing resulted in the Mark guitars—which didn't play very well.

Under new ownership in 1987, Gibson gradually reasserted its reputation. Reissues were successful, with the company restoring the basic J-200, J-45, Dove, and

1963 Gibson Everly Brothers

1960 Gibson Hummingbird
At 16 inches wide, the Hummingbird was big for a square-shouldered dreadnought. It came with mahogany back and sides and a bound body and neck.

1960 Gibson Hummingbird

1998 Gibson '60s Dove
This recent reissue is another run around the block for the bird-bejewelled flat-top. The original Dove design offered a maple body, inlaid pickguard, and oversized bridge.

1998 Gibson '60s Dove

ACOUSTIC GUITARS

2002 Gibson Sheryl Crow

Hummingbird. Gibson began promoting the J-200 as "The King of the Flat-Tops." A long line of artist models have joined the burgeoning lines of today, including guitars named for Elvis Presley, Elvis Costello, John Lennon, Pete Townshend, Sheryl Crow, Emmylou Harris, Robert Johnson, and many others.

1999 Gibson J-50

2002 Gibson Sheryl Crow

This signature model is a square-shouldered dreadnought based on Crow's own 1962 Gibson Country-Western model. The square-shouldered Country Western is in turn regarded as a variation of the Hummingbird.

1999 Gibson J-50

Gibson strongly reasserted its reputation for quality acoustics through the 1990s, thanks largely to its new factory in Bozeman, Montana. This J-50, which harks back to a guitar of the early 1950s, is one example of that effort.

1963 Gibson Everly Brothers

The Everly Brothers were rarely seen on stage without their special Gibson acoustics, in general production from 1962 to 1972, and reintroduced in the 1980s as the J-180. The curved twin pickguards, smaller on later models, make these models easy to spot.

1962 Gibson J-160E

This guitar was used on many classic Beatles recordings throughout the 1960s. Although Harrison and Lennon each owned a J-160E, they swapped guitars in the studio, and the instrument shown was used by both Beatles. Lennon later added the drawings of him and Yoko. The model was launched in 1954, with on-board pickup and controls, and lasted to 1979.

1962 Gibson J-160E

1994 Gibson ad for the Blues King L-00

ACOUSTICS

FLAT-TOPS
EARLY NORTH AMERICAN

The steel-strung flat-top acoustic guitar is such an important part of American music, particularly in bluegrass, country, and blues, it comes as no surprise to note the huge numbers of such instruments made by US companies.

The innovations of the prime American makers have already been described, and here we chart the impressive instruments of some of the smaller flat-top manufacturers that, leading by example or by providing competition, have contributed to the American acoustic guitar's evolution.

Ditson, known as the company that sold Martin's early Dreadnoughts from 1917 to 1930, was also an early player in the American guitar scene. It offered high-quality parlor guitars such as the Haynes Excelsior line from 1885 and the later Conquest and Empire lines.

Also in the 1880s, Washburn grew out of the Lyon & Healy company of Chicago, itself a subsidiary of Ditson. Its factory-made instruments were rosewood and spruce creations which owed much to Martin's designs, though they were structurally inferior. The product line contrasted highly decorated guitars, often endorsed by artists, with bread-and-butter inexpensive models often sold by mail order.

Around the turn of the century, Harmony began its rise to prominence as the world's largest mass-producer of instruments by offering solid-timber acoustics of all sizes, and proving itself more than willing to innovate. Harmony kept pace with trends and did well even during the Depression, with highly decorated "decalomania" finishes, unusual stencils, textured finishes, and artist tie-ins. Post-war, Harmony settled into a steady groove that would see it through the 1960s guitar boom and beyond.

c.1906 Ditson Model 261

c.1892 Washburn Style 108

c.1906 Ditson Model 261
Like many guitars of its day, this model sold by Oliver Ditson is in fact a flat-top, but uses a separate bridge and tailpiece. This arrangement applies less stress to the top of the guitar than today's more common integral pin bridge.

c.1892 Washburn Style 108
This beautiful specimen is a Chicago-built Lyon & Healy Washburn, one of the newly established factory's more lavish models that, like many early Washburns, owed an aesthetic debt of gratitude to Martin.

1938 Harmony-made Supertone Gene Autry Roundup

Guild catalogue of the 1970s

ACOUSTIC GUITARS

1939 Larson Jay Rich
This magnificent cutaway guitar was specially built by August Larson for country performer Jay Rich. A typed label inside reads: "7-21-39 Custom made for Jay Rich. A. Larson, Chicago. Ser #1552." It is possible this was one of the guitars made by the Larson Brothers for stars of the WLS radio show *National Barn Dance*.

c.1940 Euphonon
This superb large-body guitar, with similarities to Gibson's SJ-200 of three years earlier, has newspaper photographs of Django Reinhardt stuck inside the body. It has been suggested that the instrument may at one time have been owned by Reinhardt.

1939 Larson Jay Rich

c.1940 Euphonon

1936 Oahu Deluxe Jumbo 68

1936 Oahu Deluxe Jumbo 68
Oahu was a great marketing scheme started in 1927 by steel-guitar mogul Harry Stanley to sell Hawaiian guitar-playing courses. Despite offices in Cleveland, Ohio, Stanley advertised "Honolulu Conservatories" and "studios in all large cities." Stanley had a line of Oahu guitars made, too, like this Kay-built square-neck.

1992 Guild press ad featuring Richie Havens

1938 Harmony-made Supertone Gene Autry Roundup
The early "decalomania" on the guitar's belly shows a lasso-wielding cowboy on his horse and is one of a series of endorsements from Roy Smeck, Bradley Kincaid, and Gene Autry.

c.1965 Harmony Sovereign H-1260
This jumbo-sized Sovereign flat-top model debuted in 1958, and exhibits the square-shouldered shape that would dominate the company's flat-top output thereafter.

c.1965 Harmony Sovereign H-1260

FLAT-TOPS
MODERN NORTH AMERICAN

Heritage brands Martin and Gibson's flat-top success stories—and the companies' less glorious chapters—have inspired plenty of names to compete for headstock space. Some of the new kids on the block who have steadily risen to prominence have carved out an identity beyond mere imitation, and will continue to make acoustic guitar-buying decisions tough for years to come.

Bob Taylor began building guitars in Lemon Grove, California, in 1974, founding Taylor with partner Kurt Listug. Now employing over 550 people in two plants in El Cajon and across the border in Tecate, Mexico, Taylor's varied product line serves all manner of players, from the beginners' 100 Series to the well-heeled 8 Series flagship line. Backed up by clever production and innovations such as the proprietary Expression System pickup and preamp (see pages 70–71), and the adjustable NT neck system, its reputation for playable, dependable instruments has made the company one of America's biggest guitar producers.

Collings, started by Ohio's Bill Collings in the mid 1970s, creates high-quality fretted Americana of all types from its Austin workshop. Its line of crafted acoustics are progressive in their construction methods but traditional in their fundamental design

templates. The company is a firm favourite of the stars, and counts Keith Richards, Pete Townshend, and Lyle Lovett among its customers.

No prizes for guessing where Santa Cruz is based. And it's another 1970s upstart that quickly found favor with star guitarists such as Eric Clapton and bluegrass ace Tony Rice, whose 1981 signature model based on his legendary D-28 is still in the company's catalogue today.

Canadian Jean Larrivée began making classical guitars in 1967 in Toronto, and has expanded the business since, with sound construction techniques that include Larrivée's symmetrical bracing. Many decades and thousands of guitars later, the twin-factory operation is in rude health.

Paul McCartney and Gretchen Wilson featured in 2010 Epiphone ads

2000 Taylor Pallet guitar

1984 Larrivée C-10

2000 Taylor Pallet guitar
Bob Taylor made his original Pallet guitar in 1995 from scrap wood. The idea was to prove that it is the guitar-maker's skill rather than materials that determine the quality of an instrument. However, an experiment turned into orders—and so this 2000 limited-edition of 25 was made, also using a pine top and "pallet-grade" oak back, and now with a fingerboard inlay of a forklift truck.

2000 Collings OM2-H

This OM-H's vintage sunburst finish gives it a distinctive look among natural-wood guitars. Collings has made an art from automation in its production process, employing computer-controlled milling machines that afford engineering with high accuracy.

2000 Collings OM2-H

2009 Collings ad with Lyle Lovett

1998 Santa Cruz Tony Rice Model

This guitar is based on the famous flatpicker's original Martin D-28, once owned by Clarence White, that had a crudely enlarged soundhole. The original instrument became too fragile to use on tour, so Rice had a replica made and the design became a production model.

1999 Taylor 514ce

This cutaway guitar is a grand auditorium-sized instrument with onboard electronics and comes with a solid cedar top. Taylor's three-digit model numbering system indicates the wood used, the string complement ("1" for six-string, "5" for 12-string), and body size.

1998 Santa Cruz Tony Rice Model

1984 Larrivée C-10

The spruce-topped C-10 is one of this Canadian maker's longer-running steel-string flat-tops. It was launched in 1968, just three years after Jean Larrivée began building guitars in Vancouver. He later opened a second factory in Oxnard, California.

1999 Taylor 514ce

ACOUSTIC GUITARS

61

FLAT-TOPS
BOUTIQUE & MULTI-STRING

As influential as the designs evolved by Martin and Gibson have become, smaller modern boutique makers have nonetheless pushed the boundaries of those companies' accepted totems, as well as creating refined takes on the standards for discerning aficionados. Here on these pages are a few choice pieces that range from the classic to the bizarre.

Country and bluegrass favorite Bourgeois builds 30 guitars a month with a close-knit team of eight co-workers. Founder Dana Borgeois knows whereof he speaks: he previously worked as a luthier for Martin, PRS, and Gibson. Michael Millard founded Vermont-based Froggy Bottom in

1970. A high-end flat-top steel-string specialist, the company has an established product line ranging from small parlors to its Model B baritone. Custom orders are its forte and individual handcrafting its calling card.

Flamenco guitarist Ervin Somogyi began building guitars in 1971, and his reputation as a maker was enhanced in the 1980s when influential acoustic Windham Hill artists Will Ackermann, Alex de Grassi and Michael Hedges started to use his guitars.

Canadian luthier Linda Manzer trained with Larrivée and D'Acquisto before starting her own company in Toronto. A distinctive aspect of her designs is the Wedge body shape,

2003 Taylor Richard Sambora Double-Neck
This spectacular signature-model double-neck six- and twelve-string for Bon Jovi's Richie Sambora showcases Taylor's more exotic materials and design prowess.

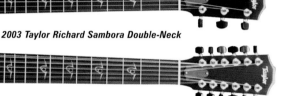

2003 Taylor Richard Sambora Double-Neck

2002 Froggy Bottom H12 Deluxe

2002 Froggy Bottom H12 Deluxe
This sunburst guitar follows the approximate shape of Martin's pre-war 00 model, with a 12-fret neck, gold-plated Waverly tuners, and an abalone soundhole ring. The diminutive 15-inch-bodied guitar is popular with fingerstylists, and it has proved the company's most popular model over the last 20 years.

1994 Valley Arts ad

c.1986 Smith 18-String

where the guitars are shallower on the bass side and deeper on the treble side. She feels this makes the guitars more comfortable to play.

LA's Valley Arts has taken a roundabout approach to the custom-building business. Starting out as a guitar repairer, moving into guitar-making, the company soon began building production models in America, Japan, Germany, and Korea—before Gibson bought the firm in 2002 and reinstated it as a custom-builder.

1995 Manzer Pikasso II
Canadian maker Linda Manzer's Pikasso model, with a mere 42 strings, originated from an order by jazz guitarist Pat Metheny for a guitar with "as many strings as possible." This second version was built in the mid 1990s for guitar collector Scott Chinery.

1995 Manzer Pikasso II

Dell'Arte catalogue from 2002

1998 Bourgeois Martin Simpson

1998 Bourgeois Martin Simpson
Designed for revered fingerstyle master Martin Simpson, this round-shouldered 16-inch Dreadnought features a 12-fret neck join, an abalone soundhole rosette, and a striking deep "fall-away" pointed cutaway.

1992 Somogyi
A cutaway, dreadnought-sized guitar from luthier Ervin Somogyi. The Oakland builder is also a flamenco guitar player of some note, and has built a number of top-quality nylon-string instruments.

1992 Somogyi

c.1986 Smith 18-String
Ralph G. Smith of Wichita, Kansas, took the 12-string concept a step further by using six three-string courses. The necessarily extra-long peghead with nine-a-side tuning machines does make the guitar head-heavy.

FLAT-TOPS
EUROPEAN

The flat-top acoustic guitars produced in Europe have tended to follow the patterns set by US makers. The direct simplicity of the designs established by Martin leave little room for innovation by other makers, so builders in Germany, Britain, Sweden, and elsewhere in Europe have created few surprises. In addition to the makers shown here, Eko from Italy produced a large range of mainly budget-priced flat-tops, principally in the 1960s and '70s.

Since the 1970s, Northern Ireland firm Lowden has built a reputation as a viable alternative to the flat-tops from the other side of the Atlantic and has developed a hand-built model line that owes less than most to the major archetypes. Lowden's distinctive construction, internal and external, and the celebrated rounded tone have earned them celebrity endorsers like Richard Thompson, Michael Hedges, Pierre Bensusan, and David Gray.

Brook, run by ex-Manson employees Simon Smidmore and Andy Petherick, is a UK maker with an outstanding

1987 Manson Slideslammer

1963 Framus 5/98 King

2000 Lowden S-25C

1987 Manson Slideslammer
This guitar, made by Andy Manson of Devon, England, has two extra fittings. At the nut is Manson's Slideslammer device, which raises the strings to a higher action for slide playing. At the bridge is a B-string bender, giving pedal steel effects and more usually associated with electric Telecasters (see page 91).

1963 Framus 5/98 King
This was a budget-priced flat-top. The King was a cutaway version, but a similar non-cutaway guitar, the 5/97 Jumbo, was also available. The King's top was made from pine, the back and sides from mahogany.

2000 Lowden S-25C
This small-bodied jumbo has the rounded style that Lowden's guitars have tended toward, with a top made of cedar—a wood the company has employed more than many. Lowden was also associated with the more budget-conscious Avalon brand.

ACOUSTIC GUITARS

reputation. One of the UK's finest luthiers, Devon's Andy Manson has been making flat-tops since the 1970s in various models, including the popular Magpie. Among his custom orders, Manson created multi-neck acoustics, including a number of mandolin-appended versions for rock legends John-Paul Jones and Jimmy Page.

A very different acoustic instrument was the Selmer guitar designed for the Parisian company in the 1930s by Italian Mario Maccaferri. Although his association with Selmer was short-lived, Mario's unusual ideas for an internal sound chamber gave the guitar a distinctive, cutting tone. This, combined with the small numbers made and their use by Django Reinhardt, has led to a rare and desirable set of models.

2001 Furch F26

2002 Brook catalogue

1972 España press ad

2001 Furch F26

The Czech Republic maker headed by Frantisek Furch began producing guitars clandestinely in 1981 as private enterprise was illegal during the Communist era. Since becoming more widely available in Western markets since the late 1990s, Furch guitars have made a name for themselves, in part thanks to artistically elaborate inlays, such as this jumbo's original twist on the abalone tree-of-life motif.

c.1978 Levin W36

c.1978 Levin W36

Sweden's Levin made 800,000 guitars—mostly Spanish models—over 80 years. A dynastic business, the US Martin company bought Levin in the 1970s, and this guitar bears clear signs of Martin influence. Martin diluted the brand name with budget releases until Levin ceased making guitars in 1979. A new owner has since produced Levin-brand guitars in Asian guitar factories.

1932 Selmer Maccaferri Jazz

1932 Selmer Maccaferri Jazz

Mario Maccaferri was an Italian "classical" guitarist turned guitar designer. The French Selmer company adopted his designs for a series of instruments in the 1930s. The type shown includes an unusual internal sound chamber to increase volume and give a smooth tone. However, a dispute meant that fewer than 300 such guitars were made. Maccaferri moved to the USA and in the early 1950s made an innovative if unsuccessful range of plastic guitars (see page 53).

ACOUSTIC GUITARS

65

FLAT-TOPS
ASIAN & AUSTRALASIAN

One of Japan's best-known guitar makers, Aria began life in 1960 when classical guitarist Shiro Arai worked with the Ryoji Matsuoka Guitar Company to create better domestic classicals. In 1968, Aria produced perhaps the first in-bridge piezo pickup. Nowadays, familiar flat-tops balance a healthy emphasis on electro-acoustic models, typified by the attractive Sandpiper.

Korea's Cort, shortened from Cortez, produces instruments for many other companies and has expanded since 1977 to become one of the world's biggest guitar makers. 1994's Earth series was a breakthrough, in OM, dreadnought, and classical styles, later expanded into 12-string and parlor models. Today, Cort offers almost every classic design, alongside quality budget options.

Renowned for its electrics, Ibanez began as an acoustic manufacturer in the early 20th century, distributing guitars sourced from Salvador Ibáñez, Spain's biggest guitar company. The '50s and '60s saw expanding exports; Ibanez entered the familiar 'copy' phase during the 1970s, running into legal pressure from Gibson; and in the new millennium 2008's radical Montage, 2009's arch-backed Ambiance, and the Exotic Wood range have bolstered the line.

Takamine, another Japanese company with a proud heritage, became synonymous with pushing the electro-acoustic to the forefront of guitarist's thoughts. Industrial behemoth Yamaha may be a corporate giant, but since 1946, it has carved its own path when it comes to guitars, balancing art, playability and value and ending up in the hands of Bert Jansch and Bruce Springsteen in the process.

Finally, Australia's Maton has produced over 300 guitar models and is endorsed by one of guitar's most outrageous talents, Tommy Emmanuel.

1998 Aria NXG-03

2003 Ibanez AEL-2012ETKS

2003 Ibanez AEL-2012ETKS
This 12-string from the popular AE series has a solid spruce top, flamed maple veneer back and sides, and is equipped with a Fishman pickup and EQ.

2007 Yamaha FG-720S

TOMMY EMMANUEL c.g.p

2007 Yamaha FG-720S
The recently updated FG series has been upgraded with some of the design features from the L series. This Dreadnought-sized guitar has a brown sunburst finish over a solid Sitka spruce front with a mahogany back and a rosewood fingerboard.

1998 Aria NXG-03
Aria's take on the semi-solid nylon-string electro format pioneered by Gibson has a solid spruce top with an unusual offset soundhole and bolt-on neck.

2007 Maton ad with Tommy Emmanuel (above)

2002 Crafter ad with Marcello Suissekind (opposite)

1999 Yamaha ad with David Pack (below)

2002 Cort Earth 1200
The Earth 1200 is a contemporary dreadnought from Korea that has proven to be a versatile staple of Cort's product line. Note the elaborate abalone "tree of life" inlay running up the fingerboard.

1998 Takamine Santa Fe Limited Edition
Featuring an evocative celestial inlay inspired by Native American motifs and made from exotic materials such as turquoise, the high-end models such as this continue to be manufactured in Japan. In 1998, Takamine shifted production of budget models to Korea.

2002 Cort Earth 1200

1998 Takamine Santa Fe Limited Edition

ACOUSTIC GUITARS

FLAT-TOPS
OVATION & THE ELECTRO

For the touring band of the 1960s, accurate amplification of acoustic guitars on-stage was a constant problem. A microphone in front of the guitar was inefficient, and tied the performer to one spot. An electric guitar pickup stuck in an acoustic guitar gave little of the original sound quality of the adapted instrument.

Connecticut company Ovation had been started by 1966 by Charles Kaman, a wealthy aeronautics engineer and keen guitarist. An electro-acoustic Balladeer model first appeared in 1970; Ovation made 100 and predicted failure. Today, "Ovation" is almost synonymous with "electro-acoustic."

In the late 1960s the Ovation company, came up with the electro-acoustic idea, and built a special type of six-way pickup into the bridge that reacted to the mechanical movement both of the strings and of the guitar's top. Amplified, this gave a sound claimed to be more like that of a regular acoustic guitar. These piezo-electric pickups, commonly known by the generic term transducers, are incorporated into many makers' acoustic guitars. Six piezo elements at the points where the strings cross the bridge saddle pick up vibration from the strings and the guitar's top, responding to mechanical rather than just magnetic movement, as an electric guitar's pickup does.

There are several modern developments to "onboard" electro-acoustic technology.

Fishman, with its proprietary Aura Acoustic Imaging preamps—which enable an acoustic guitar's pickup sound to be blended with a real-time digital EQ process called an "image" simulating different guitar models—is one of the most prominent.

Fishman has developed the idea with its Blend line of products, whereas Taylor's Expression System uses a new magnetic-sensor and pre-amp approach.

1990 Washburn EA40

1990 Washburn EA40
This Japanese electro-acoustic became popular with touring rock bands in the 1990s as a stage guitar. Note the side-mounted slider controls for altering EQ and volume.

1990 Yamaha APX-10

1990 Yamaha APX-10
This had the usual transducer pickup in the bridge but added another inside the body. It also offered stereo output.

Adamas

Glen Campbell

Nancy Wilson

Marcel Dadi

by

OVATION
INSTRUMENTS INC.
BLOOMFIELD, CONNECTICUT 06002
A KAMAN COMPANY

THINK ACOUSTIC...
LIVE ELECTRIC...
PLAY TAKAMINE

The Takamine LTD-91. Its unique Koa wood arched top and back design and advanced eq/preamp put it at the head of the acoustic/electric class in pure performance. But that's the easy part.

The LTD-91 has that elusive quality that sets it apart from the others—personality. Its elements of design and craftsmanship combine perfectly into an instrument that looks, feels and sounds just right.

Test ride a Takamine at your favorite music dealer today.

For complete information about Takamine write: Takamine Guitars, PO Box 507, Bloomfield, CT 06002

Takamine GUITARS

Dave Stewart works hard, rides a Harley and plays a Takamine LTD-91. Not necessarily in that order.
Photo by Neal Preston.

German Takamine press ad from 2003 (opposite)

1978 press ad with Glen Campbell, Nancy Wilson and the late Marcel Dadi

Dave Stewart advertises a Takamine LTD 90 (right)

1976 Ovation Custom Legend

1976 Ovation Custom Legend
Ovation's standard guitars have a wooden top and a lyrachord fiberglass bowl-back. The back on this guitar has a "shallow bowl," making it slightly thinner and more manageable on stage.

1989 Ovation Thunderbolt
This Ovation makes a strong visual statement with lightning-bolt shaped soundholes cut into the top, which is made from uni-directionally-layered fiber and spruce. The guitar has a much flatter back than other Ovations, and it is equipped with the top-of-the-line OP-24 electronics system.

1989 Ovation Thunderbolt

1978 Ovation Adamas

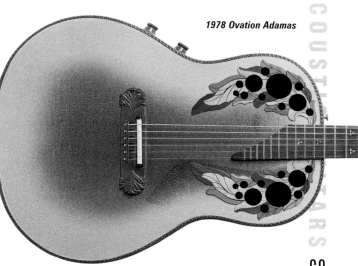

1978 Ovation Adamas
The Adamas model was added at the top of the Ovation range in 1975, furthering the company's use of synthetic materials. The top was made from a sandwich of carbon fibers and birch veneers, with 22 small soundholes replacing the usual central hole.

FLAT-TOPS
THINLINE ELECTRO-ACOUSTICS

Ovation's solution to the problem of amplifying the acoustic guitar has proved very successful, although many players argue that the amplified sound of electro-acoustic guitars still does not reproduce very accurately the pure sound of the acoustic guitar.

After Ovation, some guitarists wanted a combination of the sound of the electro-acoustic with a body based on solid electric styling. During the 1980s various makers offered the sound of the electro-acoustic in compact packages. Some produce a more natural acoustic sound, while a few are actually solid electrics with a bridge transducer; all are designed mostly for amplified use.

The success of these thinline electro-acoustic guitars relies on ease of use: they plug in just like an ordinary electric guitar, and they are styled so that players of solids will feel comfortable with them.

Before Ovation came up with their piezo-electric bridge pickup, a number of guitar makers were offering flat-top acoustic models with ordinary magnetic pickups fitted in to the sound hole. Some of these guitars even came with

controls on the body. Magnetic pickups do not usually retain the acoustic character of the guitar, so engineers would combine the output from these pickups with that of a microphone placed in front of the guitar, aiming to return some of the lost acoustic quality. The Aura system (see page 68) is an ingenious continuation of that principle.

These thinline electro-acoustic designs demonstrate the degrees by which guitar makers will vary the classic "rules" of guitar construction to try to improve performance, solve a particular problem, or meet a specific demand.

New modeling technology has produced more options for the electric guitarist looking for acoustic sounds. As an example, modeling pioneer Line 6, working with luthier James Tyler, has recently released the James Tyler Variax line: electric guitars fitted with L.R. Baggs Radiance Hex polyphonic piezo pickups built into the bridge saddles. The guitars offer 25 electric and acoustic guitar "models," and among these are acoustic sounds inspired by specific Martin, Guild, Gibson, Dobro, and National instruments—as well as some important sitar and banjo sounds.

1989 Kramer Ferrington II KFS2

1989 Kramer Ferrington II KFS2
Any guesses which decade this unassuming semi-acoustic guitar is from? This was designed by luthier-to-the-stars Danny Ferrington, and launched by Kramer in 1986. Ads featured players such as Eddie Van Halen (plus his golden retriever) and Dweezil Zappa. Kramer also made a Telecaster-shaped KFT model.

CLARITY OF SOUND
...and vision

YAMAHA

2004 ad for Yamaha SLG Silent Guitar

1989 Godin L.R. Baggs

1994 Washburn ad featuring John Hiatt

1990 Washburn SBT-21
Like the similarly Telecaster-styled Godin, this Washburn needs a second look before you can be sure it is an electric. But the six piezo elements are visible on the bridge.

1990 Gibson Chet Atkins CEC

1990 Gibson Chet Atkins SST

1990 Gibson Chet Atkins CEC
Launched in 1982, this guitar was designed by Chet Atkins and Gibson as an electric version of a classical nylon-strung guitar and was offered with standard-width finger board or a wider "classical"-width board, as shown here. The line, which Atkins first conceived to rescue his fingernails from steel-string wear, sparked interest in amplified classical guitar.

1990 Gibson Chet Atkins SST
This steel-strung version with body-mounted controls appeared in 1987. Three years later, Gibson added a 12-string model. Both were gone by 2005.

1989 Godin L.R. Baggs
This Canadian hollow-bodied guitar has a three-piece transducer under the bridge and an active circuit. Godin has also made acoustics for other brands, such as Simon & Patrick, Art & Lutherie, and Seagull.

2006 ad for Crafter Slim Arch Series

ACOUSTIC GUITARS

71

RESONATOR GUITARS
DOBRO & NATIONAL

In the 1920s and 1930s most makers responded to calls from musicians for louder guitars by building bigger-bodied instruments or by starting experiments with amplification. But a stylish, effective, portable solution was offered by the various "ampliphonic resonator" guitars made in California (later in Chicago) and commonly known as dobros. In fact, these guitars, based on the principle that a resonating aluminum cone inside the body would greatly increase their volume, were popularized by two brands, Dobro and National.

The guitars have a distinctly brash sound thanks to the aluminum resonator and, very often, a metal body as well. In general, Dobro-branded models tend to have wooden bodies and Nationals have metal bodies, but there are exceptions. Cheap resonator guitars proved popular with some blues players, and a variation with a squared neck was used for playing Hawaiian or lap-steel styles. The name Dobro was derived from the inventors, five

Czechoslovakian immigrants—the DOpyera BROthers. They started making Tri-plate resonator guitars with the National Guitar Co. in about 1927. John, Rudy, and Ed then formed the Dobro company, making "spider" resonator guitars from 1929. Dobro and National merged in 1932, splitting again a few years later.

The Chicago-based Regal company was licensed to make Dobros in 1934; Mosrite in California bought the rights to use the Dobro name in 1965; and in 1967 Ed Dopyera's son Emil started making resonator guitars for his Original Musical Instrument (OMI) company. In 1985 this set-up was sold, and until 1998 resonator guitars were being made to the original designs by National ResoPhonic Guitars of California.

Today, everyone from Fender to a slew of boutique companies offers resonators, with varying levels of quality and adornment. Necks usually join at the 12th fret; 14th-fret joins improve access but slightly detract from tone.

c.1937 Dobro/Regal No.25

c.1937 Dobro/Regal No.25
The Dobro brand began as an offshoot company from National, but the two merged in the early 1930s. Also in that decade, the Chicago-based Regal company was licensed to make Dobros. Many of the Dobro resonator guitars have wooden bodies, with f-holes or small round screen-covered soundholes.

c.1930 Dobro Model 55
Originally named for its $55 price, the model 55 typifies the spartan but now highly desirable style of the Dobro resonator guitar, particularly interesting when compared to the fancier style of National, the brand's chief rival.

c.1930 Dobro Model 55

National catalogues of the 1930s (opposite, and right)

2011 Regal press ad (above)

Japanese catalogue of the 1960s with Firstman copies of Mosrite guitars (top right)

1998 National ResoPhonic Polychrome Tricone

1998 National ResoPhonic Polychrome Tricone
This entry-level metal-bodied model had a baked-on "wrinkle" finish.

1965 Melphonic
The Chicago-based Valco company made some National guitars from the 1940s to the '60s. These plastic-bodied models were made with various brands; this one also appeared with a National or Supro logo.

1965 Melphonic

c.1931 National Style O
This is an example of the Style O, National's best-known resonator guitar. The Hawaiian scenes sandblasted onto the front (and particularly the back) suit some of the music made with these instruments. It has a single, spun resonator, and the bridge is attached to a circular "biscuit." This transfers the strings' vibrations to the floating resonator, which moves like a loudspeaker to amplify the sound. This guitar is like the one on the cover of Dire Straits' *Brothers In Arms*.

c.1931 National Style O

ACOUSTIC GUITARS

STEEL GUITARS
LAPS & PEDALS

The steel guitar is played horizontally, on the seated player's lap or on a stand with attached tuning pedals. The strings are stopped over the neck of the guitar with a sliding steel bar (hence the name) held in the player's non-picking hand (sometimes a glass bottleneck, metal comb, or knife is used). The strings are raised off the neck, and players usually wear picks on their picking fingers and thumb to achieve a hard, attacking sound.

The steel guitar style was developed in Hawaii in the late 19th century. Local musicians hit upon a drifting sound obtained by sliding a metal object across the guitar strings, which they already customarily set to various open or "slack key" tunings.

Although no one person seems responsible for the style's invention, George S. Kanahele's *Hawaiian Music and Musicians: An Illustrated History* suggests that three early Hawaiian players, James Hoa, Gabriel Davion, and Joseph Kekuku "may have discovered the technique independently." The style is also referred to as Hawaiian guitar, or slide guitar. Lap-steel guitars enjoyed a vogue in the USA during the 1920s and 1930s, during which time they were much more popular than the "normal" guitar, usually referred to as the "Spanish" type.

Fender steel catalogues from 1973 (above) and 1975 (right)

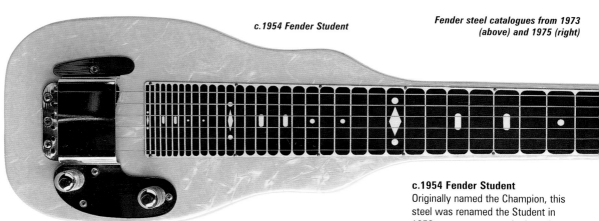

c.1954 Fender Student

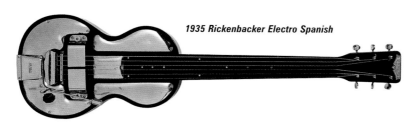

1935 Rickenbacker Electro Spanish

c.1954 Fender Student
Originally named the Champion, this steel was renamed the Student in 1952 as a come-on to the booming teaching studios of the time. They loaned steel guitars to their students for home and studio lessons, before persuading parents to invest in a better lap-steel for the talented offspring.

1935 Rickenbacker Electro Spanish
Bakelite, the first synthetic plastic, was used for the Electro Spanish (later Model B) lap steel from 1935.

c.1940 Rickenbacker Electro Model B
This guitar, also made from Bakelite, first appeared in 1935. Arguably the first "solidbody" electric guitar, it was a popular steel, lasting in various forms into the 1940s. This example, which dates from around 1940, has volume and tone controls plus Rickenbacker's regular "horseshoe" pickup.

c.1940 Rickenbacker Electro Model B

c.1958 Fender Champ
The Champ was introduced in 1955 and was sold individually or as a "set" with a matching amp for $120.

c.1958 Fender Champ

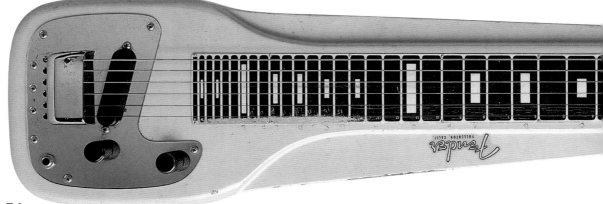

Pedal steel

A distinction of the steel guitar style is the use of a variety of open tunings. In order to change instantly from one to another, players began to use multi-neck steel guitars. In the 1940s, makers such as Bigsby added pedals to change tunings. Players would use the pedals to move to new tunings as if they had changed necks, but the idea of using the pedals to shift pitch during playing came later. Probably the first use of the "slurring" sound, now the pedal steels' trademark, was on Webb Pierce's *Slowly* (1954, by Bud Isaacs). Pitch-changing knee-levers were added later to the instrument, providing even greater versatility.

Lap steel

The earliest lap steels were simply Spanish-style guitars played on the lap, but soon musicians and guitar-makers were adapting that instrument, for example by raising the strings off the neck with a high nut so that the object used to slide across the strings did not hit the frets.

From the 1930s, players wanted louder lap steels: some used resonator guitars or the loud, hollow-necked acoustic steel guitars by Los Angeles maker Weissenborn. But soon, makers introduced electric lap steels, including the first electric guitar, the Rickenbacker "Frying Pan" (for details of which see page 79).

c.1938 Gibson Double Neck Electric Hawaiian
This was in effect a twin-neck EH-150. The 150 came with six or seven strings; the Double Neck was offered with six, seven, or eight strings per neck. Gibson also produced a now-sought-after matching amp with the same model name.

1938 Gibson EH-150
This model was, strictly speaking, Gibson's first electric guitar. The earliest examples of this lap steel appeared in 1935, just before the "Electric Spanish" ES-150 (see page 80).

c.1938 Gibson Double Neck Electric Hawaiian

1938 Gibson EH-150

c.1949 Gretsch Jet Mainliner

1949 Gretsch Jet Mainliner

"Electromatic" was the name that Gretsch gave to some electric lap-steel models, seen on the bridge cover here. This steel has the smaller, box-like body that became popular for lap steels, with some attractive if late Deco styling.

Sho-Bud catalogue (right)

Steel players Shot Jackson and Buddy Emmons started Sho-Bud in the USA in the 1950s. Sho-Bud was bought by Gretsch in 1979 but does not seem to have produced much since the 1980s. In the early 1960s, Buddy formed the Emmons company, which continues today.

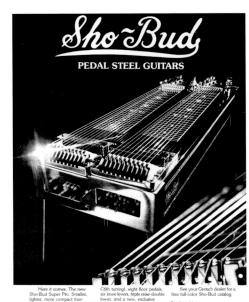

CHAPTER TWO
EARLY ELECTRICS

With the guitar's popularity blooming, it wasn't long before enterprising inventors, luthiers, and guitar players realized there was only so much volume that could be created with a purely acoustic instrument.

Electric amplification was the answer, and from the 1930s onward, makers began experimenting with materials such as Bakelite and cast aluminum instead of wood. In 1931, Rickenbacker's "Frying Pan" used a pair of horseshoe-shaped magnets as the first electro-magnetic pickup, and a new strand of guitar DNA soon followed.

The pre-war period saw rudimentary attempts at developing these ideas so that guitarists could be heard in the big-band jazz orchestras popular at the time. These solutions were mostly confined to traditional Spanish-style or archtop guitars with pickups added.

Soon after World War II was over, however, there were notable experiments, including Les Paul's prescient semi-solid Log and Clunker designs, and motorcycle-maker Paul Bigsby's one-off constructions. These predated the visual flavor of Fender's early models, and demand from players in the emerging styles of music led to a rapid evolution of these primitive forerunners of the electric guitar.

Leo Fender and his colleagues harnessed the mass-production techniques of the day, resulting in the ingenious Telecaster, Precision, Stratocaster, and Jazz Bass. Gibson's corresponding introduction of the more traditional Les Paul solidbody began a rivalry that has dominated the electric-guitar industry to this day.

RICKENBACKER
BIRTH OF THE ELECTRIC GUITAR

No one invented the electric guitar. Rather, the instrument evolved from a series of experiments and collaborations between musicians, makers, and engineers, principally in the United States during the 1930s and 1940s. These people wanted a guitar that could project a louder but tonally accurate version of the acoustic instrument. At first, some designers came up with mechanical methods to achieve this, the best known of which are resonator guitars.

Gradually, it became clear that the most practical answer was offered by the amplifications of electromagnetic pickups, an idea first put into practice by Rickenbacker. The method was applied very successfully to steel guitars. Then came the application of electric amplification to the "Spanish" guitar—a term used to identify the less popular regular guitar.

Not long after that, a handful of visionary men – among them Les Paul, Paul Bigsby, Merle Travis, and Leo Fender – replaced the guitar's traditional hollow body with a solid construction. This reduced the body's interference with the guitar's tone, simplified production, and paved the way for the electric guitar as we know it today. The Rickenbacker name often arises among the claims and counter-claims of guitar historians keen to assign the invention of the electric guitar to one company or one

inventor. Three instruments related to Adolph Rickenbacker's companies of the 1930s are of great importance in the embryonic days of the electric guitar. The "Frying Pan" was among the first electric steel guitars; the Electro Spanish contends for the title of earliest electric-acoustic guitar; and the Rickenbacker Electro Model B could well be called the first solidbody electric guitar.

By 1925, Adolph Rickenbacker, a tool-and-die-maker in his early thirties and of Swiss extraction, had formed the Rickenbacker Manufacturing Company in California. One of the jobs he picked up after meeting George Beauchamp was to make metal parts for the National resonator guitars.

Beauchamp, a guitarist and inventor, had collaborated with National's founders, the Dopyera Brothers, to produce resonator guitars (see pages 72–73).

Beauchamp toyed with another way to make a guitar louder: electric amplification. In the early 1930s he tried applying these theories to a working instrument, and with Paul Barth, who had worked for National, he put together an experimental electric steel guitar. The main result was an instrument with a long wooden neck, and a round wooden body with a large "horseshoe" pickup. Yet another ex-National man, Harry Watson, built the one-piece neck and body for Beauchamp. The guitar's most famous nickname, the "Frying Pan," reflects its shape.

*1930s Rickenbacker catalogue with
production "Frying Pan" guitar*

c.1935 Rickenbacker Ken Roberts

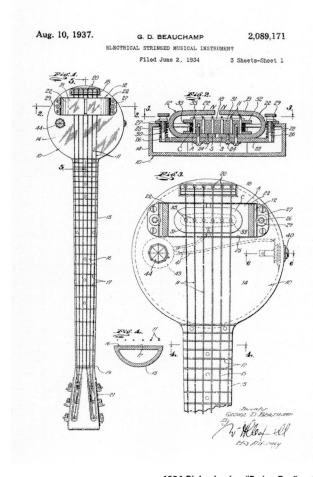

Aug. 10, 1937.　　G. D. BEAUCHAMP　　2,089,171
ELECTRICAL STRINGED MUSICAL INSTRUMENT
Filed June 2, 1934　　3 Sheets-Sheet 1

1934 Rickenbacker "Frying Pan" patent

1931 "Frying Pan"

c.1932 Rickenbacker Electro Spanish

1931 "Frying Pan"
This prototype instrument was among the world's first electric guitars, built by George Beauchamp, Paul Barth, and Harry Watson. It now resides in Rickenbacker's museum in Santa Ana, California.

c.1932 Rickenbacker Electro Spanish
This was Rickenbacker's earliest electric-acoustic guitars. The Electro Spanish model was made between about 1932 and 1935, and featured the horseshoe magnet of the "Frying Pan" fitted to a hollow body with f-holes (the body and neck were made for Rickenbacker by the Harmony company of Chicago).

c.1935 Rickenbacker Ken Roberts
The Rickenbacker Electro company made this model from about 1935, named for a local musician who has since passed into obscurity. As with its other early hollowbody electrics, Electro bought in the neck and body, supplied for this model by Harmony of Chicago. The Roberts guitar has a horseshoe pickup and a single volume control, as well as a Kauffman vibrato, a crude pitch-wobbler invented by Doc Kauffman.

Adolph Rickenbacker

THE FRYING PAN
The first electro-magnetic pickup to be used on a guitar was mounted on the original "Frying Pan": it had two large horseshoe magnets surrounding the strings, with a coil situated underneath.

The electro-magnetic pickup is based on a relatively simple principle. If a magnetic field is disturbed by the vibrations of a metal string, a current will be induced in a coil situated in that field. The coil generates a signal of electrical current as the strings are plucked and vibrated, and this signal is fed out of the guitar to the amplifier where it is boosted and fed to an accompanying loudspeaker.

The prototype "Frying Pan" electric steel guitar was adapted to a production instrument in 1932 by Ro-Pat-In, a company set up for that purpose by George Beauchamp, Adolph Rickenbacker, and Paul Barth. It was now made from cast aluminum and came in two versions—the A22 and the longer-scale A25.

During the early 1930s Ro-Pat-In changed its name to the Electro String Instrument Corporation, and the guitars began to bear the combined Rickenbacker Electro brand in 1934.

Some early instruments had Rickenbacker spelled without the anglicized k: "Rickenbacher." As far as Adolph was concerned, this was the correct (Swiss) way, and it appeared on and off through the next few years.

At first the "Frying Pan" sold poorly, according to Rickenbacker's records. The aluminum apparently caused problems with the stability of the guitar's tuning.

The instrument appeared sporadically in Rickenbacker's catalogues until the late 1950s, but during the mid 1930s, Rickenbacker had moved to a more immediately successful series of electric steel guitars. These models had small bodies of a regular guitar shape, and they were made from sheet metal or from Bakelite.

GIBSON
FIRST ELECTRICS

In the 1930s, some guitarists needed more volume. A number had even taken up the banjo, particularly in the studio where it cut through a loud band more effectively than a guitar. And so, despite the overwhelming popularity of high-action "lap steel" guitars in the USA, a number of makers began to test-market the avant-garde electric-acoustic guitar. This was a conventionally shaped acoustic guitar with normal action, but with an electric pickup and associated controls built into the body.

Rickenbacker issued its Electro Spanish electric-acoustic model in 1932, but only a handful were sold. Other early examples came from Dobro and National (with pickups by Dobro man Victor Smith). Gibson stepped toward the new electric instruments with the launch in 1936 of the ES-150, the company's first "Electric Spanish" guitar. The "Spanish" designation was used purely to distinguish these models from the then-predominant Hawaiian-style equivalents.

The ES-150's place in guitar history may have already been assured, but it was truly cemented when, in late 1939, a young Texan jazz guitar player named Charlie Christian (1916–1942) created a stir with a pioneering soloing style on his ES-150. Fellow Texan jazz guitarist Eddie Durham (1906–1987) is usually credited with being the first player to play an electric guitar solo, also on an ES-150, in 1938. But it was Christian's clear, single-note runs and fluid style, played as though he was a horn player, that established the electric guitar as a solo instrument.

1937 Gibson ES-150
This is a fine example of Gibson's first electric model, which was introduced late in 1936. The unadorned tailpiece and simple dot fingerboard inlays make for a plain appearance, inspired by Gibson's cheap L-50 acoustic, on which the ES-150 was based. The bar pickup was replaced around 1940 by a rectangular unit of more standard appearance. Note the long pickguard and the Bakelite volume and tone control knobs with arrow markers. When production re-started after World War II, the ES-150 was offered with a larger body. The model was withdrawn in 1956.

1937 Gibson ES-150

1937 Gibson catalogue
Featured are the ES-150 and accompanying amplifier. It was the last catalogue with the Nick Lucas model, and the Advanced Jumbo was introduced.

EARLY ELECTRICS

1955 press ad featuring Jimmy Raney playing an ES-150

Lloyd Loar At Gibson

Electric instruments were not completely without precedent at Gibson when it introduced the ES-150. There is firm evidence that acoustic engineer Lloyd Loar experimented with pickups and amplification while employed by Gibson from 1919 to 1924. For example, in the company's self-published *Gibson Story* (1973) by employee Julius Bellson, there is a photograph of an electric double bass made by Loar at Gibson. Loar set up the short-lived Vivi-Tone company in 1933, for which he devised some particularly peculiar guitars, including an early solidbody electric. None of the Vivi-Tone instruments were sold in any significant quantity.

1941 Gibson ES-300

This early Gibson electric guitar was among the first to bear a diagonally slanted pickup. The feature, designed to accentuate the unit's sensitivity to bass and treble, was popularized nearly ten years later on Fender's early solid electric guitars. The 300 lasted only about another year in this form; after 1945, versions with more traditional pickups appeared, and the model lasted until 1952.

1941 Gibson ES-300

Early Electric Guitar: Chronology

The history of the early electric guitar began with Rickenbacker's "Frying Pan" lap-steel of 1931 and culminated with the Gibson Les Paul Gold Top model in 1952. This chart catalogues the key events during this crucial period in the instrument's development. Dates are approximate.

1931
Rickenbacker's "Frying Pan" prototype, among the world's first electric steel guitars, is built by George Beauchamp, Paul Barth, and Harry Watson in California.

1932
Rickenbacker market production versions of the "Frying Pan" and launch one of the earliest electric acoustic guitars, the Electro Spanish.

Similar models are produced elsewhere in the US at this time by National, Dobro, and Vivi-Tone.

1935
The Rickenbacker Model B appears, an electric steel guitar with a semi-solid Bakelite body. Few solidbody guitars pre-date this instrument.

1936
Gibson's first electric guitar, the "Electric Spanish" ES-150, goes into production at its factory in Michigan. The bar pickup is later nicknamed the Charlie Christian.

1940s
Guitarist and inventor Les Paul builds prototype through-neck electrics at home, which he nicknames his Log and his Clunkers. He fails to interest Gibson in the idea.

1947–48
Country musician Merle Travis designs an early through-neck solidbody electric guitar with Paul Bigsby in California. Bigsby builds the guitar, the Bigsby-Travis, another significant early electric solidbody, and a few dozen more similar ones.

1950
In California, Leo Fender and George Fullerton design and build the world's first commercially successful solid electric guitar, the Fender Broadcaster (soon renamed the Telecaster).

1951–52
In 1951, Gibson reacts to Fender's launch by contacting Les Paul again. In the following year, Gibson markets its first solid electric, the Gibson Les Paul Model, known as the Gold Top.

LES PAUL
LOG & CLUNKERS

By the end of the 1930s, some inventors and musicians had the idea for a solidbody electric guitar. Here was an opportunity to dispose of the involved construction of the acoustic guitar and concentrate on a solid base to support the strings and pickups that would create a clear amplified tone.

Back at Rickenbacker, for example, the "normal" guitar version of its Bakelite steel, the Model B (see page 78–79) was launched in 1935, effectively one of the earliest solidbody electric guitars. The Vibrola Spanish Guitar from 1937 was a deep-bodied variant of the Model B, designed by Clayton Orr ("Doc") Kauffman and featuring a novel motorized vibrato system. But the guitar was so heavy it had to be supported on a stand attached to its amplifier. Experiments continued in the USA, but it wasn't until 1950 that a commercial solidbody electric guitar appeared.

Les Paul's inventions changed the way that modern music sounds. Best known of these is the Gibson Les Paul solidbody electric guitar, launched in 1952, but his electric guitar experiments began earlier.

Les said he first amplified a guitar when he was 12, working to entertain the customers at a local hamburger stand who had complained they couldn't hear him. So he jabbed a record player pickup into his acoustic guitar, slid a telephone mouthpiece under the strings, and wired up both to his parents' radio which doubled as an amplifier.

That prompted Les to consider a solidbody electric guitar. What he had in mind was the production of an amplified tone that accurately reproduced and sustained the sound of the strings. To this end, he would stuff rags into hollowbody guitars, and even had a company called Larson Brothers in Chicago build him a guitar with two pickups and a solid maple top. Around 1939, Les started working on a prototype solid electric guitar that he called his Log, for the central block of wood that formed its body.

Les took the Log to Gibson in the 1940s. "They laughed at the idea," he recalled later of Gibson's initial reaction. "They called it the kid with the broomstick with the pickups on," he laughed.

1934 Gibson Super 400 with added pickups
During the 1920s and 1930s, pickups and controls began to appear built into pickguards. Added to existing guitars, these guards "floated" free of the surface to avoid compromising inherent tonality.

1940s Les Paul's "Log"

*1934 Gibson Super 400
with added pickups*

Les Paul: Musician And Inventor

Lester William Polfuss, whose ideas have had a lasting effect on modern electric guitars and on the methods adopted in today's recording studios, was born in 1915 in Waukesha, about 20 miles from Milwaukee, Wisconsin.

As a teenager, Lester called himself Rhubarb Red and the Wizard Of Waukesha, and was already playing country music and rhythm 'n' blues. "Red" moved to Springfield, Missouri, then to Chicago, and on to New York, where by 1938 his trio was appearing on the Fred Waring radio show. "Red" had by this time adopted a new name, Les Paul, and The Les Paul Trio toured the country for several years.

During World War II, Les was in the armed forces radio service, playing with his various groups.

He came up with a recording method now called sound-on-sound. This involved recording onto one disc-recorder, and then transferring the first recording to another machine while adding a new part, and repeating the process to build a layered sound.

Les sometimes varied the speed of the recording to create impossibly high, fast guitar passages. He moved to tape recorders in 1951, when he recorded the classic *How High The Moon*.

Another of his important ideas was the multi-track tape recorder – the basis of all modern recording – which he eventually persuaded Ampex to produce in 1953.

Gibson had laughed at his first attempt in the 1940s to interest the company in his semi-solid electric Log guitar, which he'd put together at weekends at Epi Stathopoulo's Epiphone factory in New Jersey. About this time Les moved to California, where he continued to play the Log.

There were other players and inventors dabbling with the idea of the solid electric guitar, and three of them were then in California: country musician Merle Travis, mechanical expert Paul A Bigsby, and radio repairman Leo Fender. When Fender started his revolutionary mass-production of solid electric guitars in 1950, Gibson decided that it might now need "the kid with the broomstick with the pickups on it," as they'd described Les and his Log.

1952 Gibson ad showing Les Paul playing one of his Clunkers (above right)

1940s Les Paul's "Clunker"

Rear view of the Log
A small black painted block of wood joins the solid center section of the body to the separate neck. The two "wings" of the body, made from the spruce top and sides of an Epiphone guitar, are backed by plywood that was screwed onto the rear of the "wings".

1940s Les Paul's "Log"
This is Les Paul's prototype semi-solid electric guitar, now in the Country Music Hall of Fame in Nashville. It was the instrument that Paul took to Gibson in the 1940s in an initially unsuccessful attempt to have them build a solid electric guitar. The "log" is the solid pine block that Les used to create the center block of the body, with "wings" of an Epiphone body added to complete the shape. Les used the neck of a 1940s Gibson, and the fingerboard is from a Larson Bros guitar.

1940s Les Paul's "Clunker"
Another of Les's handmade prototypes, which he put together around the same time as the Log, has a Bigsby pickup and an early Kauffman vibrola. He regularly played this and another similar Clunker (for his partner Mary Ford), where the Log was more of an experiment.

PAUL BIGSBY
THE MERLE TRAVIS GUITAR

Paul A. Bigsby's guitar, designed by Merle Travis and built in 1948, never succeeded commercially on anything like the scale of the later Fender solid electric guitars. But the Bigsby-Travis guitar is very significant historically: it looks closer to the modern idea of a solid electric guitar than anything that had been made before.

Travis was a country musician, Bigsby a mechanically adept Californian who was keen on both racing and fixing motorbikes and a skilled woodworker. They put their heads together and came up with an astonishingly fresh design. Writing in *Guitar World* in 1980, Travis explained that he wanted an instrument with machine heads along one side of the headstock, because "reaching down to change the first, second, and third [strings] bugged me. I wished somebody would build a guitar with all the tuning pegs on the top." More importantly, Travis insisted that

the body should be "thin and solid. That way, it'll keep ringing like a steel."

Travis initially asked Bigsby to apply his mechanical skills to the vibrola on a Gibson L-10, which was always putting the strings out of tune. Instead, Bigsby built his own-design vibrato unit which worked much better. Travis then set him a more adventurous task – building a solid electric guitar – and in his *Guitar World* piece Travis estimated that Bigsby made about a dozen similar guitars for later customers, including the 1952 Grady Martin oddity seen below. It is clear that the Bigsby-Travis guitar was ahead of its time not only in its assembly: the neck extended right through the body, a method that became fashionable more than 20 years later.

There was some dispute, mainly provoked by comments from Merle Travis in the 1970s, as to whether

1948 Bigsby "Merle Travis" guitar
This was a very early solidbody electric guitar designed by Merle Travis, a country musician, and Paul Bigsby, better known for his widely-used vibrato unit. While the Bigsby-Travis pre-dates Fender's first solidbody electric by some years,

Bigsby produced similar guitars only in very small numbers. As with Bigsby's electric pedal steels, his standard solid could be bought with custom parts. The Bigsby-Travis guitar is kept today at the Country Music Hall Of Fame museum in Nashville, Tennessee.

1948 Bigsby "Merle Travis" guitar

EARLY ELECTRICS

the Bigsby-Travis guitar directly influenced the later and far more successful solid electric guitars of Fender. There's little doubt it did, especially the shape of the Bigsby-Travis headstock, which influenced Fender's 1954 Stratocaster.

Bigsby had success with electric pedal steel guitars, used by some of the leading steel players of the day such as Bud Isaacs and Speedy West. Bigsby's pedal steels were among the first to range the pedals in a line rather than arrange them in a fan shape, as for example on Gibson's earlier Electraharp model.

But most guitarists will be familiar with Bigsby because of his vibrato system. This is his more lasting contribution to the electric guitar, and despite many modern "improved" vibrato units, it is still seen on numerous guitars.

Paul A. Bigsby died in 1968. He had sold the company three years earlier to Ted McCarty, recently departed from his job as president of Gibson, and McCarty ran it until it was acquired by Gretsch in 1999.

Bigsby never embraced the mass-production ethos, never expanded his business, and never tried to speed up his production. He preferred to hand-build distinctive custom-order guitars and mandolins. Today, fewer than 25 of his guitars have survived, and it's been estimated that he made around 100 steels.

Bigsby Vibratos

Paul Bigsby designed his first vibrato unit in the 1940s. The Bigsby works by "wobbling" the string retainer with a spring-loaded handle, and is often retrofitted— that is, added to an existing guitar. Around 1950, Gibson was the first to offer Bigsby units as factory options on some guitars. Gretsch also began to use specially-made "Gretsch by Bigsby" vibratos around this time. The occasional use of the extra "bar" pulls the strings down to help maintain their tension at the bridge. While Bigsby's design offers less variation in pitch, or "travel," than most of the vibrato units that succeeded it, it has endured and thrived because its idiosyncratic shimmer is difficult to achieve in any other way.

Long-plate Bigsby without tension bar

Short-plate Bigsby with tension bar

Gretsch By Bigsby vibrato

Horseshoe-style Bigsby for solidbody guitars

Record jacket featuring Grady Martin with his Bigsby Double-Neck

1952 Bigsby Grady Martin Double-Neck

1952 Bigsby Grady Martin Double-Neck
An early example of the Bigsby vibrato bridge was fitted to this custom-order solid electric guitar-and-mandolin double-neck, which Paul Bigsby built for country musician and session man Grady Martin. Note the tuners in a line on the top of each headstock: this was one of the many features popularized by Bigsby's visionary guitar designs.

LEO FENDER
THE BROADCASTER

The Fender Broadcaster, launched in 1950, was the world's first commercially available electric guitar with a solid wooden body and bolt-on neck. Leo Fender's whole design was geared to mass production and to a simple, effective electric instrument—and it has been a great and long-lasting success.

At the end of the 1940s, Leo and his small team at Fender Electric Instruments began to design and devise their new solidbody electric guitar, soon to be known as the Fender Esquire or Broadcaster, and later the Telecaster. Leo later explained to *Guitar Player* his design criteria: "On an acoustic-electric guitar you have a string fastened to a diaphragm top, and that top does not have one specific frequency. If you play a note the top will respond to it and also to a lot of adjoining notes. A solid guitar body doesn't have that: you're dealing with just a single note at a time."

This seems in line with Les Paul's theory that the principal advantage of the solid body is to deliver a clean, amplified version of the string's inherent tone. Clearly many clever people were thinking along similar lines, and their collective inspiration led inexorably to the solidbody electric guitar.

Don Randall took the Broadcaster to a Chicago trade show in 1950, and was dismayed to find rivals dismissing the stripped-down design as a "shovel" and a "canoe paddle." It appeared on the scene for a list price of $169.95, with a built-in truss rod and the classic combination of maple neck and ash body with twin single-coil pickups. Over half a century later, all manner of star artists continue to use Fender's first and wonderfully basic solidbody design.

Even if Fender had only made that one model, the company's place in the history of the electric guitar would be assured. And yet the firm continued to create new instruments of great diversity. A year after that first Fender solidbody, it invented the solidbody electric bass guitar, and a few years after its solidbody six-string defined the mass-production solidbody electric, the company launched the stylish Stratocaster, in 1954.

There can be little doubt that the Telecaster, the Precision Bass, and the Stratocaster designs—not to mention the Jazzmaster, Jaguar, and Jazz Bass—will be around in various guises for many years to come, a testament to the quiet genius of Leo Fender and his team.

1950 Fender Broadcaster

1950 Fender Broadcaster
This was the instrument that established the idea of the modern, mass-produced, solidbody electric guitar. The California-based Fender company's revolutionary Broadcaster of 1950 was soon renamed Telecaster, and as such it is still in production 60 years and more since its introduction.

EARLY ELECTRICS

1952 Gibson Les Paul Model (Gold Top)
Gibson soon followed Leo Fender's lead and produced a solidbody electric guitar. This example from the launch year, pissibly a prototype, has unusual black-cover pickups (usually white). Nicknamed the Gold Top for its distinctive finish, the model was replaced by the sunburst Standard in 1958. The Gold Top has been reissued regularly by Gibson since then.

1952 Gibson Les Paul Model (Gold Top)

2007 Fender catalogue featuring a '51 Nocaster Closet Classic (above)
"Closet Classic" is the name Fender gives to the particular type of aging process it has applied to this brand-new guitar: "Built as if bought new in its respective year and played a few times, then put carefully away. Has a few small dings, checked finish, oxidized hardware and aged plastic parts."
Leo Fender in the factory at Fullerton c.1954 (below)
The founder of the Fender company is pictured by a punch press in his Fullerton, California, factory, probably during 1954. By this time, the Broadcaster had become the Telecaster, and the new Stratocaster model was just being launched.

1951 Fender "Nocaster"

1951 Fender "Nocaster"
The Fender Broadcaster was the shortlived production model of Fender's new revolutionary solidbody. The Gretsch drum company objected to the use of the name as they already marketed Broadkaster drums. Fender looked for a new name, but in the meantime it snipped the name from the headstock decals, resulting in what are now known as "Nocaster" models.

CHAPTER THREE
SOLIDBODY ELECTRIC GUITARS

The solidbody electric guitar is a relatively recent invention, and many contemporary makers now take advantage of modern mass-production methods in their workshops and factories so that they can produce a precisely tooled and cost-effective instrument.

The Fender company, with prime 1950s innovations such as the Telecaster and the Stratocaster, did more than any other maker to foster these production systems. Its guitars, and those of many major makers, are based on the idea of modular construction: necks and bodies can be made separately and bolted together; controls, pickups, and wiring are fitted to a pickguard, which is then screwed to a body with routed channels that will house these components; and other hardware, including the bridge, machine heads, and jack, is screwed to the body.

There are, of course, exceptions and variations. Glued-in necks are a traditional alternative to the bolt-on type, primarily on guitars made by or in the style of the Gibson company, notably the Les Paul models. Another method, known as the through-neck design, has the neck made from a single or laminated piece of wood that travels the length of the guitar. Wooden "wings" are then added to complete the body shape.

Today, the classic wooden Stratocaster and Les Paul designs remain the blueprints for the stylish, modern, mass-produced electric guitar, despite many makers' eternal experiments with different shapes and materials.

FENDER
TELECASTER

The Fender Telecaster is the longest-running electric solidbody guitar still in production, a brilliantly simple piece of design that works as well today as it did when it was introduced in 1951.

In fact, the Telecaster was simply Fender's original Broadcaster electric under a new name, the company being forced to change it when Gretsch claimed prior rights to the name. But Leo Fender and his small workforce in Fullerton, California, must have been delighted with the new Telecaster name, its thoroughly modern reference to the emerging medium of television just right for an equally innovative device like the Telecaster, the first commercially marketed solid electric guitar.

The Telecaster – usually abbreviated in discussion or print to the suitably simple Tele, a nickname so popular, Fender has registered it as a trademark – is known for its bright cutting tone and its straightforward, no-nonsense operation. For these reasons it has been used throughout its long history by players from all kinds of musical backgrounds, delivering the stinging slide lines of Muddy Waters' electrified Chicago blues, all the way through to the present-day arena-rock stylings of Radiohead and a seemingly never-ending roll call of modern acts.

However, it is with country musicians that the instrument has seen most consistent service. Its neck pickup tone has become synonymous with driving country rhythm, and its bridge pickup feels like home to countless Nashville chicken pickers. The genre's players also particularly value the Tele's ability, in talented hands, to emulate steel guitar sounds.

The secret of the Tele's sound centers on the bridge. The strings pass through the body and are anchored at the back by six ferrules, giving solidity and sustain to the resulting sound. A slanting-back pickup is incorporated into the bridge, enhancing the guitar's natural treble tone.

1959 Fender Esquire

1959 Fender Esquire (above), 1952 Fender Esquire (above right) First produced between 1951 and 1970, this was a one-pickup version of the normal Tele, minus the neck pickup (although Fender used Tele bodies for the Esquire with all the pickup routing). Controls looked identical, but the selector provided three versatile settings.

1964 Fender Telecaster with B-Bender The B-Bender device beloved of country guitarists for its steel-guitar-esque sound was originally called the Parsons/White Pull-String, and early prototypes were intended to mechanically alter the pitch of the E, B, D, and G strings.

1964 Fender Telecaster with B-Bender

1952 Fender Esquire

"You won't part with yours either"

You Won't Part With Yours Either
Fender upped its promo power when it hired a new ad agency in 1957, and with it, the vision of Bob Perine. His most famous innovation was the humorous series of *You Won't Part With Yours Either* ads, starring Fender guitars in the most unlikely situations. Two examples are shown above, while the 1959 amplification ad demonstrates that almost any Fender promo material of the Perine period could boast a dose of charm and style. Perine also refined the famous Fender logo, and his design is still in use today.

LISTEN!

1952 Fender Telecaster

1952 Fender Telecaster
Leo Fender's groundbreaking design would have set you back $189.50 in 1951—when the average family income was around $3,700. This early example sums up the elegant simplicity that lives on in today's Telecaster.

STEEL FEEL
A number of add-on gadgets have been developed for the Telecaster that take further its inherent ability to make sounds suited for country music. One of the earliest of such devices was called the B-Bender, invented in the late 1960s by two guitarists from country-rock group The Byrds: Gene Parsons and Clarence White. The Parsons/White B-Bender employs a system of levers inside the body, connecting the bridge to the top strap button. When the player "pulls" on the strap, the levers raise the pitch of the B-string, giving bends within chords to emulate sounds associated with the pedal-steel guitar.

The Bigsby Palm Pedal was simpler. Pushing one of the two levers behind the bridge raised the pitch of the B- or G-string for similar effects. A refinement of this idea is the Hipshot, which in its optional Parsons-Green version more or less combines the effects of a B-Bender and a Palm Pedal.

FENDER
TELECASTER II

The Telecaster underwent little modification during its first decades. Few guitars that have been around even half as long as the Tele have survived without some interference. But Fender evidently realized very soon that a large part of the Telecaster's success was due to its unencumbered simplicity, and made only relatively conservative alterations to the design of Leo's iconic original, which was characterized by its all-maple neck, its blonde natural finish, and its contrasting black pickguard. Changes included a rosewood fingerboard and eight-screw pickguard, from 1959 to 1965; a new neckplate in 1965; and a six-saddle bridge and neck-tilt adjuster on 1988's American Standard model.

Not that Fender has left the Tele entirely alone. In addition to the exceptions already noted, we can mention the Custom version of the Telecaster, which was made between 1959 and 1970, featuring a sunburst finish and a bound-edge body. This should not be confused with the later Telecaster Custom model, easily identified by its humbucking neck pickup.

In the 1980s, cost-cutting produced the short-lived Standard, differing most noticeably in its lack of through-body stringing, which instantly diminished the Tele sound. Gold hardware made fleeting appearances in the 1980s on the black-finish Black & Gold Tele and the Gold version of the Elite Telecaster.

1989 Fender 40th Anniversary Telecaster
Fender's fledgling Custom Shop created a limited run of 300 of these variants on the American Standard model. Deluxe touches include the bound body faced with figured maple and gold hardware. Country star Keith Urban relies on a heavily modified version as his main guitar.

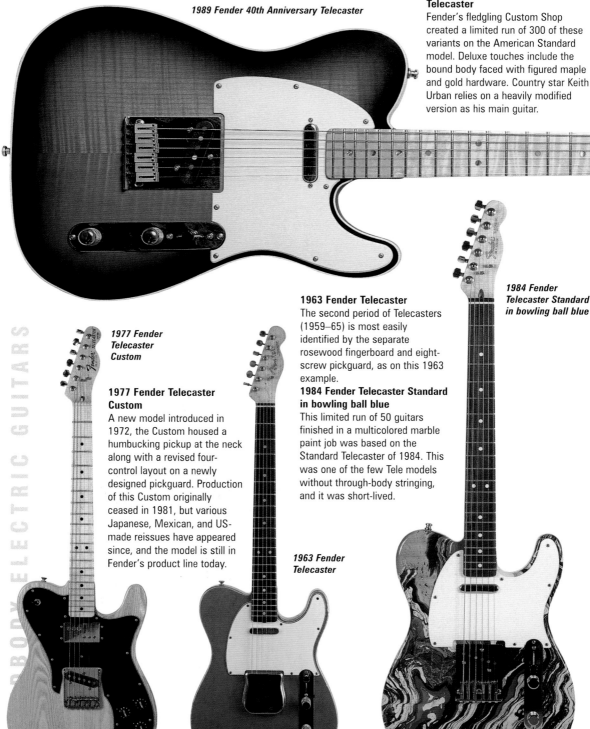

1989 Fender 40th Anniversary Telecaster

1984 Fender Telecaster Standard in bowling ball blue

1977 Fender Telecaster Custom

1977 Fender Telecaster Custom
A new model introduced in 1972, the Custom housed a humbucking pickup at the neck along with a revised four-control layout on a newly designed pickguard. Production of this Custom originally ceased in 1981, but various Japanese, Mexican, and US-made reissues have appeared since, and the model is still in Fender's product line today.

1963 Fender Telecaster
The second period of Telecasters (1959–65) is most easily identified by the separate rosewood fingerboard and eight-screw pickguard, as on this 1963 example.

1984 Fender Telecaster Standard in bowling ball blue
This limited run of 50 guitars finished in a multicolored marble paint job was based on the Standard Telecaster of 1984. This was one of the few Tele models without through-body stringing, and it was short-lived.

1963 Fender Telecaster

POSTWAR ELECTRIC GUITARS

1971 Fender Thinline Telecaster

1971 Fender Thinline Telecaster
This guitar is actually a semi-hollow Thinline (note the f-hole). The model first appeared in 1968 sporting conventional Tele hardware and a new "pearloid" pickguard. From 1971 to 1979 it accommodated two humbuckers and a six-way bridge, and the concept has inspired various recent reissues.

Blue Flower Telecaster flyer from 1968 (right)
The catalogue's cover star was a pretty far-out psychedelic Blue Flower model.

1982 Fender reissue catalogue (far right)
Fender Japan built this high-quality, highly prized '52 Reissue model in 1982.

1975 Fender ad (below)
Proving the 1970s decade was a strange one for Fender, this ad sees Goldilocks playing bass with a Tele-toting Papa Bear.

1983 Fender Gold Elite Telecaster

1990 Fender Jerry Donahue prototype

1976 Fender Telecaster Deluxe

1983 Fender Gold Elite Telecaster
This distinctly different Tele was introduced in 1983. It featured new pickups, circuitry, and hardware. However, its upscale image met with little success, and it was withdrawn the following year.

1990 Fender Jerry Donahue prototype
In the late 1980s, Fender started to make signature guitars endorsed by well-known players. This prototype for a Jerry Donahue model coupled the familiar Tele feel with custom wiring and a Strat neck pickup, offering a range of Strat-like tones as well as Tele sounds.

1976 Fender Telecaster Deluxe
Available from 1973 to 1981, this model had a Strat-like headstock, contoured body, and two humbuckers. This mid-1970s example is one of a small number that came with a Strat-style vibrato.

FENDER
TELECASTER III

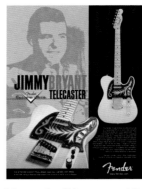

There was a time in the 2000s that every new chart-topping guitar slinger on both sides of the Atlantic was suddenly head-over-heels in love with the Telecaster. From Franz Ferdinand, Coldplay, and Radiohead in Britain to Arcade Fire, John 5, and Brad Paisley in North America, this latest resurgence in popularity has shown no signs of diminishing and is testament to the remarkably enduring design of Leo Fender and his team.

Recent Fender variations on the theme have reflected the instrument's appeal not only to the vintage-guitar aficionado but also to a new species of rock player drawn to humbucker-equipped versions of the Telecaster for their solidity and playability. The Fender Custom Shop's 2011 60th anniversary Tele-bration line stays within the classic silhouette while playfully revisiting some of the Tele's key design features and materials. Fender's retro-focused Relic and Road Worn lines have also zeroed in on the Telecaster, while reissues of the humbuckered Custom, Deluxe, and Thinline Telecasters of the 1970s have been well received.

Fender has also attempted to meet the demands of the modern rock player for richer, darker sounds by issuing signature models such as the John 5 Triple Tele Deluxe triple-humbucker model, the Blacktop Series, with their "raw humbucking power," and the envelope-pushing high-end Special Edition Customs.

1997 Fender Hellecaster Will Ray Jazz-A-Caster

2004 Fender ad for Jimmy Bryant Tribute Telecaster (top rght)
The influential 1950s country guitar hero was the Telecaster's first endorsee, and this ash-bodied Tribute has Nocaster pickups and a hand-tooled leather pickguard overlay.
2007 Fender ad for John 5 Triple Tele Deluxe (above)
Rob Zombie guitarist and solo artist John 5 combines speedy shred, twanging country picking, and behind-the-nut bending styles, and Fender has honored him with several signature Telecaster models.

2007 Fender Joe Strummer Telecaster

2002 Fender "Go Cat Go" Telecaster

2002 Fender "Go Cat Go" Telecaster
A highly decorated fingerboard and blue sparkle body make this Carl Perkins Telecaster a signature Custom Shop product. Note the Fender-licensed Bigsby vibrato.

2010 Fender American Deluxe Telecaster

1994 Fender Custom Shop Egyptian Telecaster

2010 Fender American Deluxe Telecaster

This 21st-century refit of the Telecaster features N3 Noiseless pickups, S-1 switching, and an American Tele bridge with six chromed-brass saddles.

1997 Fender Hellecaster Will Ray Jazz-A-Caster

This signature model hybrid, which has a gold foil leaf finish and a four-way switching system, is also fitted with a modified bridge incorporating a Hipshot String Bending System to bend the second string up a whole step.

2007 Fender Joe Strummer Telecaster

Based on a classic '60s Telecaster, this replica of the Clash guitarist's Tele comes complete with a distressed finish to the body and neck, "aged" metal parts, and an art customization kit designed by graphic artist Shepard Fairey.

1994 Fender Custom Shop Egyptian Telecaster

An example of the high-end "art guitars" line, this one-off guitar from Fender Master Builder Fred Stuart has snakes and runes carved by George Amicay.

2007 Fender ad for Avril Lavigne Telecaster (above)

Canadian Grammy nominee Avril Lavigne became a Telecaster endorsee in 2007, putting her name to a single-humbucker Squier model.

1992 Fender Set Neck Telecaster Country Artist

2009 Fender Special Edition Custom Spalted Maple Tele

1992 Fender Set Neck Telecaster Country Artist

This mahogany-bodied Telecaster has a glued-in "set" neck and a humbucker pickup in the neck position, and replaces the classic chrome control plate with a gold six-saddle version.

2009 Fender Special Edition Custom Spalted Maple Tele

This unusual Special Edition, with a set-neck and a carved body front featuring highly-figured timber, has two Seymour Duncan coverless humbucking pickups and the six-saddle bridge.

FENDER STRATOCASTER
EARLY MODELS

The Fender Stratocaster is arguably the most popular and most emulated solid electric guitar ever. Launched in early 1954, it was designed by Leo Fender with his colleagues at the Fender Electric Instrument Co and a number of local musicians, including country guitarist Bill Carson.

The Fender company of Fullerton, California, had already pioneered the solidbody electric with its Telecaster model. The stylish Stratocaster, epitome of 1950s tailfin-flash design, built upon the Fender team's idea of a guitar engineered for mass production rather than handcrafted for individual players. It had three pickups where most electrics had one or two, there was a vibrato unit to bend the pitch of the strings and return them more or less to accurate tuning, there was adjustment for all six strings at the bridge, a dramatically contoured body for player comfort, and an output jack recessed into the front of the body.

From the rear, a four-screw neck/body joining plate was visible, along with a plastic cover plate covering a pocket machined into the body, which contained the five tension springs of the ingenious vibrato unit.

Musicians were amazed, and have been ever since – testament to the genius of Fender in the 1950s.

1954 catalogue cover

1954 Fender Stratocaster
The Stratocaster incorporated refinements of many of the Telecaster's key characteristics, and was also strongly influenced by the twin-horned aesthetic of 1951's Precision Bass. This early Strat has a maple neck with an ash body; Fender changed the body wood mainly to alder in 1956. The single-ply pickguard is also an early Stratocaster feature. This specimen has a neck date of May, placing it in the earliest months of production.

1954 Fender Stratocaster

SOLID ELECTRIC GUITARS

1956 catalogue

Two classic Fender ads from 1956 designed by Bob Perine
Fender's early press campaigns placed guitars in the hands of daredevil skydivers, surfers, and a cast of wholesome Californians.

1954 Fender Stratocaster

1958 Fender Mary Kaye Stratocaster
A rarity for the period, this guitar has gold-plated hardware and a blonde finish more usually associated with Telecasters. Today, this model is known as the "Mary Kaye" after that musician appeared with one in Fender catalogues, starting in the late 1950s.

1958 Fender Mary Kaye Stratocaster

1954 Fender Stratocaster
This guitar has an unusual non-standard finish, an aluminum pickguard, and the serial number 0001. However, evidence suggests that it was not the first Strat made, but perhaps a special one-off model. It's now owned by legendary Pink Floyd guitarist David Gilmour, who played it at a special Fender concert celebrating the Strat's 50th anniversary in 2004.

1954 press ad

FENDER STRATOCASTER
CUSTOM COLORS

Guitarists in the 1950s were mostly a conservative lot: by and large, guitars had sunburst finishes, and that was what the players expected. But the Stratocaster design called for more—and got it.

The futuristic design of the Strat was clearly influenced by American automobiles of the 1950s, so it was hardly surprising that when Fender started to offer custom colors later in the decade, they chose Du Pont paints, originally designed for use on cars.

Early custom color Strats have become highly prized by collectors, mainly because relatively few survive in good, original condition. Some of the most alluring colors have equally romantic names, such as Lake Placid Blue, Burgundy Mist, Shoreline Gold, Surf Green, or Fiesta Red. No collection is complete without one. Even the Strat's standard two-tone sunburst finish was updated with the introduction of a three-tone blend, adding red to the original black and yellow shading.

The first major alteration to the Strat came in 1959, when Fender decided to change from the original maple neck with integral fingerboard to a two-piece construction with a separate rosewood playing surface. This revision had first appeared the previous year on the Jazzmaster model, and would soon be applied across the Fender line. The amendment also affected the way the truss-rod was installed, and the maple neck accordingly no longer needed the contrasting "skunk stripe" fillet along the back.

Until mid 1962, the fingerboard had a flat base (leading to its later "slab board" nickname), and it then changed to a curve that matched the top-surface radius. After about a year, the rosewood was thinned to almost a veneer, and this style remained until the early '80s.

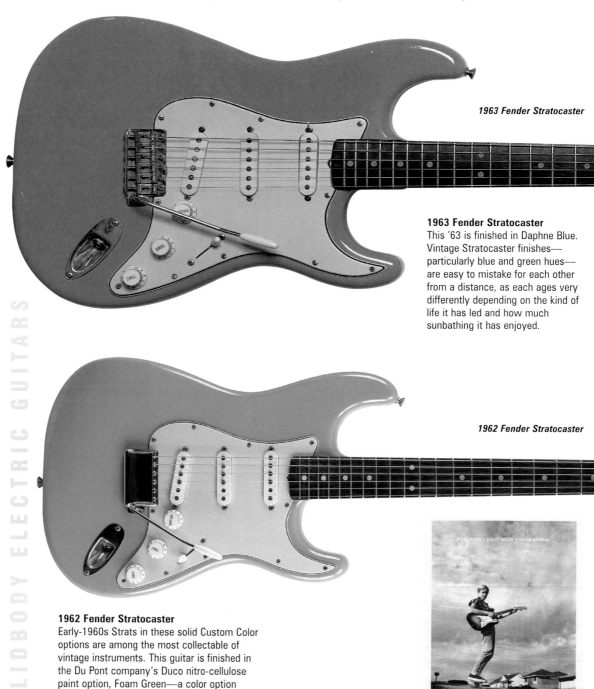

1963 Fender Stratocaster

1963 Fender Stratocaster
This '63 is finished in Daphne Blue. Vintage Stratocaster finishes—particularly blue and green hues—are easy to mistake for each other from a distance, as each ages very differently depending on the kind of life it has led and how much sunbathing it has enjoyed.

1962 Fender Stratocaster

1962 Fender Stratocaster
Early-1960s Strats in these solid Custom Color options are among the most collectable of vintage instruments. This guitar is finished in the Du Pont company's Duco nitro-cellulose paint option, Foam Green—a color option associated with Buick. Note the flashy gold-plated hardware.

1958 press ad

SOLIDBODY ELECTRIC GUITARS

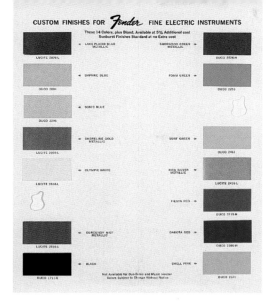

1961 Custom Color chart

1964 Fender Stratocaster

1964 Fender Stratocaster
This guitar is finished in Sonic Blue and still has the original vibrato cover. Over time, the wear on some vintage finishes gradually testifies to the fact that multiple layers of paints were sometimes applied in the Fender factory: sometimes undercoats were skipped, or poorly applied finishes served as undercoats.

1958 Fender Stratocaster

1959 catalogue cover

1961 Fender Stratocaster

1958 Fender Stratocaster
The gold finish of this 1958 specimen is set off by its matching hardware and the maple neck. Fender's rival, Gibson, had already introduced gold paints on its ES-295 and Les Paul from 1952, and while the Goldtop became an object of desire among guitarists, gold finishes on Strats never had the same impact.

1961 Fender Stratocaster
Adding a custom color to a guitar increased the retail price by five per cent, adding up to $303.97 at the time. This guitar is finished in Burgundy Mist Metallic, a color that lasted in the catalogue until 1965, and was revived most prominently in 2012 as an option on Fender's 50th Anniversary Jaguar.

1959 Fender Stratocaster
Fiesta Red was one of Fender's first custom color finishes and has since become its most famous. George Fullerton recalled that he had a local paint shop mix the first batch of what came to be known as Fiesta Red in 1957. In the UK, the influence of Hank Marvin's iconic 1959 Strat ensured that, for some time, Fiesta Red was the only color to own.

1959 Fender Stratocaster

SOLIDBODY ELECTRIC GUITARS

FENDER STRATOCASTER
CHANGING FACES

The Stratocaster has survived for nearly 60 years with very few changes, proof that Fender's original design was uncannily right. It has lent itself to every conceivable style of music, and even Leo Fender could surely not have guessed how great the demand for his Strat would become.

It peaked in popularity during the 1960s, and then again in the 1980s when its clean, cutting sound could complete with the newly popular synthesizers. Even the challenger to the Strat's world-domination, the so-called "superstrat" (see page 136), borrowed heavily from the original.

In the 1970s, noticing that many players were stripping down guitar bodies to the wood, Fender offered a range of natural finishes to meet this demand. Fender has obligingly catered since to cosmetic trends for outrageous color schemes with the likes of purple frosts and crimson bursts, right up to the present-day obsession with artificially-aged "Relic'd" finishes.

It wasn't until the 1980s that Fender made alterations to the previously sacrosanct classic Stratocaster, and even then, the variations were subtle. There was the distinctly heavy all-walnut Strat early in the decade, along with the Gold Strat's glittering finish and hardware. Later on came the Elite models, with pushbuttons to select the plain-cover pickups, and more recently the Strat Ultra, with an extra single-coil at the bridge.

Fender is faced with a tricky choice over its modern Stratocaster. The company is keen to innovate and update the model, but it seems musicians want the classic Strat—and probably always will. An update to the American Standard Stratocaster model in 2012, with its combination of modern and vintage pickup options, and aged plastic parts contrasting with a new body contour, sums up the tension between old and new that will probably always continue to define the Stratocaster.

1966 Fender Stratocaster

1966 Fender Stratocaster
During 1965, following the company's $13 million sale to CBS, the headstock of the Stratocaster was changed—officially to ease warping problems. The new broader style brought the Strat in line with the Jazzmaster and Jaguar, and it lasted until the early 1980s.

1983 Fender Standard Stratocaster
This unremarkable-looking low-budget Strat featured plenty of refinements, almost all added to make the Stratocaster cheaper to produce. It had two knobs instead of three and relocated the jack socket in the pickguard; Fender also changed the neck, truss rod, bridge, tremolo system, pickguard, and even the logo.

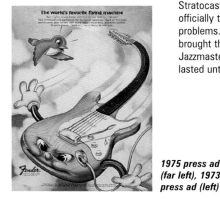

1975 press ad (far left), 1973 press ad (left)

1983 Fender Standard Stratocaster

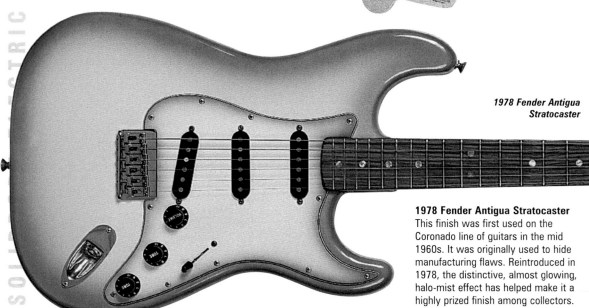

1978 Fender Antigua Stratocaster

1978 Fender Antigua Stratocaster
This finish was first used on the Coronado line of guitars in the mid 1960s. It was originally used to hide manufacturing flaws. Reintroduced in 1978, the distinctive, almost glowing, halo-mist effect has helped make it a highly prized finish among collectors.

100

1980 Fender International Color Stratocaster

Fender introduced a range of guitars in lurid colors (among them Morocco Red, Monaco Yellow, Maui Blue, and Sahara Taupe) in 1980. This example is in Capri Orange, and the range combined bright white pickguards with contrasting black pickup covers and control knobs.

1980 Fender The Strat

This model, introduced at the NAMM Show in 1980, officially used the Strat abbreviation. It reflects the trends of the time, with brass hardware, a hot X-1 bridge pickup, four additional tone selections, and color-matched heads.

1979 Fender 25th Anniversary Stratocaster

To celebrate 25 years of Strat production, this 1979 model had an "Anniversary" body logo and deluxe machine heads. The first 500 came in white, but severe cracking meant a change to a more appropriate special silver finish. Supposedly a limited edition, around 10,000 were made up to 1980.

1980 Fender International Color Stratocaster

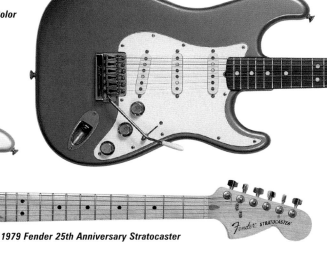

1980 Fender The Strat

1979 Fender 25th Anniversary Stratocaster

1965 catalogue

1983 Fender Elite Stratocaster

1983 Fender Elite Stratocaster

The Stratocaster received similar treatment to the Elite Tele. Three redesigned pickups were fitted to the Strat Elite, together with a hum-cancelling dummy coil and active circuit. The five-way selector was replaced by three pushbuttons. The new Freeflyte vibrato system was an operational disaster and a major contributor to the model's failure. This example has the blue Stratoburst shaded finish.

FENDER STRATOCASTER
MODERN MODELS

Fender's strength continued to grow alongside the breadth of its catalogue in the 1990s, but a studied look back over the shoulder continued to offer a reliable means of success in model development. Namely, more players than ever seemed to want guitars that not only were made like they were in the old days, but also looked like they were made 30 or 40 years ago.

After building a handful of aged or "distressed" instruments for name artists, often as replicas of much-played favorite guitars that had become too valuable to take on tour, the Fender Custom Shop formally introduced its Relic series in 1995. These guitars included intentional dings, scuffs, scratches, and "arm rubs" in the finish, along with artificially aged and tarnished hardware.

The line proved extremely popular, and in fact the Mary Kaye Stratocaster (a blonde-finish version of the 1956 Stratocaster with gold-plated hardware, on page 97) proved the Custom Shop's bestseller of the late 1990s.

Between the official launch of the Relics in 1995 and May of 1999, the aging of bodies, necks, and parts assembled at the Custom Shop was outsourced to Vince Cunetto in Bolivar, Missouri. He would go on to provide the look that came to define the Relic series.

Later, in 1998, Fender expanded the distressed line into the Time Machine series, which included the relatively well-aged Relics, the gently aged Closet Classics, and the entirely un-distressed N.O.S. guitars (N.O.S. means new old stock, a term commonly used for amp tubes made many years ago, but which have remained unused on the shelf and are therefore in "new" condition.)

In 1999, Fender moved the aging of all Time Machine models in-house, although the majority of Closet Classic guitars were already being produced in the Custom Shop itself during 1998, as of course were the non-aged N.O.S. guitars. The Relics of 1995–99, known in collector's parlance as Cunetto-era, have become collector's items.

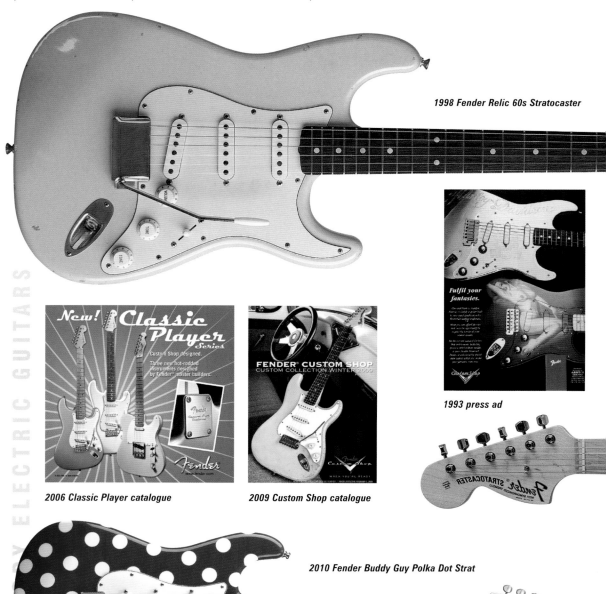

1998 Fender Relic 60s Stratocaster

1993 press ad

2006 Classic Player catalogue

2009 Custom Shop catalogue

2010 Fender Buddy Guy Polka Dot Strat

2010 Fender Buddy Guy Polka Dot Strat
This Strat originally came in white with black polka dots, but Fender added this colour combination in 2010.

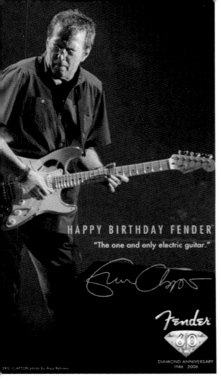

2006 press ad featuring Eric Clapton

1997 Fender Carved Top Strat

1997 Fender Carved Top Strat
This has a PRS-like carved and figured timber body, a roller nut and locking tuners, and a modern configuration of pickup layout and associated controls.

2004 Fender American Deluxe Ash Stratocaster
An ash-bodied model in the American Deluxe series, this guitar comes with staggered-height locking tuners and the recent S-1 switching system.

2004 Fender American Deluxe Ash Stratocaster

1998 Fender Relic 60s Stratocaster
This Relic Strat, with artificially aged finish, was made in the year that Fender renamed these models as part of the Time Machine series.

1997 Jimi Hendrix Stratocaster

1998 Fender Regina Del Mare Strat

1998 Fender Regina Del Mare Strat
This was the third Regina del Mare Strat made in the Custom Shop for Fender's Catalina Island Blues Festival.

1997 Jimi Hendrix Stratocaster
A reversed version of the late-1960s Strat used by Hendrix, who played regular Strats upside down. This version is a left-handed guitar turned upside down and restrung for a right-handed player.

1996 Fender Lone Star Strat
This is similar to an American Standard Stratocaster but fitted with hot pickups including a Seymour Duncan bridge position humbucker.

1996 Fender Lone Star Strat

SOLIDBODY ELECTRIC GUITARS

FENDER MODELS
VARIATIONS ON A THEME

Fender's other electric guitars tend to be overshadowed by the spectacular success of the Stratocaster and the hardly less impressive achievements of the Telecaster. Yet from the 1950s to the 1990s, Fender issued over a dozen different models in addition to their celebrated duo, some of which are excellent, and each one of which possesses its own unique sounds.

In 1965, the huge CBS Corporation paid $13 million for the Fender companies, and Leo Fender departed soon after to form CLF Research (which later manufactured Music Man guitars). Once Leo's association with the Fender brand ended, there was little innovation in design, and there was an apparent loss of quality.

In the face of increasing Far Eastern competition, mainly in the form of cheaper, well-produced copies, CBS set up Fender Japan in 1982. Initial production concentrated, naturally, on high-quality copies of the most popular Fender vintage originals, alongside cheaper versions marketed under the Squier brand name (taken from the name of a string-making company bought by Fender in the 1960s; see pages 106–109). An expanded mid-1980s range boasted new models and updated design ideas and hardware.

More copies appeared, reproducing the majority of the Fender USA range and spanning all price brackets. Fender Japan then seemed to tire of copying and tried its first original designs, the Master Series of 1984. But these were unusually unconventional and quite different from Fender's regular style, as was the quirky but equally short-lived Katana from 1985. These were followed in the same year by the angular Performer, but it also proved unpopular.

A new outlook came eventually in 1985 when the existing Fender management, headed by Bill Schultz and Dan Smith, bought the company back from CBS and successfully set about returning Fender to consistent quality production, both in the USA and the Far East.

1986 Fender Performer

1986 Fender Performer
This high-quality American design from 1985 was the projected flagship of Fender's new range. Despite being a brave departure from the company's design traditions, production problems as the company changed hands and poor reaction led to its early retirement in 1986.

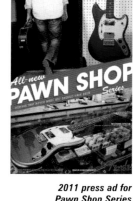

2011 press ad for Pawn Shop Series featuring a Mustang Special

1964 Fender Jaguar

1964 Fender Jaguar
With the same styling as the Jazzmaster, but with a shorter-scale 22-fret neck, and switches for pickup on/off and tonal variation, the Jaguar (1962–1975) was Fender's most expensive solid. It was never a huge success in the day but was reissued in 1986.
1971 Fender Mustang
A relatively low-end guitar for the student that became popular with 1990s grunge acts—particularly Kurt Cobain, frontman of Nirvana, whose chosen models were reissued in 2012.

SOLIDBODY ELECTRIC GUITARS

1957 press ad for the Musicmaster

1967 press ad for the Jazzmaster

c.1972 Fender Bronco

1963 Fender Jazzmaster

1963 Fender Jazzmaster

This misleadingly named guitar was Fender's top-of-the-line solid when introduced in 1958, with a new offset-waist body and a richer, deeper sound from the wide coils of the steel-guitar-like pickups. Yet another long-running Fender model, it remained virtually unchanged until dropped in 1980. It was reissued by Fender Japan in 1986.

c.1972 Fender Bronco

The Bronco was a budget-line student model with a single pickup, a 24-inch scale length, and a simple vibrato, Leo Fender's fourth design. It was initially sold as part of a package with a small Fender Bronco amplifier, a re-badged Vibro-Champ.

1966 Fender Marauder

1966 Fender Marauder

This prototype from an ill-fated attempt to introduce a new model has slanting frets and a multitude of switches. It never made it into production in its original format, but Fender did introduce a loose approximation of it with the 2011 Modern Player Marauder, equipped with a novel Triplebucker pickup.

1971 Fender Mustang

1999 press ad

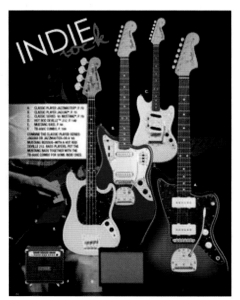

A press ad from 2010 stresses the alternatives

FENDER MODELS
GRUNGE & SQUIER

Fenders beyond the ubiquitous Strats and Teles proved popular with 1990s grunge guitarists, and once again showed the strong impact that player identification can have on a model's popularity. Seattle guitar-anti-hero Kurt Cobain of Nirvana had played Jaguars and Mustangs; Steve Turner in Mudhoney opted for a Mustang; J. Mascis of Dinosaur Jr. was often seen with his Jazzmaster. And the reason was relatively straightforward. These guitars had the comforting Fender logo on the headstock, but could be bought more cheaply second-hand than Strats or Teles. The ethics suited grunge perfectly.

Back in 1993, Cobain decided to take cut-up photos of his Jag and Mustang and stick them together, this way and that, trying combinations to see what they could look like. Larry Brooks of the Custom Shop took Cobain's paste-ups, assembled the design, and added a contour or two to improve balance and feel. After Cobain's untimely death in 1994, his family collaborated with Fender to release a Japanese-made production version of the instrument, named the Fender Jag-Stang. Cobain's guitar hit the market in 1996.

As grunge exploded, an Associated Press wire report for March 21 1991 marked a sad occasion: "Clarence Leo Fender, whose revolutionary Stratocaster was the guitar of choice for rock stars from Buddy Holly to Jimi Hendrix, died today. He was 82. Fender was found unconscious in his Fullerton home by his wife, Phyllis, and died on the way to the hospital. Fender had suffered Parkinson's disease for decades but continued to work on guitar designs." Leo had been at his bench at his G&L company just the day before, tinkering with yet another guitar improvement.

Fender Jag-Stang reissue ad from 2003 featurng Kurt Cobain

1997 Squier Jagmaster
This guitar was based on a humbuckered Jazzmaster played by Bush's Gavin Rossdale. It was one of the Vista Series of guitars, produced in Japan.

1997 Squier Venus
This guitar was based on a model from the maker Mercury that Hole's rhythm guitarist Courtney Love played. She used several Venus models on stage to avoid damaging her original much-loved Mercury.

1997 Squier Jagmaster

1997 Squier Venus

1991 Fender Prodigy II

1998 press ad for the Toronado

1996 Fender Jag-Stang

Nirvana's Kurt Cobain often played a Mustang or Jaguar, both of which he modified with humbuckers and personalised. Soon after the recording of the band's 1993 *In Utero* LP, Kurt cut up some pictures of his guitars and stuck the top half of his Jag onto the bottom half of the Mustang. Then he took his handiwork to Fender's Custom Shop, where builder Larry Brooks came up with a special customised instrument.

1996 Fender Jag-Stang

1989 ad for Japanese HM Strats

1997 Squier Super-Sonic

1997 Squier Super-Sonic

The Squier marketing manager Joe Carducci was inspired to design this third Vista Series guitar by a photograph of Jimi Hendrix playing a Fender Jaguar upside-down. Crafted in Japan, it had a reverse headstock, a 24-inch scale, and two Seymour Duncan-designed humbuckers.

1991 Fender Prodigy II

Yet another superstrat competitor was the Prodigy, with an offset body and sharper horns than a Strat, the defining two single-coils and bridge humbucker layout, and an optional locking vibrato.

The Prodigy was one of the first guitars to receive attention at Fender's new Mexican factory, located just across the California/Mexico border at Ensenada, although the model was officially US-made.

FENDER MODELS
SQUIER IDENTITY

Fender's decision to introduce a budget line of guitars in 1982, under the resurrected brand name of a string manufacturer it had acquired years earlier, proved to be a smart business move. In the 30 years since, many budding rock stars will have made their first forays into the guitar world on a Squier, and by and large, Fender's budget brand won't have let them down.

Squier originally arose as a reaction to an alarming rise in quality in Japanese copycat brands—chiefly Tokai—that were being exported around the world and snapping at Fender's heels in the early 1980s. Fender's answer was to rebrand its own line of five guitar models rolling off the Fender Japan production line as "Squier Series" and, initially at least, to sell them in Japan and import them to Europe to see off the upstarts.

Today, the Squier brand is almost as important to the Fender company as Fender itself. Squier has long been a hotbed of creativity for the company's luthiers, who have enjoyed the freedom to be more adventurous and experimental with instrument designs without Fender's

2004 Fender Cyclone II

2004 Fender Cyclone II
A derivative of the Mustang that Fender reintroduced in 1986, this version came with three single-coil pickups with unusual metal "sawtooth" sides and go-faster stripes. Jaguar-style switching was also a feature. All variations of the Cyclone had been discontinued by 2007.

2004 Fender Showmaster QBT-HH

2004 Fender Showmaster QBT-HH
Fender started using fancy timbers on the later versions of its Showmaster Series, such as carved quilted bubinga tops. These high-end superstrat guitars had set (glued-in) necks and Seymour Duncan humbuckers.

2003 Squier Showmaster H Jimmy Shine SLE

2003 Squier Showmaster ad with Sepultura

heritage hemming them in. One-off curios such as 2005's Squier '51 and 2012's Squier Vintage Modified Surf Stratocaster have turned the head of many a conventional Fender lover. Pro artists such as Chuck Prophet, Biffy Clyro's Simon Neil, Avril Lavigne, John 5, and others have lent credibility to the brand. Squier has also benefited from the Fender Custom Shop's design expertise steadily filtering down into its product lines.

Fender has also shown enthusiasm for occupying a market niche in the hinterland between Fender and Squier, producing occasional lines of instruments that either fall between both camps (such as the mass-aged Road Worn series) or stray into non-artist signature-guitar territory (like the Jimmy Shine SLE model, bottom).

Add the Custom Shop to the mix, and it's clear Fender has so many lines and potential outlets for off-the-wall designs at its disposal, it'll be keeping the traditionalists guessing for years to come.

Hello Kitty ads from 2006 (left and opposite).

2006 Squier '51

1999 Squier Stagemaster HSH

1999 Squier Stagemaster HSH

Squier was back to the superstrat theme in 1999 with the launch of the Chinese-made reverse-headstock Stagemaster models. The Stagemaster line would evolve into the Showmasters in 2002, but these would last only until around 2005.

2005 Fender So-Cal Speed Shop

Another guitar made for promotional activities at sporting events, this model is named after a specialty parts shop for hot-rod cars based in Pomona, California. Certainly an instrument to get you noticed.

2006 Squier '51

New in 2005, this guitar was a sensation. Justin Norvell wanted a guitar based on the '51 Precision Bass. The result was a guitar cheap enough and modular enough to satisfy a craze for modifying and adapting the wildly popular '51.

M-80 Master Series ad from 2007

2003 Squier Showmaster H Jimmy Shine SLE

Squier reached out to younger rock players with a mobile roadhouse that travelled to sporting events. This promotion featured the Jimmy Shine model, an incongruous tribute to a custom motorcycle maker.

2005 Fender So-Cal Speed Shop

LEO AFTER FENDER
MUSIC MAN & G&L

Despite selling the Fender companies to CBS in 1965, Leo Fender stayed on as a consultant, contributing new ideas and designs (such as the Mustang Bass) until 1970. He then became a partner and major shareholder in Music Man, which had been set up in 1970 by former Fender men Forrest White and Tom Walker. Leo provided two new guitars for Music Man, made by his own company, CLF Research. First was the StingRay, soon followed by the Sabre.

In 1984, Music Man was acquired by the Ernie Ball company, probably best known for its guitar strings. Demand from players meant that the Music Man basses were the first to be revived. The first guitar was launched in 1987.

This first Ernie Ball/Music Man instrument was the Silhouette, an all-new model designed by Dudley Gimpel and developed with the help of country guitarist Albert Lee. The Fender tradition was still apparent, but there were a number of refinements, including a 24-fret neck giving the player a full two octaves per string, a six-bolt neck/body

fixing, a small body, interchangeable pickup/pickguard assemblies in various formats, and a distinctively compact four-and-two headstock. Still in production at the start of the 2010s, this line has enjoyed increasing popularity. In 1987, the Silhouette was joined by the Steve Morse model. This incorporated a multiple-pickup layout along with other individual features requested by this respected guitarist.

Leo established the G&L company in 1980 with George Fullerton (the initials represented the forenames of its two founders). In 1986, Fullerton sold his share to Leo, after which the G&L logo indicated guitars by Leo Fender, although Fullerton continued to work at the factory. The first G&L solid, the F-100, was similar to previous Music Man instruments. More models appeared subsequently, some reflecting changes in players' needs, others trying to introduce rather than follow trends. All have borne typical Leo Fender touches, combining innovation with further refinement of proven features.

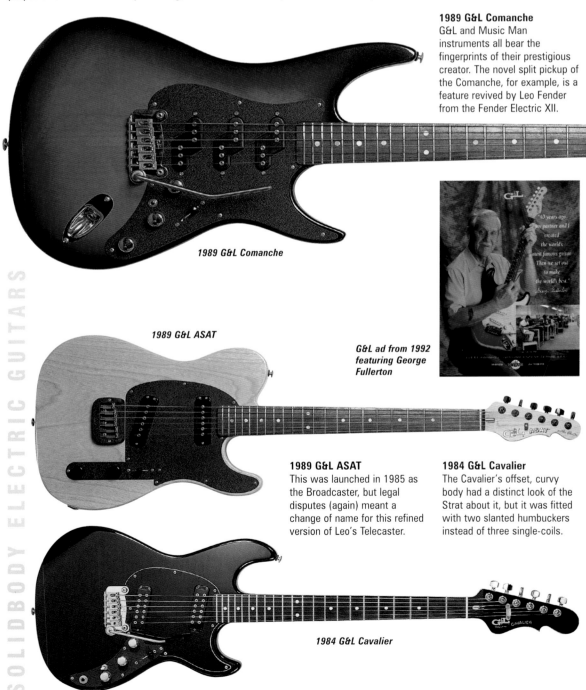

1989 G&L Comanche
G&L and Music Man instruments all bear the fingerprints of their prestigious creator. The novel split pickup of the Comanche, for example, is a feature revived by Leo Fender from the Fender Electric XII.

1989 G&L Comanche

1989 G&L ASAT

G&L ad from 1992 featuring George Fullerton

1989 G&L ASAT
This was launched in 1985 as the Broadcaster, but legal disputes (again) meant a change of name for this refined version of Leo's Telecaster.

1984 G&L Cavalier
The Cavalier's offset, curvy body had a distinct look of the Strat about it, but it was fitted with two slanted humbuckers instead of three single-coils.

1984 G&L Cavalier

SOLIDBODY ELECTRIC GUITARS

110

G&L ads from 1996 and 2007

c.1978 Music Man StingRay

This versatile Leo Fender design was produced between 1976 and 1980, but it never matched the game-changing success of his earlier guitars. Humbucking pickups replaced Fender's familiar complement of single-coils, and in keeping with 1970s trends there was no vibrato.

1993 Music Man Albert Lee

Music Man has made impressive signature guitars, including this odd Albert Lee model.

2000 Music Man Axis Super Sport

The Super Sport comes with the option of P-90-like MM90 pickups, which were the first to be made in-house at the company. Later models of the Super Sport followed the hybrid trend and offered piezo pickups.

1988 Music Man Silhouette

Th Silhouette was the first guitar model from Music Man's new owner, Ernie Ball. This one has a special one-off finish.

*1988 Music Man
Silhouette*

*c.1978 Music Man
StingRay*

*1993 Music Man
Albert Lee*

*2000 Music Man Axis
Super Sport*

1988 Music Man ad with Steve Morse

SOLIDBODY ELECTRIC GUITARS

GIBSON LES PAUL
GOLDTOP

In the early 1950s, the very traditional Gibson company recognized the growing popularity of the revolutionary Fender solidbody electric guitar. It decided to collaborate with Les Paul (1915–2009), a leading guitarist of the time and a keen inventor. The resulting instrument bore his name and some of his ideas, and the first version hit American music stores in 1952.

The styling was pure Gibson: the heavily carved top and classic symmetrical headstock were borrowed from its established archtop guitars, as was the scaled-down yet much heavier solid body. These aspects of the Les Paul

guitar's design, together with features such as the glued-in neck and ornate fingerboard inlays, conveyed Gibson's craftsmanship. They were almost certainly intended to contrast with Fender's slab-bodied instruments and mass-production approach.

Gibson's Les Paul started life as the company's first tentative step toward a modern solidbody instrument, yet the design has remained virtually unchanged throughout its 40-year history. Together with Fender's Telecaster and Stratocaster designs, the Les Paul is among the most popular and emulated electric guitars ever made.

1994 Gibson Les Paul Classic Centennial

1994 Gibson Les Paul Classic Centennial
The Centennial models came with gold hardware, diamond appointments, and a specially inscribed gold pickguard. On the rear of the headstock was a medallion with a portrait of founder Orville Gibson.

1958 Gibson Les Paul Goldtop

1958 Gibson Les Paul Goldtop
Technically known as the fourth version, this Goldtop had Seth Lover's legendary "Patent Applied For" humbucking pickups fitted, from 1957 (the patent was awarded in 1959).

1957 Gibson Les Paul Goldtop
This is a rare factory-made left-handed Goldtop owned today by Paul McCartney. Vintage Goldtops are of course big game

among guitar collectors. For the less wealthy, Gibson's Historic Collection has lovingly recreated various milestones in the development of the Goldtop.

1952 Gibson Les Paul
Goldtop

1954 Gibson Les Paul
Goldtop

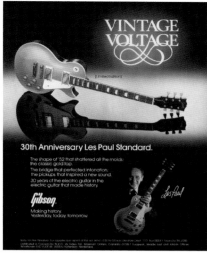

1982 Goldtop anniversary ad

1952 Gibson Les Paul Goldtop
This was the first version of the model, with
two P-90 pickups and associated selector
switch, and with the first trapeze-style
bridge/tailpiece. A similar early specimen
belonging to Les Paul and autographed by
him was auctioned by his estate in 2012,
following Les's death in 2009.
1954 Gibson Les Paul Goldtop
Between 1953 and 1955, the Goldtop had
an angled one-piece bridge/tailpiece. After
1955, it had a new six-saddle Tune-o-matic
bridge patented by Ted McCarty and a
separate stop-bar tailpiece, an innovation
which helped with the individual adjustment
of each string's intonation.

1952 press ad

2010 press ad

1957 Gibson Les Paul Goldtop

GIBSON LES PAUL
CUSTOM

The Custom, which debuted in 1954, had an all-mahogany body, as favoured by Les Paul himself, rather than the maple-mahogany mix of the Goldtop, giving the new guitar a rather mellower tone. Les insisted that Gibson got the timber arrangements the wrong way around, and that as far as he was concerned the cheaper Goldtop should have been all-mahogany, while the costlier Custom should have benefited from the more elaborate maple-and-mahogany combination. The Les Paul Custom was promoted in Gibson catalogues as the "Fretless Wonder" because of its very low, flat fretwire that was different to the wire used on other Les Pauls at the time. Some players favored this style for the way it helped them play more speedily.

In addition to its conventional P-90 at the bridge, the Les Paul Custom featured a new style of pickup at the neck. It was soon nicknamed the Alnico, a reference to the aluminum-nickel-cobalt alloy used for its distinctive rectangular magnetic polepieces (although alnico is used in many other pickups). The new pickup was designed by Seth Lover, a radio and electronics expert who had worked on and off for Gibson in the 1940s and early 1950s, while also teaching and doing installation jobs for the US Navy. Lover rejoined Gibson's electronics department permanently in 1952.

Since the original version of the Custom was announced in 1954, Gibson has produced several versions and reissues in both two- and three-pickup formats.

Since 1997, signature models have been added to the lines, including guitars named for Ace Frehley, Jimmy Page, Steve Jones, and Randy Rhoads. The black Jimmy Page Custom model comes with an optional Bigsby vibrato.

Press ad from 1954

*1974 Gibson Les Paul Custom
20th Anniversary*

1974 Gibson Les Paul Custom 20th Anniversary
This was Gibson's first guitar that celebrated an anniversary at the company, a sign of a growing awareness of the value of its history. This two-humbucker version of the Custom has "Twentieth Anniversary" inlaid into the position marker at the 15th fret.

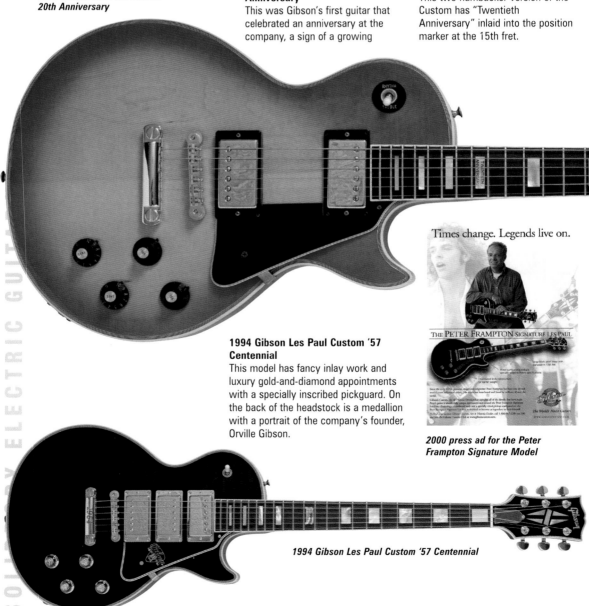

1994 Gibson Les Paul Custom '57 Centennial
This model has fancy inlay work and luxury gold-and-diamond appointments with a specially inscribed pickguard. On the back of the headstock is a medallion with a portrait of the company's founder, Orville Gibson.

2000 press ad for the Peter Frampton Signature Model

1994 Gibson Les Paul Custom '57 Centennial

1954 Gibson Les Paul Custom

1954 Gibson Les Paul Custom
The guitar named the "Black Beauty" has a Tune-o-matic bridge and plastic-covered P-90 and "Alnico" single-coil pickups. The instrument's gold-plated hardware and cream binding to the body and fingerboard help to provide it with a look of restrained quality.

1957 Gibson Les Paul Custom
In 1957, the Custom gained three new Seth Lover-designed humbucking pickups with gold-plated matching covers. The model retained the standard three-way pickup selector, however, so not all pickup selections were available: the middle selection gave middle and bridge together.

1957 Gibson Les Paul Custom

Ad from 1957

1968 Gibson Les Paul Custom
This model has two humbucking pickups instead of three, along with a body that has a maple cap—like the original Goldtop—instead of the solid mahogany body of the original Custom.

1968 Gibson Les Paul Custom

Ad from 1997 featuring Ace Frehley

SOLIDBODY ELECTRIC GUITARS

GIBSON LES PAUL
STANDARD

In 1958, Gibson replaced the Les Paul Goldtop with the Standard model, an identical guitar except for its more conservative three-tone sunburst finish; at last the maple top could be seen, sometimes to stunning effect. Demand for the Les Paul had dwindled, so perhaps Gibson was trying to attract customers with more traditional tastes who had been deterred by the earlier model's garish gold paint.

Gibson gave up on this model in 1960, and soon launched the SG-style guitar instead. However, later in the decade, players discovered that a Les Paul at high volume produced a desirably thick, sustaining sound, ideal for blues-based music. This renewed interest led to the reintroduction of some Les Paul models in 1968, but surprisingly the Standard didn't appear again until 1975, since when it has remained in continuous production at Gibson.

The sound of the Les Paul Standard depends to a great extent on the timbers used in its construction. The original concept was for a mahogany body to provide depth of tone, with a maple front adding brightness. The combination offered good sustain without being too heavy, and these woods have remained consistent throughout the Standard's production history. The glued neck and the large

1958 Gibson Les Paul Standard

1958 Gibson Les Paul Standard
This is a fine example of a '58, with the sunburst finish undimmed by age. The maple tops or caps on these guitars were bookmatched to produce a sometimes beautiful near-symmetrical pattern in the timber of the maple top.

1959 Gibson Les Paul Standard (below)
The figure or grain pattern on sunburst-finished Les Pauls from this era vary widely. This example's very rare cherry-colored finish covers the grain of the maple on this guitar. The necks on Standards made in 1958 and 1959 had a chunky round-backed profile.

1959 Gibson Les Paul Standard

SOLIDBODY ELECTRIC GUITARS

humbucking pickups also contribute to natural sustain and wide tonal range, elements that meet Les Paul's own original requirements and are responsible for the instrument's continuing and wide-ranging popularity.

In the hands of a few players such as Eric Clapton in Britain and Mike Bloomfield in the USA, the Les Paul Standard reached unprecedented levels of popularity in the late 1960s. The Les Paul's thick, sustained sound featured by Clapton on John Mayall's *Blues Breakers* "Beano" album (1966) and by Bloomfield on the *Super Session* album (1968) was an influence on contemporary players.

These sought-after sunburst Standards were made between 1958 and 1960, but only about 1,500 were produced during this period. Demand has, therefore, always outstripped supply by some distance. Prices shot up during the Les Paul boom of the late 1960s and has subsequently reached such high levels that, ironically, mere musicians are rarely able to afford these instruments, many of which have ended up locked away in bank vaults or private collections, sometimes as purely financial investments.

1959 Gibson Les Paul Standard

1959 Gibson Les Paul Standard
This rare example (top right) has a factory-fitted Bigsby vibrato, and the top displays contrasting "tiger stripes." This alone makes it desirable among collectors and adds substantially to its value ... aside from its previous ownership by Keith Richards.

1960 Gibson Les Paul Standard
A rare example of a left-handed version of the Standard, which is owned today by Paul McCartney. Eric Clapton's legendary "Beano" Les Paul was, reputedly, also made in 1960, which is why Gibson released the Eric Clapton 1960 replica in 2010.

1959 Gibson Les Paul Standard

1960 Gibson Les Paul Standard

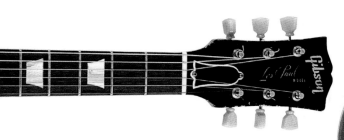

1959 Gibson Les Paul Standard (right)
This well-used guitar, once owned by Paul Kossoff, has replacement Grover tuners and has lost its pickguard and much of the sunburst finish. This effect is termed as an "unburst" finish, but it still has a wonderful honey-colored hue and a fine tightly-packed, tiger-striped grain visible in the maple of the top.

GIBSON LES PAUL
STANDARD REISSUES

Despite its popularity with many players, the sunburst Les Paul Standard, complete with humbuckers, was absent from the Gibson catalogue in the early 1970s, although the model was available as a special order. A dealer in Memphis put in a small order for Standards with custom specifications that brought them a little closer to the 1950s original, and this short run of custom Les Pauls made between 1975 and 1978 is recognised as one of the first attempts to recreate the now hallowed '59 Standard.

In 1991, Gibson started to get serious about recreating a more accurate reissue of the Les Paul Standard. By 1993, the new revised and improved Les Paul Standard '59 reissue had arrived, followed by the Standard '58 Plaintop in 1994. A year later, Gibson introduced signature-edition Les Pauls starting with a Jimmy Page Standard. This was followed by signature models from Aerosmith's Joe Perry

and Slash of Guns N' Roses. Not to be outdone, Zakk Wylde had his unmistakable bullseye-finish model introduced in 1999. The trend has continued to this day, with the latest Les Paul-wielding hero Joe Bonamassa earning a number of signature models at various price points and specs.

Gibson followed the trend for creating aged "relics" that sought to conjure up the indefinable appeal of an original vintage instrument, and there is now a large range of variations on the original Standard.

The tremendous variation in flame and the natural ripple effect found in maple can be seen in the four reissue guitars on the right-hand side of the facing page. Gibson gave its customers the opportunity to select the timber for the tops of their custom orders in the 1980s, and the grades and types of grain were reflected in a baffling range of model names and variations.

1979 Gibson Les Paul KM

1979 Gibson Les Paul KM
The Kalamazoo Model—an early attempt to recreate a 1950s Burst—is now seen as a half-hearted stab. The headstock was considered to be too big and the body lacked the "dish" on the top that the originals had.

1997 ad

1983 press ad

2010 Sammy Hagar Red Rocker Les Paul
This is a slightly new take on the Standard theme, matching a cabernet finish over a flame-maple top with "chickenfoot"

rectangular peace symbol at the headstock. It has a rock-ready configuration of a '57 Classic pickup in the neck and a BurstBucker 3 in the bridge.

2010 Sammy Hagar Red Rocker Les Paul

2001 Gibson Les Paul Standard '58 Figuredtop

2008 Gibson Les Paul Historic Standard 60

2001 Gibson Les Paul Standard '58 Figuredtop
One of a series of Les Paul reissues where different grades of top are available, albeit at a pretty price. This is a striking example of a broadly figured top.

2008 Gibson Les Paul Historic Standard 60
The Historic Collection line from Gibson was not a set of Custom Shop-style recreations. The guitars have their roots in a historic model with some modern features. This example is based on a 1960 Standard, with the thinner neck profile associated with that period.

1982 Gibson Les Paul Guitar Trader Reissue

1980 Gibson Les Paul Heritage Standard 80 Elite

1983 Gibson Les Paul Standard Reissue

1993 Gibson Les Paul Standard '59 Flametop

Les Paul Studio Premium Plus ad from 2006

1982 Gibson Les Paul Guitar Trader Reissue
In the early 1980s, Gibson and the Guitar Trader store worked on reissues designed to recreate the fabled '59.

1980 Gibson Les Paul Heritage Standard 80 Elite
Not considered overly close to the 1959 originals, the Heritage Standard 80 Elite had a severe, wide cutaway and other non-original specs.

1983 Gibson Les Paul Standard Reissue
In 1983, Gibson began officially reissuing the Standard, with highly figured tops and features closer to the '59 than before.

1993 Gibson Les Paul Standard '59 Flametop
The Historic Reissue series was upgraded at this time, and this example has an eyecatching flame to rival almost any other.

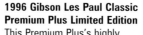

1996 Gibson Les Paul Classic Premium Plus Limited Edition

1996 Gibson Les Paul Classic Premium Plus Limited Edition
This Premium Plus's highly figured maple top is matched symmetrically, and the contrast is enhanced here by the green finish. Gold-plated hardware further reinforces the Limited Edition tag of this gorgeous example of Gibson's work.

GIBSON LES PAUL
JUNIORS & SPECIALS

As well as having the Custom and Goldtop models in the mid 1950s, Gibson also had a simple slab-bodied model in its catalogue. The budget Junior was designed for and aimed at beginners. It did not pretend to be anything other than a cheaper guitar.

The outline shape was the same as the Goldtop and Custom, but the most obvious difference to its Les Paul partners was a flat-top solid mahogany body. It had a single P-90 pickup, governed by a volume and tone control, and there were simple dot-shaped position markers along the unbound rosewood fingerboard. It was finished in Gibson's traditional two-colour brown-to-yellow sunburst and it had the wrapover bar-shape bridge-tailpiece (or stopbar) like the one used on the latest Goldtop.

In 1955, Gibson launched the Les Paul TV, essentially a Junior but with a finish that the company referred to variously as "natural," "limed oak," and (more often) "limed mahogany." Surviving original TV models from the 1950s reveal a number of different colors, with earlier examples tending toward a rather turgid beige, while later ones are often

distinctly yellow. No one knows for sure where the model's TV name came from. One theory has the TV name coined in order to tie in with Les Paul & Mary Ford's very popular TV series of the time.

Also in 1955, the original line of Les Paul models was completed with the addition of the Special, effectively a two-pickup version of the Junior, finished in the TV's beige colour (but not called a TV model—a cause of some confusion ever since). The following year, Gibson added a Junior Three-Quarter model. It had a shorter neck, giving the model a scale-length some two inches shorter than the normal Junior. Gibson explained in its brochure that the Junior Three-Quarter was designed to appeal to "youngsters, or adults with small hands and fingers."

Some 30 years later, the Junior became fashionable again and was well used by the punk fraternity. Gibson reissued the Junior in 1988, and signature models were added to the line later, with John Lennon and Billie Joe Armstrong models. An upscale high-tech self-tuning Robot model joined the line in 2009.

1956 Gibson Les Paul TV

1956 Gibson Les Paul TV
This model was finished in striking yellow/beige paintwork. There are many theories as to why this model was named "TV": it is possible the name alludes to Les Paul's and Mary Ford's popular 1950s television show. The 1958 Gibson Les Paul TV (opposite) has the later revised double-cutaway body.

1954 Gibson Les Paul Junior

2006 Billie Joe Armstrong Les Paul Junior

2009 Gibson Robot Les Paul Jr Special

2006 Billie Joe Armstrong Les Paul Junior

This signature guitar for the lead guitarist of punk band Green Day has a single humbucking pickup disguised as an original single-coil P-90, for a look in keeping with the original Junior. His own original model dates from 1956.

2009 Gibson Robot Les Paul Jr Special

This revision combines the classic P-90s, TV yellow finish, and solid mahogany construction with a self-tuning mechanism. Servo-powered Robot Tuners, an onboard CPU, a Tune Control Bridge, and a Data Transmitting Tailpiece are activated via a Multi-Control Knob, which can store user-defined custom tunings.

2002 Les Paul Bob Marley Special

This single-cut Special is a copy of the much-customized instrument played by the reggae star. It has an aluminum pickguard and an elliptical washer on the pickup selector switch, plus an aged "stripped" cherry finish and small-block fingerboard markers.

2002 Les Paul Bob Marley Special

1959 Gibson Les Paul Special

1958 Gibson Les Paul TV

1959 Gibson Les Paul Special

The Special was a two-pickup version of the Junior. This double-cut version is finished in cherry, with separate tone and volume controls for each pickup and a pickup-selector switch.

1958 Gibson Les Paul TV

The TV went double-cut along with its fellow students: the Junior and TV gained high-fret access in 1958, and the Special followed a year later.

1954 Gibson Les Paul Junior

This guitar is in the original sunburst finish and sports a simple unbound fingerboard and straightforward pair of tone and volume controls. The stripped-down no-nonsense ethos appealed to guitarists ranging from Johnny Thunders to John Lennon and contributed to the model's later resurgence in popularity with punk players.

SOLIDBODY ELECTRIC GUITARS

GIBSON LES PAUL
LES PAULS & SGs

By 1961, Gibson had decided on a complete redesign of the line in an effort to rekindle interest in the Les Pauls. The company had more than doubled the size of its Kalamazoo plant, and among the first models to benefit were the revised Les Pauls. The SGs had a completely new highly-sculpted double-cutaway design. At first, Gibson continued to call them Les Paul models, so guitars of this new style made between 1961 and 1963 with suitable markings are now known as SG/Les Pauls. But by 1963, the Les Paul name was gone, and the models officially continued as SGs. The SG name stands for Solid Guitar.

The main reason that Les Paul's name was dropped from Gibson guitars in 1963 relates to his divorce. Les did not want further royalties derived from Les Paul models to be tied up in his divorce from Mary Ford.

The pointed-horn SG shape proved popular and has been reissued over the years. Many signature models have emerged, from Tony Iommi to Angus Young and Pete Townshend to Robby Krieger.

As well as recreating the classic original 1950s Les Paul Standards, Gibson has designed many variations of Les Pauls, from the 1970s Professional and Recording, with their low-impedance pickups, to the more recent Studio-style models. In 1976, Gibson introduced The Les Paul, a guitar with wooden pickup-surrounds, pickguards, and control knobs, all exuding a feel of pure luxury.

1980 Gibson Les Paul Artist

1980 Gibson Les Paul Artist
This guitar's electronics—the control knobs and additional switches that controlled the expansion and compression features of the model—were borrowed from Gibson's RD series. The model also came with a fine-tuning tailpiece.

2007 Gibson Les Paul BFG
This radical and brutally stripped-down model has a Burstbucker 3 pickup at the bridge plus a P-90 single-coil. The wooden control knobs, kill switch instead of a toggle switch, and distressed gun-metal hardware further emphasize the utilitarian design.

2007 Gibson Les Paul BFG

1978 Gibson The Les Paul
This luxurious limited production version of the Les Paul—not to be confused with the 1979 model The Paul, a plain, mid-price walnut-finish variant—substitutes wood for many of the components that are usually metal or plastic. It was an expensive addition to the line, costing $3,000 at the time.

1978 Gibson The Les Paul

SOLID ELECTRIC GUITAR

63 SG ad

1990 Gibson SG Les Paul Custom

2000 Gibson Angus Young SG

1990 Gibson SG Les Paul Custom
This is a reissue of the original 1961 model that came with a block of three humbucking pickups. That model enjoyed exalted company, being a favorite of Sister Rosetta Tharpe and even ending up in the arms of Fender icon Jimi Hendrix.

2000 Gibson Angus Young SG
The AC/DC guitarist's signature model is based on the SG Standard with two humbucking pickups (one is custom-wound on this model). As well as the artist's signature on the truss-rod cover, the guitar has some startling lightning-bolt position markers on the fingerboard.

2009 Gibson SG Zoot Suit

2009 Gibson SG Zoot Suit
Evoking images of Eric Clapton's iconic psychedelic SG, nicknamed The Fool, the body of this attention-seeking model is made from multi-laminated birch, with each laminate dyed a different color. Coverless humbucking pickups have clear plastic coils, and there are also clear-plastic control knobs.

1993 40th anniversary ad

townshend. that's who.

2000 ad featuring Pete Townshend

1961 Gibson SG/Les Paul Standard

1961 Gibson SG/Les Paul Standard
This slab-bodied twin-horned guitar has the short-lived sideways-action vibrato, operating with an in-and-out action, rather than the customary up-and-down motion. It was replaced with the Gibson Vibrola unit on the SG Standard in 1962.

GIBSON MODELS
ODD SHAPES

Until the late 1950s, Gibson's solidbody guitar designs had been very traditional. All that changed with its "modernistic" guitars: the Flying V, the Explorer, and the Moderne. Before these designs, solid electric guitars had reflected established acoustic styling: a waisted body with small top bout balancing a larger bottom. But Gibson's oddball trio featured original and boldly adventurous styling.

Gibson president Ted McCarty encouraged the new shapes as his team used "modern" straight lines rather than "traditional" curves—a very radical move for the time. So radical, in fact, that the response from both retailers and players was negative. Despite Gibson's high hopes, none of these unusual guitars sold well, and production stopped within two years.

Many years later, these rare guitars became very desirable, and the renewed interest led to other makers adopting the Flying V and Explorer styling. Gibson itself has offered reissues.

In 1963, Gibson launched the first series of Firebird models, its first through-neck instruments, devised with the help of car designer Ray Dietrich and clearly intended to compete with Fender. The four models—I, III, V, and VII—used specially designed humbuckers, and all but one featured a vibrato tailpiece. Sales were disappointing, and the design was drastically revised in 1965.

Gibson played safe with the new "non-reverse" Firebirds, disposing of that innovative back-to-front look. A conventional glued neck replaced the more expensive through-neck construction of the originals.

Despite the changes and the longer production run, these Firebirds were unpopular, although the "reverse" versions did enjoy later success, prompting copies and Gibson reissues ever since.

1958 Gibson Flying V

1963 Gibson Firebird VII "reverse"

1958 Gibson Flying V
This first version is rare as only around 100 were made before production ceased in 1959, and it is highly sought-after. It was replaced by revised versions (1967–82) with a different control layout and normal hardware. An authentic Gibson reissue first appeared in 1982.

2009 Gibson Tribal V

1982 Gibson Moderne Heritage

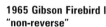
1981 Gibson Flying V V-2

1965 Gibson Firebird I "non-reverse"

1982 Gibson Moderne Heritage

The Moderne, with its shark-fin bass-side bout and curiously angular proportions, was announced in 1958 along with the Flying V and Explorer models, but it did not go into production until 1982, when it was finally launched as the Moderne Heritage. A reissue made an appearance at the Gibson booth at California's NAMM 2012 show.

1981 Gibson Flying V V-2

This reworked Flying V model, released in 1979, had odd boomerang-shaped pickups and a five-layer maple/walnut body with beveled top and back body edges. In 1982, the pickups were replaced with conventionally shaped Dirty Finger humbuckers.

1965 Gibson Firebird I "non-reverse"

Chastened by poor sales, Gibson changed its later-model Firebirds to a less radical body shape and a standard glued-in neck, with the tuners mounted on the bass side of the headstock. The Firebird V came with two pickups and the VII had three as standard.

1962 Gibson Explorer

Gibson assembled a few leftover Explorers and Flying Vs until about 1963 and, as this example shows, used period hardware.

1962 Gibson Explorer

1963 Gibson Firebird VII "reverse"

The neck-through-body design and the slightly offset waist of this first "reverse" version gave the Firebird a distinctive look. This example is owned today by Phil Manzanera.

Ad for the Explorer from 2001

2009 Gibson Tribal V

This recent Limited Run Series Flying V (one of 350 produced) has distinctive black abstract art on a Satin White background, with uncovered 496R and 500T humbuckers and a black-finish Kahler 2215K tremolo unit.

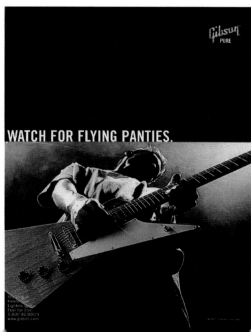

GIBSON MODELS
GOOD, BAD, UGLY

In the early 1960s, more and more teenagers began to buy electric guitars, but Gibson's rather staid instruments proved unattractive to these youthful guitarists. Even the new SG guitars suffered in comparison to Fender's flashy, colorful Jazzmasters, Jaguars, and Stratocasters.

Later in the 1960s, serious musicians emerging from the teenage pop scene began to rediscover Gibson instruments, and so the pendulum of fashion swung back in Gibson's favor over the next ten years.

The Stratocaster-dominated early 1980s proved to be a lean time for Gibson: its traditional thick-sounding, humbucker-equipped guitars didn't mesh with the new synthesizer-based music. Even the normally Gibson-toting heavy metallers were playing Fenders. Given historical precedent, Gibson must have expected fashion to swing back in its favor. But in the mid 1980s came a new trend, the Fender-inspired superstrat, and again Gibson lost out. At the start of the musically diverse 1990s, Gibson found

more success by returning to its classic designs. The company is firmly rooted in tradition, and this has made it hard for them to sell new ideas. Guitarists are conservative and usually want early classic designs rather than those Gibson produced to keep pace with modern trends.

There was a period during the 1970s and early 1980s when Gibson was trying hard to update its image, but unfortunately this coincided with a drop in quality at the factories. For this reason, none of the new guitars from this period met with success, and they are not collectable.

It was not until new ownership early in 1986 that attitudes changed at Gibson, and since that time Gibson has capitalized on the need for affordable "new oldies" by sensibly reissuing its classics and mostly avoiding fashionable or oddball designs. However, recent high-tech models such as the Dark Fire, Dusk Tiger, Firebird X, and Robot have incorporated groundbreaking self-tuning, modeling, and onboard-effects technology into classic outlines. Gibson seems to have learned the lessons of previous decades, and now it acknowledges its past in a commercially successful manner.

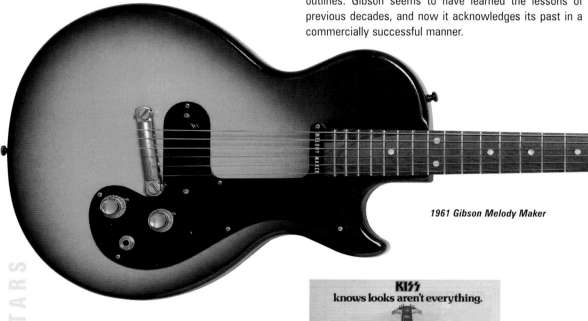

1961 Gibson Melody Maker

1961 Gibson Melody Maker
This was Gibson's first economy solid, launched in 1959 as a single-cutaway design with one or two pickups, altered to a double-cut style in 1961. This example has the optional short-scale neck, another feature aimed at beginners. In 1965, the Melody Maker adopted SG body styling, which lasted until its demise in 1970 and subsequent reissue in 1986 and 2007.

1976 Gibson S-1
Produced between 1976 and 1979, this model, unusually for Gibson, had a bolt-on Flying-V-look maple neck. Pickup specialist Bill Lawrence designed the special circuitry, and, like the Marauder model, the S-1 featured single-coil pickups.

1976 ad for the Marauder featuring Paul Stanley of KISS

1976 Gibson S-1

SOLIDBODY ELECTRIC GUITARS

126

*1983 Gibson
Corvus III*

1983 Gibson Corvus III
This model escaped in 1983. Quite what market Gibson was aiming at remains a mystery; the Corvus sank without trace two years later.

2011 Gibson Joan Jett Melody Maker
Jett may be Gibson's first female signature artist, but her Melody Maker bears little resemblance to the original double-cut model from the 1960s or the reissue from 2007. It has a custom-designed slim-tapered neck profile and a single Burstbucker 3 pickup.

1979 Gibson RD Artist
This series, launched in 1977 after collaboration with the synthesizer company Moog, incorporated complex active circuits. Ultimately, it was an unhappy marriage of traditional and modern design.

2011 Gibson Joan Jett Melody Maker

1979 Gibson RD Artist

1993 Gibson Nighthawk Special
This guitar, with its unusual Fender-like 25½-inch scale-length and more Fender-esque tonal range, won a design award from *The Music Trades* magazine in 1994 (Gibson's centennial year) and featured a multitude of push-pull pickup options. It was reissued in various forms from 2009.

1993 Gibson Nighthawk Special

As with many brands, Gibson serial numbers sometimes offer only a rough indication of the production period of a particular guitar. Often it becomes necessary to examine specific construction and hardware to pinpoint more accurately the date of a guitar, requiring specialist knowledge and experience.

Gibson solidbody guitars from 1953 to 1961 can be dated by the first number of the five- or six-digit serial. For example: 5 8274 = 1955; 910857 = 1959; 0 0195 = 1960; 1 2602 = 1961; and so on.

From 1961 to 1975, there was no specific chronological scheme, but much confusion and duplication. As a very rough guide, check the table in the next column.

1–99999 = 1961–63
000001–099999 = 1967
100000–199999 = 1963–67
200000–299999 = 1964–65
300000–599999 = 1965–69
600000–999999 = 1966–69
Confusingly, numbers 000001–999999 were used again between 1970 and 1975.

From 1974 to 1975, six digits prefixed with C, D, E, or F were used. Next came an eight-digit system, where the first two numbers indicated the date: 99 = 1975; 00 = 1976; and 06 = 1977.

From 1977 onward, a simple system was at last adopted, where the first and fifth numbers indicate the year. For example, 1XXX1XXXX indicates a guitar made in 2011.

The Eagles advertising the Nighthawk in 1995

1997 Gibson Les Paul DC Standard

1997 Gibson Les Paul DC Standard
This is the most radical design change to the Les Paul model: a double-cut body with extended horns and a carved top, a design that was seen by some as reminiscent of PRS models (see page 138–139).

SOLIDBODY ELECTRIC GUITARS

OTHER AMERICAN MAKERS
THE FIFTIES

Now we look beyond Fender and Gibson to other American makers who started producing solidbody instruments in the 1950s and 1960s. They range from better-known names like Epiphone, Rickenbacker, and Gretsch, to smaller companies such as Premier.

Many other manufacturers flourished during this period, meeting the huge demand for guitars. Harmony and Kay were Chicago-based firms producing a wide range of instruments under a variety of additional brand names, such as Silvertone, Regal, Airline, and Old Kraftsman.

Gibson bought the Epiphone company in 1957 and soon produced an Epiphone equivalent of its own Melody Maker model, the Olympic Special. A new-design solidbody was later added, with features roughly corresponding to Gibson's SG series. USA production of Epiphones ceased in 1970; solidbodies made since then originated from Japan and, later, Korea and China. From 1989, some Epiphone solidbodies have been produced once again in America, and in recent years, the line has continued to be used by Gibson to appeal to the budget end of the market, including versions of classic Gibson models.

A number of Gretsch solids were made in the 1950s and 1960s, and collectors avidly seek these guitars. They include the 6121 Chet Atkins and its G-brand relative, the 6130 Round Up, the very rare 6134 White Penguin, and the 6132 Corvette with its pastel partner, the 6106 Princess.

1959 Epiphone Crestwood Custom
The Crestwood at first had one or two "New York" pickups, with distinctive plastic end-caps, and then from 1961 had two mini humbucekrs. The model was discontinued in 1970.

1959 Epiphone Crestwood Custom

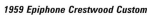

1996 Epiphone Coronet ad featuring Stacie Jones

1961 Epiphone Crestwood Custom
In the early 1960s, Epiphone launched a line of solids sharing one body style. Top of this line was the three-pickup Crestwood Deluxe, followed by the Crestwood Custom, Wilshire, Coronet, and Olympic models. Epiphone's Worn 1966 Wilshire model proved a popular budget reissue in 2010.

1961 Epiphone Crestwood Custom

2009 Epiphone "Emily The Strange" G-310

2009 Epiphone "Emily The Strange" G-310
Epiphone has been making a line of budget versions of classic Gibson guitars, and this psychedelic-inspired SG is a typical example. The graphics are inspired by the Cosmic Debris company's comic character.

128

Later Gretsch solids do not share this appeal; consequently, it was the 1950s solids that Gretsch chose for Japan-made reissues at the end of the 1980s. In 2003, Gretsch formed an alliance with Fender, which developed and marketed Gretsch. The sumptuous G6128T-GH George Harrison Signature Duo Jet of 2012 reminded the guitar-buying public of the company's heritage.

Rickenbacker, the California-based company, is best known for its electric-acoustic instruments, but its first electrics predated these by several decades. Rickenbacker has produced numerous solidbody guitar models, only a few of which have succeeded in capturing the best of the brand's character and image, albeit in a more manageable package than Rick's bulkier electric-acoustics. Most successful in this respect has been the distinctive 600 series, produced from 1962 onward. These models share the "hooked" body shape of the 400 series that was made between 1958 and 1985.

1957 Rickenbacker Combo 800

1957 Rickenbacker Combo 800

The Combo series marked the first modern electric guitars from Rickenbacker, appearing in 1954 with two basic versions. The Combo 600 had a single pickup. The Combo 800, like the one shown here, had a twin-coil unit, despite appearing to have one "horseshoe" pickup. Later versions have two separate pickups. The various Combos did not last into the 1960s.

c.1960 Premier Scroll

1957 Rickenbacker Combo 450

c.1960 Premier Scroll

This was a brand name of the Multivox company of New York. Premier solids of the 1950s and 1960s had a distinctive scroll-shaped bass horn. Others, such as the model shown, sported crushed-plastic pickguards bearing a large array of controls. Later Premier solidbodies featured a six-on-one-side headstock, imported hardware, and plastic-finished bodies.

1957 Rickenbacker Combo 450

This is a launch-year example of the two-pickup version of the Combo 400. The through-neck section is clearly visible at the body end, beyond the gold-anodized metal pickguard with two "cooker" knobs.

1960 Gretsch Jet Fire Bird

In 1955 Gretsch launched their Jet models, featuring three colored tops: the black Duo Jet, silver-sparkle Silver Jet, and the red Jet Firebird (shown here). Later versions came in other sparkle colors.

1960 Gretsch Jet Fire Bird

2003 Gretsch White Penguin

This is a later reissue of Gretsch's "Holy Grail" guitar, which was introduced as the solidbody companion to the semi-solid White Falcon in 1955. It still has the DeArmond pickups, the Penguin logo on the pickguard, and a gold-sparkle truss-rod cover. It's estimated that fewer than 50 original White Penguins were made between 1955 and 1962, and survivors are highly valued.

2003 Gretsch White Penguin

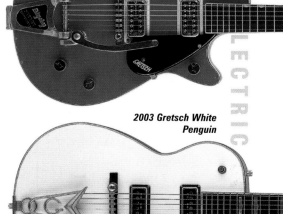

OTHER AMERICAN MAKERS
THE SIXTIES & SEVENTIES

During the 1960s and on into the 1970s, the number of electric guitar producers in the USA mushroomed. Even established acoustic-makers entered the market, alongside a multitude of new brandnames from companies of all sizes. The increased competition meant that makers had to establish their own identities, leading to the appearance of many original designs. But most failed to make any significant impact on players' tastes, and many brands disappeared from the scene.

Of those that made some fleeting impression, experimental California-based guitar-maker Semie Moseley's Mosrite made plenty of waves in the mid 1960s, thanks to a band/brand association with The Ventures. The surf-instrumental combo was wildly popular with US teenagers, and the Ventures Model endorsed by them for around five years in that decade resembled an inverted Stratocaster, with a lengthy treble horn. Mosrite made some otherworldly models for Strawberry Alarm Clock after The Ventures association ended, and Moseley stopped and restarted his business regularly until his death in 1992, aged 57.

Hamer, established in 1973 by guitar builder Jol Dantzig and business partner Paul Hamer in Wilmette, Illinois, was a forward-looking venture that recognised the nobility of the production principles of the past. Noticing the price of vintage instruments, the pair created upscale equivalents of Gibson-style instruments, and, after some custom orders from established musicians, began taking their wares to gigs. Thus, almost by accident, began one of the earliest examples of the boutique electric-guitar maker: Hamer offered a catalogue of established models such as the Standard and Sunburst, and would vary them according to demand. The company was acquired by Kaman Music in 1987, resulting in rock-orientated designs following the trends of the era.

By the 1960s, Guild had already established itself as a maker of acoustic, hollowbody and semi-hollowbody instruments, but when it moved into the solidbody realm in 1963, the results were a break with convention. The Thunderbird was the flagship: its peculiarly compelling body shape, complex circuitry, and even a built-in stand offered a viable alternative to Fender's Jazzmaster. The 1970s saw the Gibson-influenced M and S Series, and a collaboration with Brian May had the company producing various copies of the Queen guitarist's Red Special guitar, beginning in 1984.

2001 Hamer ads featuring Vernon Reid (left) and Michael Fath (above)

1979 Hamer Sunburst
This guitar has a double-cut bound body with a high-quality flamed maple top and two humbucking pickups. The neck unit sports the classic Les Paul "zebra" effect, with one black bobbin and one cream.

1979 Hamer Sunburst

SOLIDBODY ELECTRIC G

1994 Guild Brian May BHM-1
Guild collaborated with Brian May for a series of guitars based on his famous home-made instrument, Red Special, beginning with the BHM-1. This Brian May signature guitar was much closer to the original, with custom-made Seymour Duncan pickups and a custom vibrato. The guitar was available in a red or green woodgrain finish.

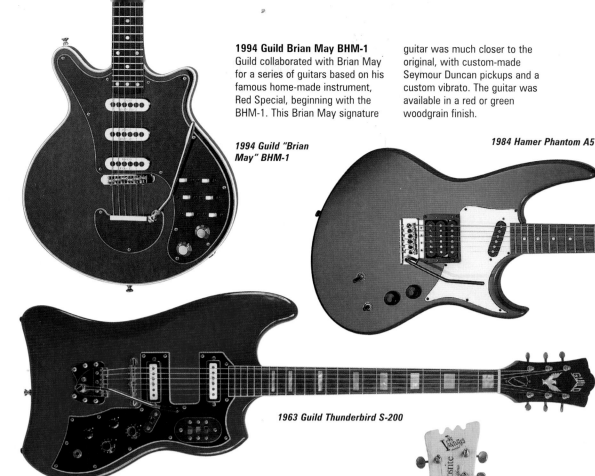

1994 Guild "Brian May" BHM-1

1984 Hamer Phantom A5

1963 Guild Thunderbird S-200

1963 Guild Thunderbird S-200
The offset-shaped body of this model, reminiscent of its namesake, the Gretsch Jupiter Thunderbird Bo Diddley, designed in 1959, had a guitar stand built into the rear of the body.

1984 Hamer Phantom A5
This guitar exhibits an unusual triple-coil pickup first used by Hamer on its early prototype for this model. The instrument went through quite a few design revisions, and a version with interchangeable magnetic fingerboards was built for Andy Summers of The Police.

c.1966 Mosrite Ventures Mark I
Semie Moseley founded his peripatetic Mosrite company in the 1950s and enjoyed great success in the following decade with the classic lopsided Ventures model. Business waned, but Moseley attempted many comebacks, with little success.

1966 Mosrite ad

c.1966 Mosrite Ventures Mark I

OTHER AMERICAN MAKERS
THE EIGHTIES

The lurid, demonic, none-more-pointy metal machines that delivered crushing tones from the darker end of the 1980s rock spectrum often came courtesy of US company B.C. Rich. Its founder, Bernardo Chavez Rico, began his guitar-making career not in the smoldering forges of Hades, but rather as a flamenco and classical guitarist creating acoustic instruments in Bernardo's Guitar Shop, his father's LA workshop, in the 1950s.

The first B.C. Rich electrics from 1969 were emulations of "modernistic" Gibson models. He followed these with the handcrafted, thru-neck, single-cutaway Seagull model around 1971 or 1972. Bernie then expanded his business, and as he did so, he and his team explored the angular "shape" designs that have since become synonymous with the B.C. Rich brand and the music it inspired.

The run of models that appeared between 1976 and 1983 set the tone, including the Mockingbird, the ten-string Bich, Ironbird, Warlock, Wave, and Stealth. Guitar warlords such as Tony Iommi, Blackie Lawless, Paul Stanley, Mick Mars, Lita Ford, Slash, Kerry King, and legions of others—including some hair-metal guitarists—

gravitated to the guitars' devastating looks and sleek playability. In 1994, Rico resumed control of his trademark, having licensed it out in 1988. He made a line of new designs such as the Ignitor, and fancy versions of classic models. He died in 1999, leaving the company in the capable hands of his son, Bernie Jr.

The superstrat may have been almost ubiquitous in the 1980s, but another US company's designs dared to differ from this format, and with enduring success. Dean Guitars was started by Dean Zelinsky in Evanston, Illinois, in 1977, and its triumvirate of Gibson-flavored models—the Explorer-like Z, the V, and the hybrid ML—was soon joined by Fender-esque lines, including 1983's Bel Aire, whose H-S-H configuration helped usher in the superstrat revolution.

Famous Dean endorsees include Billy Gibbons, the Schenker brothers, Dave Mustaine, Leslie West, and the ill-fated "Dimebag" Darrell Abbot, who designed the Razorback model subsequently played by Trivium's Corey Beaulieu.

Zelinsky left Dean in 2008 and set up DBZ Guitars in Houston, continuing to innovate across a varied and expanding product line.

1979 B.C. Rich Mockingbird Standard

1979 B.C. Rich Mockingbird Standard
This intimidating guitar is constructed on the thru-neck principle, with a solid block of wood making up the neck and the center body section of the instrument. Contrasting wood stripes between the center section and the added wings are part of the design.

1996 BC Rich Ignitor

SOLIDBODY ELECTRIC GUITARS

1982 Dean ad (above), 2004 Dean ad featuring Trivium (below)

1980 Dean Golden Elite

Following the Gibson Explorer model, this instrument sports the recognisable Dean wishbone-shaped headstock and a slightly less radical body shape with uncovered humbucking pickups and black-and-white-colored "zebra" bobbins.

1985 Dean Hollywood Z

This Explorer-like model was manufactured in Japan, and, unlike earlier models that have glued-in necks, this has a traditional bolt-on neck.

1980 Dean Golden Elite

1985 Dean Hollywood Z

Two B.C. Rich ads from 2003

1996 B.C. Rich Ignitor

Sharing the same construction principles as the Mockingbird, the Ignitor has a more extreme "pointy" body shape. The 1980s saw no end of mean-looking metal guitarists willing to undergo the odd painful stab in the kidneys from a guitar body in exchange for the aggressive vibe imparted by the company's axes.

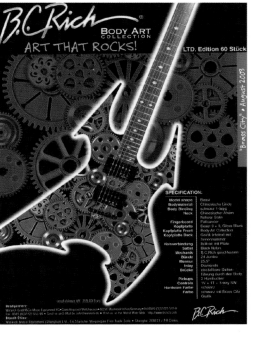

133

OTHER AMERICAN MAKERS
THE EIGHTIES II

Peavey was already well-established as an amplifier and PA manufacturer when it made its first forays into guitar manufacture in the late 1970s. By the early 1980s, the T-series guitars (so-called because they were designed by Chip Todd) were incorporating innovative ideas: the T-15 was a student instrument with a 23-inch scale, which company founder Hartley Peavey believed would make guitar-playing easier to get to grips with. The T-15 also came with an amp built into the case. Buoyed by the best-selling Bandit amp line, guitar models flowed thick and fast from the company's R&D department in the years that followed.

The T-series expanded as the decade progressed, and it was joined by pioneering shapes such as the Razor, Mystic and Mantis, alongside the more familiar Strat-like Impact, Nitro, and Falcon lines. Peavey's first Signature guitar, a design collaboration with Whitesnake's Adrian Vandenberg, appeared in 1988 in shocking Rock-It Pink. Hot-rod rock guitars were added to the line as Peavey

1984 Washburn Stage A-20V (opposite)
Shaped like a truncated Gibson Explorer with a chunky slanted headstock, this Japanese-made guitar has a bolt-on neck, although the top-of-the-line A-20s came with a glued-in set neck. It has brass washer-shaped inlays in an ebony fretboard.

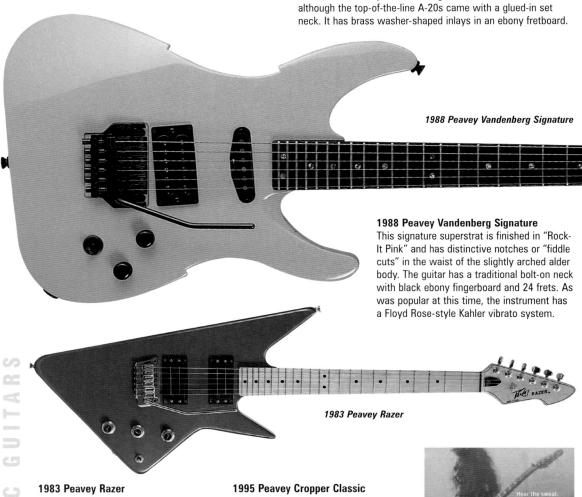

1988 Peavey Vandenberg Signature

1988 Peavey Vandenberg Signature
This signature superstrat is finished in "Rock-It Pink" and has distinctive notches or "fiddle cuts" in the waist of the slightly arched alder body. The guitar has a traditional bolt-on neck with black ebony fingerboard and 24 frets. As was popular at this time, the instrument has a Floyd Rose-style Kahler vibrato system.

1983 Peavey Razer

1983 Peavey Razer
The Razer has a bi-laminate maple neck with the laminates running in different directions, in an attempt to improve stability. The Peavey-made humbucker-style pickups have twin blade magnets instead of the usual six single cylindrical polepiece magnets. This unusual guitar was one of a trio Peavey introduced in 1983: the other models were the T-60 and the Mystic.

1995 Peavey Cropper Classic
This Steve Cropper endorsement has an unusual aluminum neck/body joint and is fitted with dual-blade humbucking pickups. The body shape is in the Telecaster tradition but made from mahogany with a figured maple top.

2002 Peavey Wolfgang ad with Eddie Van Halen

1995 Peavey Cropper Classic

SOLIDBODY ELECTRIC GUITARS

134

followed fashions, including the Tracer series. The 1990s would see a further proliferation of successful models, and a major coup: the 1996 EVH Wolfgang series, designed by guitar god, Eddie Van Halen.

At the same time as Peavey was making its forays into the guitar market, the brand name of 19th century US guitar company Washburn was revived and used on a range of Japanese-built guitars called the Wing series.

In no time, the Hawk, Falcon, Raven, and Eagle were joined by the Stage, Force, and Tour models, covering most of the rock bases from humbucker-loaded superstrat to V shape. A fruitful celebrity endorsement deal was struck in the 1990s with ex-Extreme guitarist Nuno Bettencourt—and the N series continues today. The Washburn solidbody electric line has evolved into the rocky Idol, shred-ready XM, and the stylish RX.

1983 Washburn Stage ad

1984 Washburn Stage A-20V

1988 Washburn EC-36

1990 Washburn ad with Nuno Bettencourt

1988 Washburn Force G-40V

1988 Washburn EC-36
This guitar has a 36-fret neck, but there was also a modest 29-fret version available. It comes with a deep cutaway on the lower side and a "shattered bone" finish, with a hand-hold cut through the body and a single humbucking pickup, plus active electronics and a midrange boost.

1988 Washburn Force G-40V
The Force line began its adventure as a Stratocaster-esque infant but progressively evolved into a pointy headstocked hot-rodded rock instrument.

1991 Robin Machete Custom

1991 Robin Machete Custom
This is another Gibson Explorer-inspired guitar, certainly in the headstock department. The body has unusual layered wood construction, using exotic timber.

OTHER AMERICAN MAKERS
SUPERSTRATS

Grover Jackson's California-based company can lay claim to the invention of the so-called superstrat, which refined and updated Fender's Stratocaster design. The Strat's 21 frets were expanded to 24, increasing the playing range, and cutaways were deepened to allow access to these extra frets, giving the body longer horns.

High-end superstrats used a thru-neck rather than Fender's bolt-on type with its bulky joint, facilitating top-fret access. The superstrat then added the power of a humbucker to the Strat's pickup layout, and the simple Fender vibrato gave way to a heavy-duty locking system.

The first Jackson superstrat was the Soloist, introduced around 1980. It embodied all these improvements, together with a newly designed "droopy" pointed headstock. Since then, Jackson has added US-built variations, plus Far Eastern lines under its Jackson Pro, Charvel, and Charvette brand names. The success of these designs led virtually every other guitar manufacturer in the world to copy the superstrat.

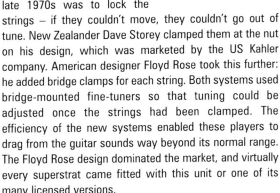

Early vibratos did not always return to accurate pitch after they had been used. The solution that emerged in the late 1970s was to lock the strings — if they couldn't move, they couldn't go out of tune. New Zealander Dave Storey clamped them at the nut on his design, which was marketed by the US Kahler company. American designer Floyd Rose took this further: he added bridge clamps for each string. Both systems used bridge-mounted fine-tuners so that tuning could be adjusted once the strings had been clamped. The efficiency of the new systems enabled these players to drag from the guitar sounds way beyond its normal range. The Floyd Rose design dominated the market, and virtually every superstrat came fitted with this unit or one of its many licensed versions.

Guitarists have often wished their Strats—and particularly the bridge pickups—would give more powerful, Gibson-like sounds. The superstrat catered for this need by replacing the bridge single-coil with a humbucker. A further refinement provided this pickup with a coil-tap facility, switching out ("tapping") one coil of the two in the humbucker. This approximates the single-coil sound, and a superstrat so equipped can deliver all the classic Fender tones, plus the thicker, louder humbucker sounds, in any combination.

Joey Z advertises Jackson in 1997 (above)

2009 Jackson ad with Matt Tuck

1992 Jackson Stealth TH2

1992 Jackson Stealth TH2
The guitar has a bolt-on neck and, unusually for a superstrat, a vintage-style tremolo, with a straight string-pull headstock. This refinement of the line featured Jackson's newly designed pickups and new satin finishes.

1990 Jackson Custom Shop Soloist

SOLIDBODY ELECTRIC

136

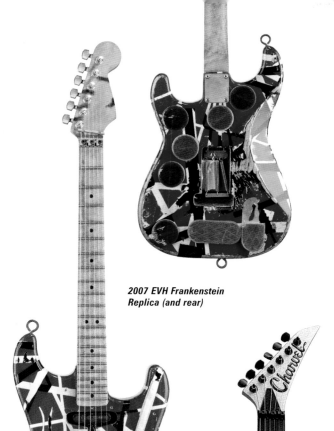

2007 EVH Frankenstein
Replica (and rear)

1983 Kramer ad with Eddie Van Halen

2007 EVH Frankenstein Replica
Fender and Eddie Van Halen produced a 300-edition limited run of copies of Eddie's iconic, modded, superstrat archetype, Frankenstein, in 2007. The original was created from a $50 factory-second body, but the clones sold for significantly more: tens of thousands of dollars more.

1986 Charvel Model 5
This superstrat is fitted with one regular humbucker and two stacked humbuckers, with active electronics. The construction method is neck-thru-body. Charvel, now owned by Fender, has made a comeback in recent years.

1986 Charvel Model 5

1995 Charvel
San Dimas

1990 Jackson Custom Shop Soloist
The Soloist featured neck-thru-body construction and was an inspiration to subsequent superstrat creators. This one sported a fetching example of Jackson's graphic-finish front, available as a standard option on the USA production models. This design is Californian Sunset.

1995 Charvel San Dimas
The earlier San Dimas models were made in Japan, but when Wayne Charvel sold the brand to Grover Jackson in 1978, production of the model continued in the USA. The So-Cal and San Dimas Style 1 returned in 2009.

OTHER AMERICAN MAKERS
PAUL REED SMITH

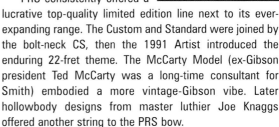

Paul Reed Smith started out in the guitar business during high school in the 1970s. He left a job as a guitar repairman to go to college in his home state of Maryland, where he built a guitar for an independent study project. Bitten by the bug, he negotiated some commissions from star players—including an all-mahogany double-cutaway guitar for Peter Frampton. This 1976 instrument, with its 24-fret neck, abalone bird inlays, twin humbuckers, Les Paul Junior-like shape, and Les Paul Standard-esque carved top, was a blueprint for his subsequent designs.

In 1980, Smith secured a dream ticket—to build several guitars for Carlos Santana. The legendary player's subsequent association with Smith's instruments was to help secure worldwide recognition for the guitar and the brand.

In 1985, a decade on from building his first guitar, Smith took the plunge and opened PRS Guitars with his partners in Annapolis, Maryland. His first model, the PRS Custom, was a hybrid "third-way" design, combining classic properties of both Gibson and Fender solidbodies and providing some effective compromises between them.

PRS consistently offered a lucrative top-quality limited edition line next to its ever-expanding range. The Custom and Standard were joined by the bolt-neck CS, then the 1991 Artist introduced the enduring 22-fret theme. The McCarty Model (ex-Gibson president Ted McCarty was a long-time consultant for Smith) embodied a more vintage-Gibson vibe. Later hollowbody designs from master luthier Joe Knaggs offered another string to the PRS bow.

Sensible refinements to pickups, materials, and model styles, a commitment to quality control, and clever expansion meant there was no stopping PRS's rise. Today, the company is one of the world's largest guitar manufacturers, and it has added acoustic guitars and amplifiers to the catalogue.

2002 press ad with Sum 41

1980 PRS

1980 PRS
Paul Reed Smith's third maple-topped guitar was a custom order from Carlos Santana, who used this guitar for many years live and in the studio. PRS went on to produce many Santana-endorsed production models.

2004 ad featuring Linkin Park

2001 PRS Private Stock #235

2001 PRS Private Stock #235
The design for this special one-off guitar using prime-grade timber finished in charcoal became the basis for one of the popular McCarty production models.

SOLIDBODY ELECTRIC GUITARS

2006 PRS Standard 24 Satin

2006 PRS Standard 24 Satin
The 20th anniversary of PRS inspired a new satin finish, applied to the Standard 24-fret model. It had the by-now famous "bird" inlays in the fingerboard, and the body had a "vintage" cherry finish over mahogany.

1991 PRS Artist I
This was the high-end model where only the most exclusive materials were used. The design and construction principles used to create this instrument are now considered as classic Paul Reed Smith.

1991 PRS Artist I

1999 PRS Custom 22 Soapbar
PRS became known for maple-bodied guitars with humbucking pickups, but this model has a solid mahogany body and single-coil P-90-style pickups. The P-90s came from Paul Reed Smith's association with ex-Gibson man Ted McCarty, and a number of PRS models bear his name.

1999 PRS Custom 22 Soapbar

1985 PRS Metal

1985 PRS Metal
The unusual graphics for the body of this guitar came from Bud Davis, a custom-car and motorcycle painter. They were not a success at the time and were only produced for a year, but they have subsequently become sought-after collector's items.

2004 PRS Tremonti Tribal
The company made several signature models for guitarist Mark Tremonti, and this single-cut model with striking graphics was put on hold during a legal dispute with Gibson about the single-cut design. PRS won the case and the various single-cut models went into full production.

2004 PRS Tremonti Tribal

2009 PRS Starla

2009 PRS Starla
PRS also now produces more basic guitars, often from mahogany, including this single-cut retro-styled model. These guitars compete with many budget-priced instruments from other manufacturers.

OTHER AMERICAN MAKERS
HIGH-END INSTRUMENTS

Today's affluent guitarists on the lookout for a top-quality modern refinement of classic electric designs are spoilt for choice, with a wellspring of bespoke workshops and established acoustic makers lining up to spec the electric guitar of their dreams.

In the US, acoustic heavyweights Taylor and Collings have expanded into the electrified realm with fully featured and meticulously crafted alternatives to the dominion of the Big Three makers, Fender, Gibson, and PRS.

Taylor's electrics include solidbody models such as the Classic with its elegant single-cutaway body and original all-aluminum bridge. The mix-and-match SolidBody platform and semi-hollowbody T3 and T5 epitomize the versatility prized by modern players. Texas-based acoustic specialist Collings began making electrics in 2006, and the 360 was developed with a thinner body to take on the City Limits model. Its current product line is a Gibson-flavored affair, with a build quality to match that of any other maker.

High-end US boutique makers have steadily carved out distinctive niches for themselves. California-based maker Tyler Guitars combines fine playability and unusual visuals: that unique headstock, as well as some mindbending finishes. Suhr offer a similarly Fender-esque high-end experience: not surprising, perhaps, as founder John Suhr worked at Pensa-Suhr in New York City, leaving in 1991 and joining Fender four years later. In 1997 he set up on his own, currently based at Lake Elsinore, California.

Tom Anderson began his Guitarworks in 1984 in California, making high-quality upscale instruments that cover all the solidbody bases in some style. Upholding the Zemaitis tradition of metal manufacture, James Trussart's steel creations blur the distinction between musical instrument and fine art. Daisy Rock is a different proposition: with its range of eyecatching "girl guitars" redressing the guitar world's traditional male bias, while Schecter's Vintage models bring retro styling and quality at an affordable price.

Daisy Rock ads from 2004 and 2005

2009 Collings 360
The regular 360 comes with an all-mahogany body, but the custom model pictured here was made with a koa top (maple is also an option). The unusual offset body shape and a rear contour is intended to make the 360 comfortable to play seated or standing.

2009 Collings 360

2008 Taylor Classic SB1-X

2008 Taylor Classic SB1-X
There are many options, easily previewed online: the example here is finished in an arresting color that Taylor calls Purple Flake, and this guitar has two mini-humbuckers—one of ten available pickup layouts.

SOLIDBODY ELECTRIC GU

2010 James Tyler Studio Elite HD-P

2010 James Tyler Studio Elite HD-P
The Studio Elite—this one is finished in outrageous Malibu Beach Shmear—was named to reference the top LA studio players. The model's compound-radius neck has excellent high-fret access and was one of the first so-called boutique superstrats.

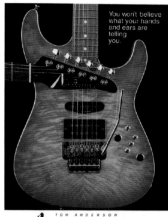

1994 Tom Anderson ad

2008 Suhr Custom Classic

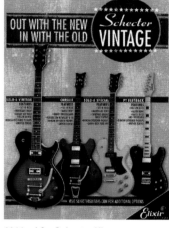

2011 ad for Schecter Vintage

2010 Tom Anderson Atom

2008 Suhr Custom Classic
The Classic is typical of Suhr's quality and style, with the intention of adding comfort, feel, and functionality to familiar originals. Vintage-voiced pickups and the 60-cycle-hum-eliminating SSC System are just two of many refinements on this model.

2010 Tom Anderson Atom
Tom Anderson began his Guitarworks in 1984 in California, making high-quality upscale instruments. The Atom is a recent design that has the now-classic combination of a mahogany body with a variety of exquisite tops, including book-matched flame or quilted maple, walnut, and koa options.

SOLIDBODY ELECTRIC GUITARS

141

BRITISH MAKERS
JIM BURNS

From small beginnings as Burns-Weill in 1959, Jim Burns's company became the most successful British guitar-making organization at its peak in the 1960s, exporting high-quality instruments throughout the world and making some important contributions to the evolution of the electric guitar.

Jim Burns and his team were never short of original ideas, which were often later claimed as firsts by other companies. The 1960 Artist had a heel-less glued-in neck with 24-fret fingerboard. The 1961 Bison had a truss-rod gear box for effective neck adjustment, and low-impedance pickups for greater clarity. The 1963 Burns TR2 was the first guitar with tone-boosting active circuitry. The 1964 Marvin used a knife-edge vibrato, and the 1965 Virginian had a stacked-coil pickup.

In 1965, the American Baldwin company bought the Burns companies, having been beaten by CBS in its attempt to acquire Fender. This signaled a change in fortune, and by 1970 all guitar production ceased. But the Burns name was not dead, and after a brief flirtation in 1969 with the British Hayman company, the new Burns UK outfit was launched in 1974 with an odd-looking assortment of solid electrics. This lasted until 1977, but the guitars were not well received.

Two years later, Jim Burns made another comeback with a new company and a new range of guitars, mixing reissues with yet more oddball designs. Again, reaction from players was less than enthusiastic and this, combined with poor management, led to the collapse of Burns in 1983. The name was revived in 1991 by Barry

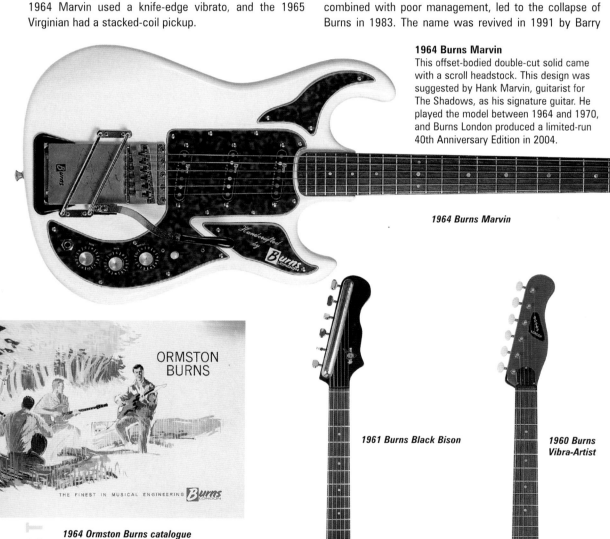

1964 Burns Marvin
This offset-bodied double-cut solid came with a scroll headstock. This design was suggested by Hank Marvin, guitarist for The Shadows, as his signature guitar. He played the model between 1964 and 1970, and Burns London produced a limited-run 40th Anniversary Edition in 2004.

1964 Burns Marvin

1964 Ormston Burns catalogue

1961 Burns Black Bison

1960 Burns Vibra-Artist

1961 Burns Black Bison
This magnificent early four-pickup Bison (1961) was succeeded by a three-pickup version and then a restyled model with a scroll head. It was reissued in 2003, with both headstock styles available.

1960 Burns Vibra-Artist
This was the first Burns production solid (1960–62), with a 24-fret short-scale neck and complex controls. If those pickups look familiar, it's because they're the same Tri-Sonic design you may have seen in Brian May's homemade Red Special guitar.

ORMSTON BURNS

THE FINEST IN MUSICAL ENGINEERING **Burns** LONDON

Gibson as Burns London, with Jim Burns's involvement, and among the offerings from the new firm was the Club range of Korean-made reproductions of a number of classic Burns models of the 1960s (see next page).

These days, the 1960s Marvin is the most sought-after Burns guitar. This design was suggested by Hank Marvin, guitarist for The Shadows, and only around 350 were made, so today's demand far exceeds supply. The various Bison models come next on the Burns collector's list, while most of the many remaining Burns instruments are less desirable. But many of these 1960s models have strong nostalgic appeal for older British guitarists, who may have started their playing careers on instruments such as the Sonic, Jazz Split Sound, and Vibraslim, or the Vista Sonic.

Baldwin catalogue from 1967

1977 Burns UK Flyte
The Burns UK incarnation of the company lasted between 1974 and 1977, and its guitars were manufactured near Newcastle upon Tyne in the northeast of England. This design was apparently inspired by the Concorde supersonic airliner.

1965 Baldwin Baby Bison
In 1965, Burns designed a cheaper, smaller version of the Bison for export only, and most carried the Baldwin name. A later type appeared with a different, more scroll-like headstock.

1979 Burns Scorpion
The name refers to the peculiar body shape of this model. It was reissued as the metal-slanted Gothic Scorpion in 2002, part of the Club Series.

1977 Burns UK Flyte

1965 Baldwin Baby Bison

1979 Burns Scorpion

BRITISH MAKERS
THE BURNS CONNECTION

There is an interesting contrast between the huge impact of British music throughout the world over the past 30 years and the comparatively low-key nature of the UK guitar-making scene. During the 1960s, only a handful of British guitar brands made any significant impact on their home market. Most guitarists seemed to prefer the imported competition.

Although UK-made guitars have sometimes offered better value and quality, they apparently lack the mystique of leading USA instruments. The discovery of the caliber of British guitars seems limited mostly to beginners or British enthusiasts. Only Burns and Vox had any noticeable success with the exporting of guitars.

A few brave makers have produced models with original designs, trying to compete with the irresistible tide of imported guitar models by offering something different.

Ex-Burns man Jack Golder established his company in the late 1960s, supplying instruments and parts for British brands like Hayman, Burns UK, and Ned Callan. Jack's own Shergold range of the 1970s and early 1980s included the Meteor, Modulator, Cavalier, and Activator. Shergold was the last company to make electric guitars in quantity in the UK. Golder, regarded as the godfather of the British electric guitar, concentrated on custom work until he died in 1992.

Another British manufacturer with its focus very much on craft is Gordon-Smith. Started in 1979 by Gordon Whitham and John Smith, and based in Partington near Manchester, the company is proud of its status as "the longest-running contemporary guitar company in England." The Gordon-Smith product line is packed with instantly recognisable designs, and the brand enjoys a reputation for good-value, decent-sounding workhorse instruments.

1999 Burns Marquee

1996 Burns Nu-Sonic

1999 Burns Marquee
This bestselling Club Series design is heavily based on the Fender Stratocaster with three single-coil pickups. Its distinctive feature is the three-piece pickguard. The guitars are now manufactured in the Far East.

2004 Burns Marquee ad

144

c.1968 Wilson Sapphire III

1973 Hayman 3030H

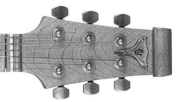

c.1964 Watkins Rapier 33

c.1968 Wilson Sapphire III
Wilson, a sub-brand of the Watkins company, made a range of cheap semis and solidbody guitars. This instrument has a strong Burns look about it. The company ceased trading in 1985.

1973 Hayman 3030H
The Hayman brand was owned by the UK distributor Dallas Arbiter. This model was one of four instruments in the series, and was a simplified version of the three-pickup 1010. Jim Burns was involved in the designs with Bob Pearson, and many of the parts were made by Jack Golder.

c.1964 Watkins Rapier 33
Known for making guitar amps and effects, Watkins also produced a line of guitars and basses. They were cheap and were often used on the early beat-group scene in Britain.

1980 Shergold Custom Masquerader
This guitar has similarities to the Burns range, which is not surprising as Shergold's founder, Jack Golder, previously worked at Burns. Golder wound down his guitar production in 1982, but began making new Shergolds again in 1991, producing limited-edition Masquerader models until his death the following year.

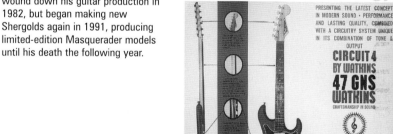

Watkins catalogue from the early 1960s

1996 Burns Nu-Sonic
This guitar came with either two or three Nu-Sonic pickups, designed by Jim Cairnes to work with the Rezo-tube system, where the bridge has six resonator tubes mounted underneath, another unique Burns feature.

1999 Burns Drifter
This guitar is virtually identical to the Club series Marquee, but with Kinman pickups, and came in fiesta red or duck-egg blue.

1999 Burns Drifter

1980 Shergold Custom Masquerader

BRITISH MAKERS
VOX & THE NEW BREED

As one of the few big UK guitar names of the 1960s, Vox produced some models that have since become classics of the period. Best known are probably the coffin-shaped Phantom models, and the Mark VI, which was nicknamed the Teardrop. Vox were not limited to one price bracket, and its large, ever-changing line included many original designs and features. Vox instruments came from various sources, the name first appearing on imported models during the early 1960s. British-made guitars followed, and later in the decade production moved to Italy.

Although Burns and Vox both contributed to the export of guitars, the majority of UK-made models were destined for home use. The influx of competing instruments, mainly from the Far East, led to the demise of all quantity makers in the UK. These have been replaced by numerous small-scale operations building limited numbers of mostly hand-

made upscale guitars. Tony Zemaitis (1935–2002) made small numbers of high-profile instruments for the rock aristocracy, especially in the 1970s and 1980s. He is best known for his Les Paul-shaped instruments with either pearl or metal fronts. His son, Tony Zemaitis Jr, continues the legacy from Zemaitis's Tokyo factory.

Patrick James Eggle is now an Oswestry-based craftsman specialising in fine acoustics, but during the 1990s his Patrick Eggle Music Company in Coventry produced the PRS-influenced Berlin model. More electrics were developed until 1993, at which time business problems resulted in a merger with Gary Levinson's Blade company, based in Switzerland. Another change of ownership in 2002 revived the brand, and the company currently provides a mix of established Eggle models and some new designs.

1991 Eggle Berlin Pro

1991 Eggle Berlin Pro
Although plain in design, the Berlin was a guitar made from expensive timbers: Brazilian mahogany faced by a contoured maple top. The guitar had a glued-in set neck, and several versions of the Berlin were produced throughout the 1990s.

Ads from 2007 and 2010 for Fret-King and Italia modern retro-style guitars.

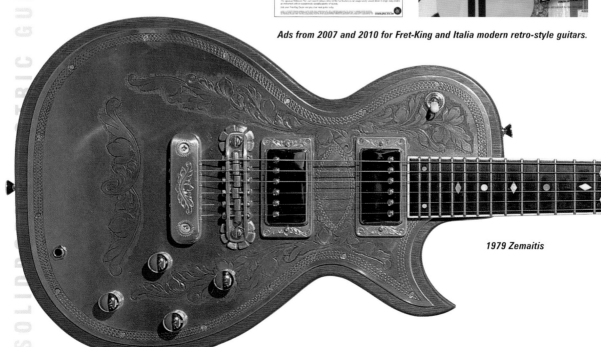

1979 Zemaitis

SOLID & ELECTRIC GUITARS

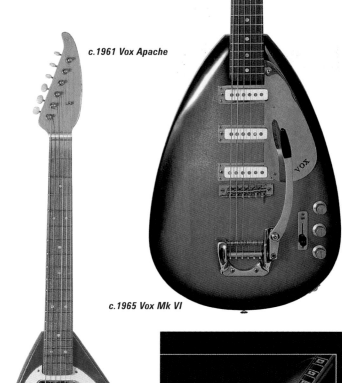

c.1961 Vox Apache

c.1965 Vox Mk VI

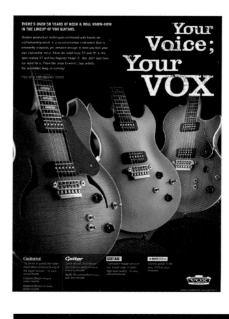

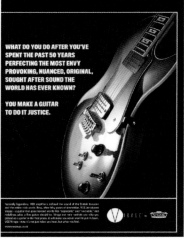

c.1961 Vox Apache
Some Vox models were made in very limited quantities, like this rare 1960s Apache. Cheap and oddly shaped, it had typically basic Vox materials and construction.

c.1965 Vox Mk VI
This guitar was nicknamed the Teardrop and became a classic of the mid-1960s beat scene, famously played by Brian Jones. It was accompanied at the time by nine-string and 12-string models.

Vox ads from 1981 and 2011, and a Vintage ad from 2005

1984 Bond Electraglide

1979 Zemaitis
Rock stars from Eric Clapton to Ronnie Wood have owned ultra-rare and collectible Zemaitis instruments. This wonderful example has engraving from Danny O'Brien, who usually engraves fine English shotguns.

1984 Bond Electraglide
This graphite guitar with control read-outs and stepped fingerboard was the brainchild of Scotland-based luthier Andrew Bond. An impressive launch in early 1984 was followed by a series of

production hiccups, and an ever-increasing retail price effectively negated the initial promise. Despite considerable financial investment, the company folded in 1986, having sold very few production instruments.

EUROPEAN MAKERS
GERMANY

The influence of rock'n'roll was felt in West Germany earlier than in other parts of Europe, thanks mainly to the American armed forces stationed there who brought their music with them. US instruments were either unobtainable or unaffordable, and so domestic guitar makers were faced with an increasing demand in the late 1950s from German guitarists who wanted to produce the sounds they were hearing on American rock'n'roll records. This gave German companies a significant head start over other European makers, and they were soon exporting guitars to many other countries—including, ironically, the United States.

Most of the major German makers—Hofner, Framus, Klira, and Hoyer—were concentrated in the Bubenreuth and Erlangen areas, and overall production continued to expand to match the demand generated by the thousands of groups active in the beat boom of the 1960s.

After that peak came the era of the copy guitar, a 1970s phase when virtually every guitar-maker produced versions of famous Fender and Gibson originals. Because of dwindling demand for homegrown products, over the next decade some major names disappeared. Currently, German companies still produce high-quality guitars but in smaller quantities, finding it hard to compete with competition from America and the Far East.

Hofner embraced the changes and in recent times has augmented its lines with Chinese-made equivalents of its older models, along with some all-new ideas. Framus officially disappeared in the late 1970s, and the brand was replaced by Warwick. In 1995, Framus reappeared on a line of upscale six-string instruments, and today, models such as the Diablo and Panthera, backed up by the company's custom shop, have restored Framus as a leading German maker.

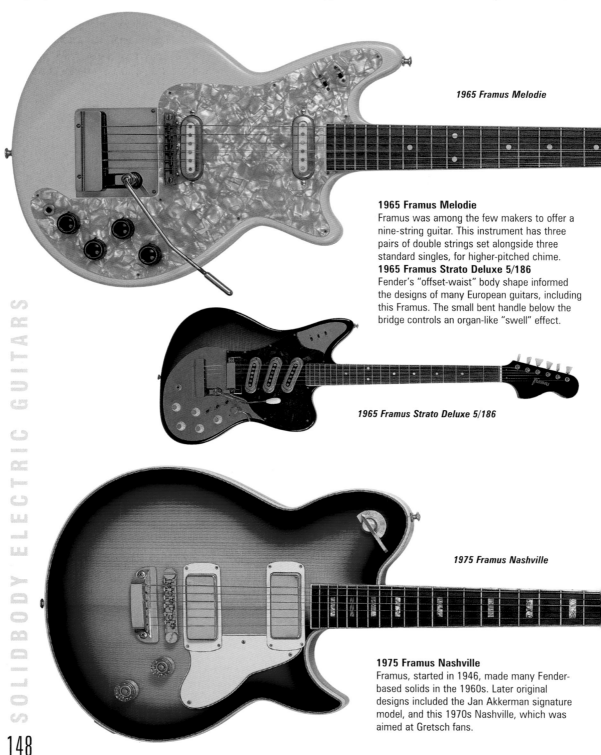

1965 Framus Melodie

1965 Framus Melodie
Framus was among the few makers to offer a nine-string guitar. This instrument has three pairs of double strings set alongside three standard singles, for higher-pitched chime.

1965 Framus Strato Deluxe 5/186
Fender's "offset-waist" body shape informed the designs of many European guitars, including this Framus. The small bent handle below the bridge controls an organ-like "swell" effect.

1965 Framus Strato Deluxe 5/186

1975 Framus Nashville

1975 Framus Nashville
Framus, started in 1946, made many Fender-based solids in the 1960s. Later original designs included the Jan Akkerman signature model, and this 1970s Nashville, which was aimed at Gretsch fans.

SOLIDBODY ELECTRIC GUITARS

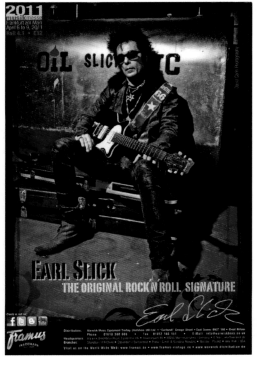

*Framus ad from 2011 (above);
Hofner catalogue cover (below
right) from the 1960s*

c.1968 Hofner 175
A special version of this model had a vinyl-covered body and red pearloid pickguard. In the 1960s, demand for guitars was so great that some companies expedited production by using vinyl instead of time-consuming paint.

c.1965 Hofner Galaxie
European players who couldn't afford real Fenders were attracted to Hofner's 1960s solids, which offered the visuals, if not the sounds, of the American originals. The Galaxie was a classic mix of Hofner features and Fender influence.

c.1968 Hofner 175

c.1965 Hofner Galaxie

1963 Hopf Telstar Standard
Hopf began as an acoustic maker in 1906, and made solidbodies such as the Telstar and semis such as the Saturn in the 1960s. The company chose to imitate rather than innovate during the 1970s, and production ceased in the mid 1980s.

c.1959 Framus Hollywood 5/132
The maker looked to Gibson for influences for this guitar. Heavily based on the Les Paul, it has an extra pickup, and the control knobs are reminiscent of an old-fashioned radio, along with a rather primitive trapeze-style tailpiece.

Elektro-
gitarren

Hofner

1963 Hopf Telstar Standard

c.1959 Framus Hollywood 5/132

EUROPEAN MAKERS
GERMANY II

Most German guitar-makers were content to work within their native country, and one such craftsman was Wenzel Rossmeisl, an established maker who named his company after his son, Roger. But Roger Rossmeisl (1927–79) decided he was an exception to the rule, and in the 1950s took his skills to America, initially working for Gibson in Michigan. He soon moved to Rickenbacker in California, and while employed there was responsible for making many custom designs, as well as production models such as the Capri and Combo. He left Rickenbacker in 1962 to join Fender, developing its first acoustic line as well as the later Montego and LTD archtop electrics.

Rossmeisl's work was a major influence on Semie Moseley, an apprentice to Rossmeisl at Rickenbacker who later founded his own Mosrite company of California. The Rossmeisl trademark was the "German carve" originally used by his father, a sort of indented "lip" following the outline of the guitar's body. This innovative contour was adopted by many other makers, particularly in Japan, where Mosrite enjoyed great popularity.

Quite why such an influential craftsman never set up his own guitar-making company remains a mystery. Instead, Roger Rossmeisl brought the benefits of German guitar craft to some very important American instrument manufacturers.

1978 Rockinger Lady

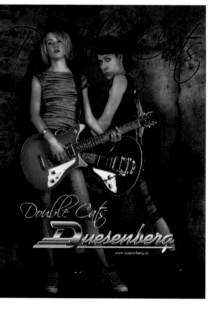

2006 Duesenberg ad

1978 Rockinger Lady
Started in 1978, Rockinger makes high-quality spares and complete guitars. This guitar has a feel of Rickenbacker design about it.

1966 Klira Tornado
Klira was the brandname of maker Johannes Klier, who set up the company in 1887. During the 1960s there were numerous original Fender-inspired solids, including this Tornado from 1966.

1966 Klira Tornado

1982 Huttl Star
The Star model of 1982 was one of the stranger-looking solids from this lesser known maker. The quality of Huttl guitars was certainly inferior compared to the major German brands.

1982 Huttl Star

SOLIDBODY ELECTRIC GUITARS

150

1988 Marlin Masterclass

1982 Musima Eterna Deluxe

1988 Marlin Masterclass

In the mid 1980s the Marlin logo replaced Kay on these East German-made electrics. The model was later made in Korea and marketed under the Marlin By Hohner brand.

1965 Hoyer 35

1982 Musima Eterna Deluxe

Musima was East Germany's major instrument manufacturer, producing a range of Fender-influenced solids.

c.1965 Hoyer 35

This guitar is a fusion of Fender-like features with distinctively German ideas. Hoyer changed hands in 2009 and currently offers a revitalised product line of six-strings and basses.

1999 Teuffel Birdfish

This strange modular metal-frame instrument from Ulrich Teuffel won three design awards and has been used by players such as Billy Gibbons. The guitar was limited to a run of 500, and many of the instruments now reside in private collections.

1999 Teuffel Birdfish

EUROPEAN MAKERS
ITALY

Like every European country, Italy experienced the pop-music boom of the 1960s, and this led to a great demand for electric guitars. Many Italian models were supplied by accordion makers, and the results were unlike anything being produced anywhere else.

Two examples of Italian plastic whackiness from the 1960s came courtesy of Bartolini and Crucianelli, the latter bearing the Elite brand name. Both have the accordion-style heat-molded plastic covering so typical of the period. Other features influenced by the accordion include the row of pushbutton selectors and the generally colorful presentation. The Eko company, started by Olivero Pigini, was one such example of a maker whose sparkle finishes

and pushbuttons were the result of the transition between accordion and guitar production.

Later, in line with the guitar-making industries in other European countries, Italian-made instruments began to reflect American design influences. By the 1970s, much of the accordion flavor had, sadly, disappeared and, as in most other countries, copies of famous brands became commonplace and accepted.

Crucianelli was itself copied, however, when the Italia brand debuted in 2000 (see page 146). The Korean-built instruments, designed by British luthier Trevor Wilkinson, embraced all things retro – including the Modena, based on a 1960s Crucianelli.

1964 Eko 700/4V

1964 Eko 700/4V
The triple-cutaway 700/4V is from the major Italian maker Oliviero Pigini & Co of Recanati, which exported its Eko brand to 28 countries. This was the top of Eko's line of plastic-covered solids. Eko's literature proclaimed "necks made from warp-proof Jong-Kong wood from Thailand" and the use of "five-ply proxylin guardplate."

SAY
IT
WITH
AN
EKO

Eko Jazz bassist Lee Burrows

EKO

Write for EKO 52-page color catalog. Send 25c in coin to: EKO SALES, Dept. GP-4, Division of Lo Duca Bros. Musical Instruments Inc., 9034 W. Walnut St., Milwaukee, Wisconsin 53208

1969 Eko ad featuring bassist Lee Burrows

1984 Stonehenge Model II
This novel instrument, with its tubular metal body frame, was designed and built in 1984 by Alfredo Bugari of Castelfidardo. The model name derives from his theories about the sound properties of the ancient English stone circle.

1964 Gemelli 195/4/V

SOLIDBODY

1964 Bartolini

1982 Melody Blue Sage

1965 Crucianelli / Elite

1964 Bartolini
This is a wonderful example of the accordion-influenced plastic-covered guitar. In fact, the switches probably came from an accordion. They didn't stop Hubert Sumlin, who occasionally played one in the 1960s with Howlin' Wolf.

1982 Melody Blue Sage
Made by a decidedly conservative company, this model is of much higher quality than most Melody guitars. It has a wooden-covered humbucker and a piezo pickup in the bridge.

1965 Crucianelli / Elite
These guitars, marketed in the US under the Elite name, and sometimes elsewhere with the Crucianelli brand, include countless configurations of the eight basic models made from stockpiled components.

1964 Wandre Dura

1964 Wandre Dura
A novel feature of this 1960s brand was the "Duraluminum" metal neck and headstock, predating the American trend by several years. The hardware is reminiscent of motorbike parts.

c.1961 Wandre Rock Oval
Antonio "Wandre" Piolli made through-neck guitars with a unique aluminum neck design, incorporating unusual laminate materials and multi-colored finishes on his more exotic models. Bob Dylan can be seen eyeballing one of these peculiar models in a London store window in his 1967 movie *Don't Look Back*.

1964 Gemelli 195/4/V
This brand was made by Benito and Umberto Cingolani in Recanati. According to the company catalogue, the 195 featured "volume and tone plunger commands" giving functions such as "Acute," "Bass Acute," and "Closed."

1984 Stonehenge Model II

1961 Wandre Rock Oval

SOLIDBODY ELECTRIC GUITARS

153

EUROPEAN MAKERS
NORTH & EAST EUROPE

Many European guitar-making companies started in the early 1960s boom. Often one domestic brand per country was enough to cater for the demand, offering cheaper alternatives to the imported competition. Naturally, many of these guitars have been based on the big-name American brands, but some European makers added distinctive features of their own that lent some local character—and avoided the copying so widely practiced by Far Eastern companies in the 1970s. Ironically, as we have seen in the preceding pages, the waves of cheaper imports that resulted from this copying would sound the death knell for many European makers.

Even in Eastern Europe, the solid electric guitar made an early impression. Although there were far fewer makers than in the West, large numbers of instruments were produced, and many of these were exported.

European instruments have never enjoyed the same level of worldwide success as the American originators, but some brandnames did enjoy limited success and a reasonable lifespan. Circumstances changed again as standardized products from the USA and the Far East supplanted most of the local varieties.

Smaller makers that have survived usually do so based on the enduring popularity of a particular heritage model, such as the Hofner 500/1 Violin Bass, or by focusing efforts on small runs of high-quality guitars, which sell to a select and often elite minority of relatively well-off players.

c.1975 Defil Jola 2

2007 ad for French maker Lag, featuring Babyshambles

c.1975 Defil Jola 2
The only company mass-producing guitars in Poland, Defil was responsible for a wide range of solidbody and semi-acosutic electrics.

1965 Egmond Model 3

1965 Egmond Model 3
Dutch-built Egmond instruments, produced from the early 1960s to the mid 1970s, were aimed at beginners—with quality and construction to match. The vinyl-covered 3 from 1965 carries a brandname of UK importer Rosetti.

c.1960 Futurama

c.1960 Futurama
This was a brandname of UK importer Selmer, first appearing around 1959 on these crude solids made in Czechoslovakia by Horovice. This one is similar to the model used by a young George Harrison, and many other early British beat-group guitarists.

SOLIDBODY ELECTRIC GUITARS

1984 Vigier Arpege V6-V

1968 Goya Rangemaster

1984 Vigier Arpege V6-V
Patrice Vigier designed this guitar with a trapezoidal thru-body neck and a fretboard reinforced with carbon fiber underneath. Since introducing the Arpege in 1980, this French maker has designed guitars with unique features and some original hardware.

1968 Goya Rangemaster
Levin in Sweden imported acoustic guitars into the USA branded as Goya. Later, the Rangemaster was manufactured in Italy and imported under the same brand, along with sparkle-topped Hagstrom guitars.

2011 Vigier ad

c.1966 Muzicka Naklada Special 64

1959 Hagstrom P46 Deluxe

2005 Lag catalogue

c.1966 Muzicka Naklada Special 64
The three-pickup solid shown here was built in the mid 1960s by the Muzicka Naklada company in Yugoslavia. It's crudely made and of poor quality, but there is no mistaking the Fender inspiration.

1959 Hagstrom P46 Deluxe
This was the first solid from Hagstrom, a Swedish company operating between the late 1950s and early 1980s, revived in 2004. A two-pickup version was offered along with this four-pickup model, in various colorful plastic finishes.

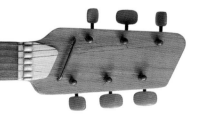

SOLIDBODY ELECTRICS

155

JAPAN
ORIGINALS & EARLY COPIES

The Japanese began to produce solidbody electric guitars in the late 1950s. Looking at the instruments of that period and of the early 1960s, the Japanese makers had clearly absorbed Western influences, incorporating them into their own relatively original designs. These early instruments are significant, because it is often wrongly assumed that the Japanese guitar industry was founded on the production of copies.

The copy era actually came later, starting around 1970, and the Japanese took to the exercise with great enthusiasm. The principal targets were the best-known US models, such as the Gibson Les Paul and the Fender Stratocaster, but virtually every original was flattered by a Japanese imitation.

Lack of technical knowledge meant early efforts were often of poor quality, making "Japanese copy" a derogatory description. But expertise and understanding improved, and so did the product, eventually presenting Western makers with a very real challenge. With the great success of their copies, many of the well-established Japanese makers felt confident enough to produce original designs once again. Western influences were still there, but during the 1970s, a distinct Japanese visual style emerged.

Some designs were radical, and in the 1980s a number of makers experimented with synthetic materials. The Japanese popularized several construction methods during this period, including the laminated through-neck style, creating a distinctive striped center-section on the body.

Increasing US production costs in the early 1980s encouraged various American makers to have some of their guitars built in Japan, most significantly Fender. The Stratocaster design and its modern "superstrat" derivatives became the dominant guitar style of the 1980s. However, Japanese companies were also hit by an increase in production costs, and major guitar companies began to shift production to other countries in the Far East. Modern Japanese-built guitars now sell for prices similar to those of American competitors.

1963 Teisco SD-4L

1959 Guyatone LG30

1963 Teisco SD-4L
Leading Japanese guitar maker Teisco adopted the European-sounding Teisco Del Rey brandname and produced its most stylish creation yet with the curvaceous SD-4L.

1959 Guyatone LG30
A guitar-maker since 1933, Guyatone introduced original-design solid electrics in the late 1950s. These were imported into the UK under brandnames such as Star, Guyatone, and Antoria (as used by Hank Marvin in his early pre-Strat days).

1992 Starfield Altair SJ Custom

1992 Starfield Altair SJ Custom
Originally making copies of Gibsons in the 1970s, Starfield was re-launched in 1992 by Hoshino, the parent company of Ibanez. The guitars were all made in Japan to a high standard until cheaper Korean-made guitars were added to the lines in 1994.

1966 Teisco Del Ray catalogue

1968 Tokai Humming Bird

This early original-design solid electric from the Hamamatsu-based Tokai company was strongly influenced by Mosrite. The big Japanese success of the Mosrite-toting Ventures had made this US maker very popular in Japan during the 1960s.

1984 Maya Model 8029

This Japanese-made model appeared in the mid 1980s. In an unusually styled package, it combined the portability of a travel mini-guitar with the convenience of the self-contained guitar's built-in amp and speaker.

1968 Norma EG-400

Norma guitars were Japanese models imported into America during the 1960s. Many were made by the Tombo Accordion company, which explains the Italian influence.

1968 Tokai Humming Bird

1984 Maya Model 8029

1968 Norma EG-400

c.1968 Kawai Concert

c.1968 Kawai Concert

By the end of the 1960s, Kawai was one of the biggest guitar makers in Japan, producing instruments for the domestic market with its own brandname as well as supplying many export customers in the US and Europe. The Concert, looking more like some kind of strange weapon than a guitar, was one of Kawai's most distinctive models.

1985 Tokai MAT M602

This guitar was part of Tokai's Most Advanced Technology series. These Fender-influenced models were available with graphite or fiberglass necks or bodies, in any combination. The example shown is all-fiberglass and features active circuitry.

1985 Tokai MAT M602

1984 Tokai Talbo A80D

Original thinking is evident in the design of the Talbo (Tokai ALuminum BOdy). The material was chosen for its sustaining and tonal properties. Tokai added a pair of Blazing Fire humbuckers to complete the Talbo's rich, ringing sound.

1984 Tokai Talbo A80D

SOLIDBODY ELECTRIC GUITARS

JAPAN
ARIA

Shiro Arai, chairman and founder of the Nagoya-based firm that made Aria guitars, was smitten by the classical guitar in post-war Japan. He imported Japan's first classical guitars in 1954, and a few years later, seeing a rise in demand, he founded his company. Electric guitars followed in 1963, originally made by Guyatone but improving in quality when production switched to Matsumoko, a company whose guitars would subsequently feature a variety of brandnames around the world.

Aria's turning point came when Arai created a bolt-neck copy of the Gibson Les Paul, formally beginning the "copy era" that characterised Japanese guitar output in the 1970s, and in which Aria would play a significant role. Copies of almost all significant Western models followed. The firm focussed on a new brand, Aria Pro II, in 1975. A year later, Aria introduced its first original design, the PE

models. These carved-top single-cut guitars, with their sweeping curve, set or bolt-on necks, DiMarzio pickups, and vibrato options, were made by Matsumoko, and they ushered in a wave of original Aria designs.

The quality of Aria's late-1970s models would do much to change global perceptions of Japanese guitars for the better, along with brands such as Yamaha and Ibanez.

In 1982, increasing popularity of hard-rock styles saw the addition of exotic shape guitars, such as the B.C. Rich-inspired Urchin, the V-shaped XX, and the Explorer-like ZZ series. Then came the superstrat craze, and Aria was in the thick of it throughout.

Aria's story has always been at the forefront of the larger tale of globalization in the guitar industry (see page 168), and it moved part of its production to Korea in the 1980s, and later to China and even the USA.

c.1968 Aria Diamond ADSG-12T

c.1968 Aria Diamond ADSG-12T
This guitar has the Fender-inspired "offset waist" body shape, and it shows that the craze for electric 12-string guitars lasted longer in Japan—by 1968, in America and Europe, the popularity of the jingle-jangle sound was in decline.

1985 Aria Pro II ZZ Deluxe

SOLIDBODY ELECTRIC GUITARS

158

1979 Aria Pro II RS-850

1979 Aria Pro II RS-850
The guitar has an ash body with walnut stripes and a five-ply maple-and-walnut neck. Its unique Quick-Hook tailpiece was specifically designed for quick string changes.

1984 and 1985 press ads

1982 Aria Pro II Urchin Deluxe
Many of the best Aria models, like this Urchin, were made at the Matsumoku factory between 1977 and 1987. The Urchin was the first odd-shaped guitar from Aria, and its sales did not match those of the brand's more traditional instruments.

1977 Aria Pro II PE-160

1999 Aria Pro II M-650T

1982 Aria Pro II Urchin Deluxe

1985 Aria Pro II ZZ Deluxe
Equipped with two "hot" blade pickups and a Kahler tremolo, this guitar has a red/black version of the zebra stripe on the ultra-pointy body style.

1977 Aria Pro II PE-160
Made in the Matsumoko factory, this copy of a Stratocaster has a unique solid-walnut body with a dragon carved into the front. Two different dragon designs and an eagle were available.

1999 Aria Pro II M-650T
The sparkle finish on this guitar was available in red, gold, or silver over an agathis wood body. It had a bolt-on neck with two humbucking pickups.

159

SOLID BODY ELECTRIC GUITARS

JAPAN
IBANEZ–THE EARLY YEARS

No Japanese maker has had such an impact on the global guitar industry as Hoshino Gakki Ten and its primary brandname, Ibanez. Since the 1960s, Ibanez has been associated with acoustic and electric guitars that have enjoyed immense popularity with generations of players all around the globe.

The guitar business began around 1908 as the musical instrument division of the Hoshino Shotena book and stationery store in Nagoya. It began importing Western instruments in 1921, and began exporting its own acoustic instruments in 1929 with the Ibanez brand (which it bought from the Spanish classical maker Salvador Ibáñez).

The company's buildings were destroyed during World War II and production resumed in 1950. By the late 1950s, Hoshino was creating and exporting guitars under a variety of brandnames, soon from its new factory, and while it's an oversimplification, Ibanez's output can be characterized into three stylistic categories: the Burns-influenced 1960s; the Gibson-dominated 1970s; and the Fender-influenced 1980s and beyond.

Throughout most of the 1960s, Ibanez focused on acoustic guitars, but it did release two notable solidbody shapes aimed at the beginner and student market. One was inspired by the Burns Bison, the other the Fender Jazzmaster (which was revised after a while to a more Stratocaster-like model).

Hoshino's serious interest in electric guitars was stimulated after Shiro Arai returned from the USA in 1968 and began making bolt-neck Les Paul copies. Ibanez joined in with its 1969 Les Paul copy and, in 1971, a see-through Lucite Ampeg Dan Armstrong copy. The new Japanese "copy era" had begun, and Ibanez was to play a defining role.

1963 Ibanez Model 882

1963 Ibanez Model 882
In 1962, the company opened the Tama Siesakusho plant and made a range of solidbody guitars bearing the Ibanez name. Shaped like a Fender Jazzmaster, this guitar is an early example.

1975 Ibanez ad featuring Bob Weir

1978 Ibanez Musician MC500

1978 Ibanez Professional 2671 Randy Scruggs

SOLIDBODY ELECTRIC GUITARS

1979 Ibanez Iceman IC-210

1964 Ibanez Model 2103

1976 Ibanez press ad with Carl Perkins and Randy Scruggs.

1979 Ibanez Iceman IC-210
The first weirdly shaped guitar from Ibanez, it has hints of Rickenbacker and the Gibson Firebird. The unusual-looking pickup was controlled by the black four-way rotary tone selector, plus normal volume and tone knobs. Other Icemen from this period came with two humbuckers or a single sliding pickup.

1964 Ibanez Model 2103
This is a virtual copy of the Burns Bison, with its three-piece pickguard, three pickups, and solid-looking side-mounted vibrato arrangement. The rocker-style switches add a touch of Eastern originality.

1984 Ibanez Destroyer II DT555
The futuristic Destroyer DT series was endorsed by Phil Collen of Def Leppard. It has what Ibanez described as three "sizzling Super 70 pickups" plus the road-tested Ibanez tremolo bridge system.

1981 Ibanez Artist 2618
This model from the Artist series has a German-carve top of maple over a mahogany body, and it's fitted with two Super 70 humbuckers.

1984 Ibanez Destroyer II DT555

1978 Ibanez Musician MC500
This model has a neck-through-body design with a center section of laminated maple and walnut. It comes with specially designed Tri-Sound Super 88 humbuckers, active electronics, a brass nut, and the Ibanez Gibraltar model bridge and tailpiece.

1978 Ibanez Professional 2671 Randy Scruggs
This single-cut design has a German-carve body of solid ash, reminiscent of the Rickenbacker "lipped top" style. It has the luxury appointments of gold-plated hardware and orante tree-of-life fingerboard inlays.

1981 Ibanez Artist 2618

Hoshino's interest in electric guitars was stimulated after Shiro Arai of Aria returned from a trade show in the USA in 1968, full of new ideas, and began making bolt-on-neck Les Paul copies. Ibanez soon joined in with its 1969 Les Paul copy, and, in 1971, a see-through-plastic Ampeg Dan Armstrong-alike. The new Japanese copy era had begun, and Ibanez was to play a defining role.

Japanese makers continued to produce full copycat lines of Fender, Gibson, Martin, and other US brands. This strategy of wholesale copying of American designs was a successful one, especially for Ibanez, and copies became progressively closer to the originals. The quality of the designs was improved based on advice from export customers in the UK and USA, and by 1974, the line had exploded, with instruments resembling the Les Paul, SG, Explorer, Flying V, Moderne, ES-345, and ES-175, not to

mention a full complement of Fender lookalikes. Ibanez did release designs of its own, including the respected Artist series in the mid 1970s, which ran until 1982, as well as 1975's collectable Custom Agent, Artwood Nouveau, and the Artwood Twin. The pointy Iceman appeared in 1976, and it was recreated in reverse form as the Ibanez Fireman by longstanding Ibanez endorser Paul Gilbert in 2009.

Back in the 1970s, however, the US companies were increasingly alarmed by the quality of the copies flooding the market and threatening their share of it. So it was that in 1977, Gibson's parent company, Norlin, claimed that the Ibanez-owned US distributor Elger had infringed its copyrighted headstock design. The case was settled out of court. Copy guitars from this era are sometimes known as lawsuit instruments.

After this, at the dawn of the 1980s, Ibanez's designs would shift toward a distinctly Fender-like template, in time for the birth of the superstrat craze.

1989 Ibanez Maxxas MX3

1989 Ibanez Maxxas MX3
Despite coming from the age of the superstrat, this design evoked a 1950s rocket ship with its sleek body lines, spaceman knobs, and optional Black Hole "reverse sunburst" finish. American DiMarzio pickups were mounted on a body with acoustic cavities. The Maxxas was a brave but unsuccessful departure from contemporary style.

1986 Ibanez Roadstar II RG240

1998 Ibanez JS 10th Anniversary

1986 Ibanez Roadstar II RG240
The Roadstar series of guitars had the obligatory locking nut and a new knife-edge vibrato system. It became one of the most fulsome of the Ibanez ranges. The later RG designation began here, standing for Roadstar Guitar.

1987 Ibanez Pro Line PL2550

1990 Ibanez Universe UV7BK

1987 Ibanez Pro Line PL2550
The Pro Line series had a new preset switching system, making many preset sounds available at the flick of a switch. With neck-through-body construction, this instrument also shared the new trend for oil-finished necks.

1990 Ibanez Universe UV7BK
This seven-string superstrat was developed for Ibanez with help from Steve Vai. It has two Blade II humbuckers flanking a single-coil unit, all from DiMarzio, on a black-finished basswood body, and with green pickups and knobs.

2000 Ibanez ad with seven-string fans Korn

1985 Ibanez Axstar AX45

1985 Ibanez Axstar AX45
In the mid 1980s, Ibanez produced a large range of unconventional pointy-bodied guitars aimed at the shred-metal guitar fraternity.

Joe Satriani and Ibanez in 1990

1998 Ibanez JS 10th Anniversary
Guitar virtuoso Joe Satriani is a long-time Ibanez player, having endorsed the 540R model which formed the basis for signature models in the JS series. This 10th anniversary model has a body of synthetic "luthite" which is finished in chrome.

Jennifer Batten and Ibanez in 1989

SOLIDBODY ELECTRIC GUITARS

JAPAN
IBANEZ TODAY

The Roadster offered budget Strat style in 1979, and was replaced by the Blazer, then the Roadstar II—a model which became the most prolific of all Ibanez electrics. The late 1980s saw the company approaching rock players in earnest with the Radius and Saber, developing a series of viable alternatives to US superstrats (the Power, JEM, and RG among them) that would find favor with fleet-fingered shredder endorsers such as Steve Vai and Joe Satriani.

Ibanez was more visible than ever, but alongside its trendsetting rock models, it still provided semi-solid and hollowbody instruments to cater for more traditional tastes. Into the 1990s, Ibanez added to its healthy list of signature endorsers from varied musical backgrounds, and there were signature models for players such as Frank Gambale, Reb Beach, Paul Gilbert, Pat Metheny, and John

Petrucci. Into the new millennium, and Ibanez consolidated its lines at all price-points. However, its catalogue of the 2000s did continue to look much as it had at the end of the previous decade. There's the reassuring pointiness of the RG and S series, with a wealth of rock-ready appointments including seven and eight-string models. The company has produced reissues of much-loved Ibanez oldies, including the Artist and the Destroyer, and regularly updated the perennially popular JEM. Meanwhile, the retro Jet King maintains this nostalgic strand, while Hoshino has used Korean, Indonesian, and Chinese sources to aid its production.

2003 German Ibanez ad

2003 Ibanez JEM 77FP

2003 Ibanez JEM 77FP
From early in the model's life, Ibanez producied the JEM 77 in a variety of multi-colored finishes, some with a painted "swirl" effect. This one is a 15th anniversary reissue of the floral-pattern model that was first released in 1988.

1998 Ibanez JEM 90th Anniversary

2008 Ibanez SHRG1Z

1998 Ibanez JEM 90th Anniversary
The JEM was first produced in 1987, and several anniversary models followed. This model celebrates the 90th anniversary of Hoshino, the parent company of Ibanez. It came with a special paint finish and a high-polished aluminum pickguard. The model was limited to a run of around 760 guitars.

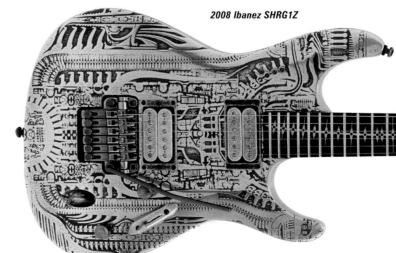

SOLIDBODY ELECTRIC GUITARS

164

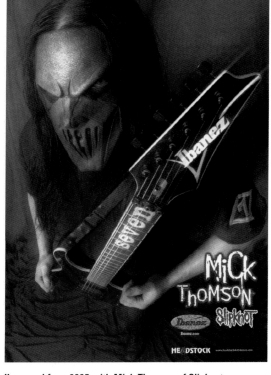

Ibanez ad from 2005 with Mick Thomson of Slipknot

1999 Ibanez S-Classic SC240

1994 Ibanez Talman TV750

2008 Ibanez JS20S

2008 Ibanez JS20S
Emblazoned on the body of this JS series guitar is the artwork from Joe Satriani's classic 1987 album, *Surfing With The Alien*.

2008 Ibanez SV5470F Prestige
The Prestige series of guitars boast hand-finished necks and fingerboards giving that give a played-in feel to the instrument.

1999 Ibanez S-Classic SC240
The S series of instruments was introduced in 1987, and the models came in a wide variety of forms, although they all share a super-thin mahogany body.

1994 Ibanez Talman TV750
The Talman series has various combinations of humbucker-style and Kent Armstrong-designed epoxy-sealed lipstick pickups. These units are mounted on the pickguard over a routed sound chamber, intended to increase resonance. This model has a traditional-looking maple top and gold-plated hardware.

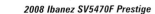

2008 Ibanez SV5470F Prestige

H.R. Giger Ibanez
ad from 2005

2008 Ibanez SHRG1Z
Alien-designing visionary H.R. Giger joined with Ibanez for a series of signature models. This one features a

Biomechanical Matrix graphic finish on a metal-coated mahogany body, and it has Giger fretboard inlays on a Wizard II neck.

SOLIDBODY

165

JAPAN
YAMAHA

Yamaha is of course a big conglomerate, manufacturing many different kinds of products. But it has been making musical instruments for well over 100 years, and with guitars it began by making acoustics, and produced its first solid electric guitars in the mid 1960s, a range of models with strong American character.

Even early Yamahas are distinguished by particularly high-quality craftsmanship. A major milestone was reached in 1976 with the release of the SG-2000, a model from Yamaha's third series of SG electrics (renamed SBG in the US). More than any other guitar, the SG-2000 convinced musicians that the Japanese could produce an instrument comparable to the best from the West. Its attractive double-cut shape helped seduce endorser Carlos Santana, and the model continued to be exported to the US until 1988 (although it's available today as a high-end model from Yamaha's Music Craft workshop based at the company's headquarters in Hamamatsu).

Having established a healthy acoustic line, and produced the successful SA-60 and SA-90 semi-hollowbodies, Yamaha's RGX Series embraced the superstrat trend in 1987. These sleek, offset-double-cutaway rock machines had evolved into the RGZ line by 1990. The company's Pacifica model debuted at this time, and became one of the best-value and most successful starter electrics, although fancier versions were also added to the line-up.

Yamaha has risen to become the world's largest manufacturer of musical instruments, and its electric line today ranges from the retro and the classic right through to the high-end and the high-tech.

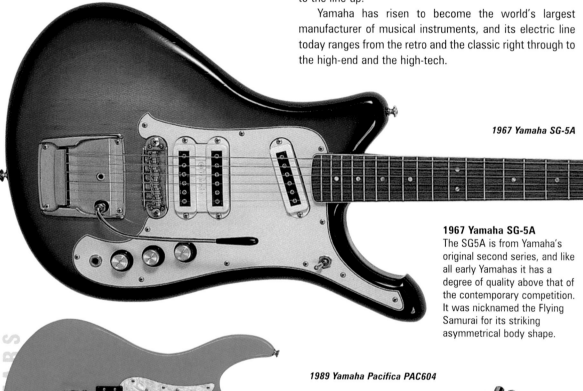

1967 Yamaha SG-5A

1967 Yamaha SG-5A
The SG5A is from Yamaha's original second series, and like all early Yamahas it has a degree of quality above that of the contemporary competition. It was nicknamed the Flying Samurai for its striking asymmetrical body shape.

1989 Yamaha Pacifica PAC604

1989 Yamaha Pacifica PAC604
The model was designed by the Yamaha Custom Shop in California in the late 1980s. The line has a wide variety of grades, including the high-end

Mike Stern signature model with Tele-style single cutaway body. The 604 variant was an entry-model guitar but was available with higher spec in the 604W.

1989 Yamaha RGX Custom

1999 Yamaha AES500

JONNY ROCKER
PLAYS AES920

AES920
Flamed maple/mahogany
body – Seymour Duncan
'59 pickups – available
in Charcoal Grey and
Honey Burst – RRP £1199

YAMAHA
GUITARS

www.yamahamusicsesion.co.uk

2007 Yamaha ad

1999 Yamaha AES500
The AES models had sound chambers
cut into the body with a solid block
under the bridge and the tailpiece area.
This 500 came fitted with two Alnico V
humbucking pickups.

2007 Yamaha SG2000
This model was from Yamaha's third SG
series, and in the mid 1970s it
combined modern performance with
vintage character. These SGs were
Yamaha's longest-running solids, built
from 1973 to 1988 and reissued later.

Major in social studies.

YAMAHA

1986 Yamaha ad

1989 Yamaha RGX Custom
The Taiwan-made RG series was introduced in 1987. The RGX
model had 24 frets and a bolt-on neck, although some high-
end variants have a neck-through-body design. The model
was upgraded in 2003 with a three-a-side headstock and a
piezo bridge option for acoustic-like tones.

2007 Yamaha SG2000

OTHER ASIAN MAKERS
KOREA & CHINA

Guitar players seem unwilling to spend the amount of money on their instruments that many other musicians take for granted. So when the cost of producing guitars in the United States and Japan began to climb during the early 1980s, the major makers in those countries had to look elsewhere for cheaper manufacturing sources. A few chose Taiwan, but the more suitable climate in Korea made it the most popular option.

The prime requirement from the Korean makers was a guitar built down to a price, and almost inevitably this caused compromises in the materials used in many of the production facilities. The result was often a guitar where fashionable features and a good paint job took precedence over quality and durability. However, standards gradually rose—but so did prices.

Ironically, companies ended up once again looking for cheaper production bases, resulting in the rise since the late 1990s of Indonesian and particularly

Chinese-made guitars, reflecting global product trends. Many well-known companies used Korean sources for their cheaper brands back in the day: for example, Harmony, Gibson's Epiphone, and Fender's Squier have all been made in Korea. Leading Japanese names such as Washburn, Westone, Aria, and Hondo also capitalized. Korea created its own brands, too, such as Samick and Cort. Today, the booming industrialization of China has led to a concentration of export-focused OEM (Original Equipment Manufacture) factories in the Guangdong Province, creating instruments for the established brands.

Some companies have set up their own bespoke production facilities in China, such as Gibson's Qingdao factory, which has been busily creating Epiphone models since 2002. As OEM margins diminish, it seems possible that Chinese manufacturers will increasingly export their own products back to the Western and Japanese markets.

c.1989 Starforce Model 8007

c.1989 Starforce Model 8007
The Korean brand produced Fender lookalikes in bright finishes and later used a more rounded body shape similar to the US maker Spector.

1999 Samick DCV9500

Alexi Laiho promotes ESP in a 2007 ad

1989 Encore SE1

1993 Fernandes FR5S

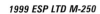

1989 Encore SE1

The Korean-made Encore brand has always been a source of budget copies for the UK. This 1989 model shows the company keeping up with modern trends by borrowing the style of one of the hottest USA makers, Paul Reed Smith. But the good finish covers a plywood body.

1993 Fernandes FR5S

This Strat-style guitar with pink see-through acrylic body was made in Korea by Fernandes, now one of Japan's major guitar manufacturers. Fernandes today produces guitars in Korea and China as well as in Japan.

1999 ESP LTD M-250

Japanese firm ESP introduced the Korean-made LTD brand in 1996. This typical superstrat, with HSH (humbucker-single-humubcker) layout, is from LTD's budget line.

1999 ESP LTD M-250

Ad for James
Hetfield's Snakebyte
Signature Series
from ESP

1999 Samick DCV9500

Samick, founded as a piano maker in 1958 in Korea, started making guitars in 1965 and by the late 1990s had an enormous line ranging from "copies" to more original designs, like this quilted maple-topped double cut-away with abalone trim. American luthier Greg Bennett recently designed a line of guitars for Samick.

NEW MATERIALS
SYNTHETICS & ALUMINUM

Guitars have traditionally been made from wood, but makers have occasionally tried out alternative materials. Sometimes this has been for economic reasons, sometimes to improve the guitar's sound, strength, or appearance.

Metals and plastics have been tried since the 1920s for their apparent improvement of rigidity and sustain. Some plastics also offered potentially faster production. But working with these materials often presented new problems to the makers, and some players found that metals felt cold and plastics appeared cheap.

To combat the instability of wooden necks, Travis Bean developed his aluminum alternative in California in 1974. Despite increasing volume and sustain, the neck's cold feel made Bean's expensive, high-quality guitars unpopular. Production ceased in 1979.

It was not until the 1980s and the advent of new materials such as "graphite" that musicians eventually accepted more alternatives to good old wood. The Parker Fly, which appeared in 1993, was at first made from a composite of carbon fiber, glass, and epoxy, showing one possible avenue for experimentation.

In the future, guitar makers may be forced to find more alternatives to wood. Quality timbers are already scarce, and the use of certain woods in quantity is out of step with modern ecological thinking. Some woods have already been embargoed, while other rare types are too costly for mass-produced guitars. Cheaper varieties including bass wood are now in common use. The trend today is to combine woods with synthetic materials, such as ebonol plastic (fingerboards) and carbon graphite (necks).

1990 Vaccaro Stingray

1990 Vaccaro Stingray
Henry Vaccaro, who was the principal of Kramer, attempted to revive the aluminum neck guitar in 1990. The Stingray had a wood-sheathed T-bar neck and various fancy sparkle finishes.

1964 National Glenwood 95

1964 National Glenwood 95
Valco owned the National name in the 1960s and made a range of fiberglass-bodied models intended for speedy, cost-effective production. But they ended up more expensive than planned. There were also Newport fiberglass guitars and similarly styled wood-body Westwood models, plus a line of slightly cheaper and less ornate Supro-branded versions.

1969 Dan Armstrong/Ampeg See-Through

1969 Dan Armstrong/Ampeg See-Through
Armstrong designed this model for Ampeg, using clear plastic to improve sustain, hence its commonly used See-Through name. It was made between 1969 and 1971.

SOLIDBODY ELECTRIC GUITARS

1977 Kramer 450G

c.1965 Airline JB Hutto Montgomery

Goulding aluminum-body guitar from a 2012 ad

1977 Kramer 450G

Gary Kramer, previously a partner of Travis Bean, started his own company in New Jersey in 1975. Guitars appeared from 1976 as Kramer continued and refined the idea of the aluminum neck. In 1985, Kramer guitars changed completely to normal wooden necks, and met with more success.

c.1965 Airline JB Hutto Montgomery

Another example of a "Res-O-Glass" bodied guitar from Valco, this one sold through the Montgomery Ward mail-order firm. A lookalike reissue is made by Eastwood, although its chambered mahogany body gives a more traditional electric-guitar sound than that of the original.

1996 Parker Fly ad

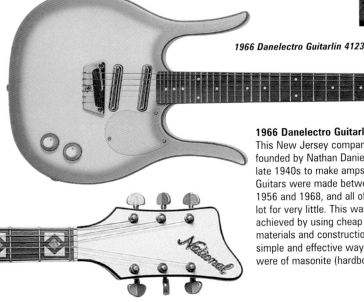

1966 Danelectro Guitarlin 4123

1966 Danelectro Guitarlin 4123

This New Jersey company was founded by Nathan Daniel in the late 1940s to make amps. Guitars were made between 1956 and 1968, and all offered a lot for very little. This was achieved by using cheap materials and construction in a simple and effective way. Bodies were of masonite (hardboard) on a wooden frame, fitted with basic hardware and pickups made from lipstick cases.

1999 Danelectro 56-U3

This popular reissue has higher output pickups, master tone, and volume knobs as opposed to the original and distinctive stacked concentric controls. However, the materials and construction methods are virtually identical.

1999 Danelectro 56-U3

1972 Veleno

John Veleno built his unusual guitars in Florida in the early 1970s. They were made almost entirely from aluminum, including the body, neck, and fingerboard. There were pickup and finish options, and the peculiar headstock was inlaid with a ruby.

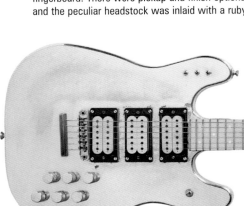

1972 Veleno

SOLIDBODY ELECTRIC GUITARS

BEYOND SIX STRINGS
TWELVE-STRING GUITARS

Most guitarists find six strings more than enough to cope with, but some brave players favor instruments with extra strings, usually added to the existing strings to form pairs or "courses." The intention is to expand the range of the standard guitar, bolstering the sound with the additional higher-pitched strings and making an effective boost for some styles of rhythm playing and melody lines.

Sometimes for solo work, single strings are added to the regular six. An early pioneer of this scheme was jazz guitarist George Van Eps, whose 1960s Gretsch was based on his old seven-string, custom made for Van Eps by Epiphone. Latter-day rock and metal players have also gravitated towards models with extra bass-side strings to accommodate their aggressive, down-tuned styles.

Ironically, using fewer strings than normal can provide new sounds, and probably the best-known exponent of this technique is Keith Richards. The Rolling Stones guitarist often uses a five-string instrument—usually a six-string with the low E removed—for his powerful rhythm parts. David Bowie took the idea to its minimal conclusion on his 1990 tour by "playing" a one-string guitar.

On a 12-string guitar, the regular six strings are doubled up. The lower four pairs each consist of a normally-tuned string plus a string an octave higher, while each of the top two pairs are tuned in unison. This strengthening of the guitar's sound through octave and unison doubling produces the classic 12-string jangling sound, almost as if two guitars were playing together.

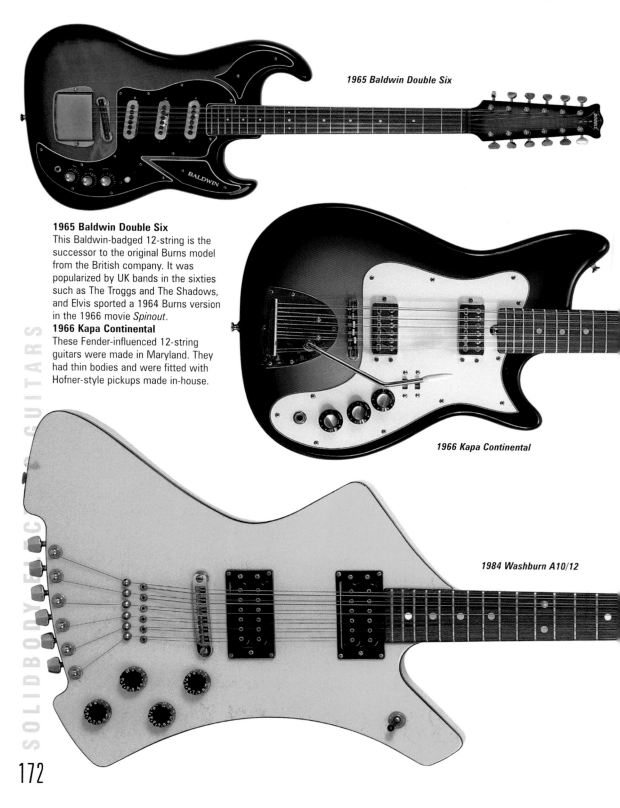

1965 Baldwin Double Six

1965 Baldwin Double Six
This Baldwin-badged 12-string is the successor to the original Burns model from the British company. It was popularized by UK bands in the sixties such as The Troggs and The Shadows, and Elvis sported a 1964 Burns version in the 1966 movie *Spinout*.

1966 Kapa Continental
These Fender-influenced 12-string guitars were made in Maryland. They had thin bodies and were fitted with Hofner-style pickups made in-house.

1966 Kapa Continental

1984 Washburn A10/12

SOLIDBODY ELECTRIC GUITARS

172

*1966 Fender
Electric XII*

Fender R&D office, from a 1965 catalogue

1966 Fender Electric XII
Fender USA's first and only electric 12-string solid of the time was launched in 1965. The distinctive "hockey stick" headstock (see left) was a typical Fender touch. Overall styling echoed its six-string Fender predecessors such as the Jazzmaster and Jaguar. During 1966, the Electric XII gained a bound fingerboard with block inlays. Production stopped in 1969.

2004 PRS Custom 22/12
The first production PRS 12-string came with newly designed pickups and PRS's unique adjustable stop-tail wrap-over bridge.

2004 PRS Custom 22/12

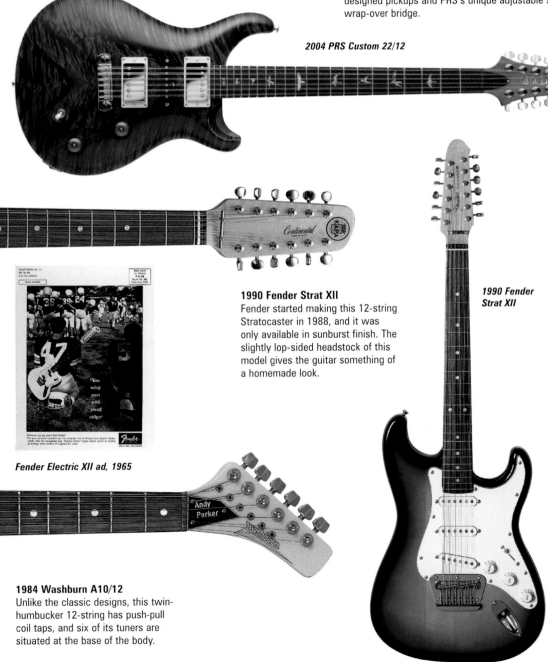

Fender Electric XII ad, 1965

1990 Fender Strat XII
Fender started making this 12-string Stratocaster in 1988, and it was only available in sunburst finish. The slightly lop-sided headstock of this model gives the guitar something of a homemade look.

*1990 Fender
Strat XII*

1984 Washburn A10/12
Unlike the classic designs, this twin-humbucker 12-string has push-pull coil taps, and six of its tuners are situated at the base of the body.

BEYOND SIX STRINGS
TWELVE-STRING GUITARS II

The chiming electric 12-string sound is closely associated with one era in music—the mid to late 1960s when bands such as The Beatles, The Byrds, and The Who filled the airwaves with their resonant arpeggios and ringing chords. The model is also synonymous in the guitarist's mind with one particular manufacturer, though it wasn't the first to produce a 12-string electric—that honor goes to Missouri's Stratosphere, which produced one in 1954. However, despite Danelectro and Vox also beating it to the punch, it was Rickenbacker's models that provided the benchmark for all subsequent makers' attempts at 12-string design. Despite the ebb and flow in popularity of the 12-string sound, the California company has kept models in constant production since the 1960s.

Rickenbacker's success began with three prototype 12-strings developed in 1963, featuring employee Dick Burke's ingenious headstock design, with its extra tuners placed at right-angles to the existing six tuners, which occupied their traditional position. The second of these prototypes ended up with Beatle George Harrison, after a masterstroke of marketing saw the band awarded various Rickenbacker guitars at a meeting in New York City. In 1964, Harrison used his new 12-string 360 on *A Hard Day's Night*, and the craze for Rickenbackers began in earnest. The company's two-pickup 330/12 and deluxe 360/12, as well as the three-pickup 370/12, provided timeless 12-string cool from that moment on, with signature versions added to the line since the late 1980s.

Rickenbacker's success didn't go unnoticed among the other major manufacturers, and Fender, Gibson, Epiphone, and Gretsch have all produced variants on the theme.

1984 Rickenbacker 360/12V64

1984 Rickenbacker 360/12V64
This vintage reissue is based on the 1963-period original, complete with "toaster"-style pickup covers and the slash-shaped soundhole and triangular position markers that are unique to Rickenbacker.

1967 Rickenbacker 360/12 L/H
Left-handed versions of any regular guitar are necessarily less common than right-handers, but this Rick looks especially unusual, given the reversal of familiar features, including a logo that slopes in the "wrong" direction.

1967 Rickenbacker 360/12 L/H

1967 Vox Starstream XII

2006 Rickenbacker catalogue

1967 Vox Starstream XII
A 12-string "Teardrop" semi from the active-electronic series of the late 1960s, made by Eko in Italy. It featured a built-in tuner, distortion, treble and bass boosts, repeat percussion, and, behind the bridge, a novel hand-operated wah-wah.

HOLLOW & SEMI-SOLID ELECTRIC GUITARS

*1965 Gibson ES-335
12-string*

1966 Gretsch 12-string

*1965 Epiphone Riviera
12-string*

1965 Gibson ES-335 12-string
Gibson introduced the 12-string version of the classic ES-335 in 1965, and it was discontinued in 1971. Instead of the stop-bar tailpiece used on the standard six-string models, this guitar has the older-style trapeze tailpiece.

1966 Gretsch 12-string
After making a prototype 12-string for George Harrison in 1964, Gretsch instead put this model into production in 1966, and it was famously used by Mike Nesmith of The Monkees.

1965 Epiphone Riviera 12-string
This guitar is very similar to the Gibson ES-335 12-string except for a narrower and more curved Epiphone headstock, which is extended to accommodate the extra tuners.

*Roger McGuinn with his signature model in a
Rickenbacker promotional shot from 1988*

1968 Fender Coronado XII
Fender introduced the Coronado line in 1966 as competition to its arch-rival Gibson's ES-335 models. Although these guitars looked like conventional semis, they retained Fender's bolt-on neck, and the 12-string version has the "hockey stick" headstock design.

1968 Fender Coronado XII

BEYOND SIX STRINGS
DOUBLE-NECK GUITARS

Why use two guitars when one will do? That is the reasoning behind the double-neck guitar, a design that incorporates two necks on one body. By no means a new idea, the double-neck provides fast changeover between two entirely different instruments, most commonly a six-string and a twelve-string. We'll break into our hollowbody theme for a few pages to investigate the two-neck world.

It's a combination that's been used to notable effect by some of rock's best-known players. The image of Jimmy Page cradling his 1971 Gibson EDS-1275 during live renditions of 'Stairway To Heaven' is one of stadium rock's most memorable sights. It surely inspired many of the

Cerberus-like beasts that both paid tribute to and gently parodied it, including Rick Nielsen's famous Hamer five-neck models and Steve Vai's custom-made heart-shaped triple-neck, built by luthier Joe Rolston.

However, there are drawbacks, the most obvious being the weight and general awkwardness of the resulting object. The body usually has to be larger than normal to accommodate the two necks, the extra controls, pickups, and related hardware. Playing a double-neck can be difficult—when one neck is in the ideal playing position, the other is often too high or too low. A double-neck guitar is thus a compromise between comfort and convenience.

1989 Fender Custom Shop 12/6 Stratocaster

1989 Fender Custom Shop 12/6 Stratocaster
Made in Fender's Custom Shop, this double-neck was built for exhibition purposes. It combines the looks of a vintage XII and Strat with noiseless Fender Lace Sensor pickups.

c.1965 Carvin 2-MS
California's Carvin introduced a mail-order catalogue in 1954, and throughout the 1960s, double-necks were a regular feature. This 2-MS model combines mandolin and six-string necks and even adds a Bigsby.

c.1965 Carvin 2-MS

c.1962 Otwin
This East German double-neck was built specifically for a music trade show in the early 1960s, to show off the abilities of the manufacturer, Musima. Note how the necks angle outward from one another to assist access.

HOLLOW & SEMI-SOLID ELECTRIC GUITARS

1964 Gibson EDS-1275 Double 12

1955 Stratosphere Twin

c.1961 Danelectro Short Horn 3923

1964 Gibson EDS-1275 Double 12

The original Gibson double-necks were hollowbodies, but in 1962 they were changed to solidbody construction, adopting the chamfered slab body of the SG series. These solid mahogany bodies often had a cherry red finish, but this example looks well in white. Famously used by Jimmy Page, the model has been reissued and signature models are also available.

1955 Stratosphere Twin

This production-made double-neck guitar came out under the short-lived brand started by brothers Russ and Claude Deaver. As it was the first electric 12, they had to invent a tuning for it, and they enlisted the help of a friend who played pedal-steel.

2005 PRS 20th Anniversary Dragon

c.1961 Danelectro Short Horn 3923

This is a combination of six-string guitar and four-string bass. It is constructed in the classic Danelectro manner, with laminated masonite tops and backs, covered in vinyl, over a wooden frame.

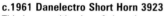

1996 Washburn Nuno Bettencourt N-8

c.1962 Otwin

2005 PRS 20th Anniversary Dragon

This stunner from PRS has exactly 863 pieces of inlay, including abalone, mother of pearl, silver, gold, ebony, and coral. The original design was the work of Jeff Easley, the famous *Dungeons & Dragons* artist.

1996 Washburn Nuno Bettencourt N-8

The Extreme guitarist has been a faithful endorser of Washburn. This N-8 has a 12-string neck with six tuners on the headstock and six on the body. The double-neck was derived from the N4 model that Washburn developed with Nuno and Stephen Davis.

SOLID & SEMI-SOLID ELECTRIC GUITARS

BEYOND SIX STRINGS
DOUBLE-NECK GUITARS II

Some of the world's major guitar makers have built double-neck hollowbody instruments, perhaps in a valiant attempt to keep the weight down. Gibson originally popularized the concept. To avoid excessive heft, Gibson's first double-necks had a carved spruce top with maple back and sides, although the necks were mahogany. There were two humbuckers per neck, and the control layout offered volume, tone, and three-way select for each neck, plus a master neck-selector above the 12-string bridge. Gibson's Tune-o-matic bridges were fitted, but with special string anchors instead of the normal stop-bar tailpiece. Gretsch introduced two double-neck models in the late 1990s. The Gretsch Nashville 6120-6/12 double-neck instrument was joined in the catalogue a year later by a double-neck Duo Jet.

Rickenbacker has released various double-neck models, too, with the 362/12 below and, reflecting its successful heritage with both instruments, the rare 4080/12 bass-and-12-string combination, for rarefied prog-rock moments.

The idea of a guitar with more than one neck is perhaps easier for the smaller custom builder, who is used to fulfilling unusual orders. A good example was the triple-neck solid built by UK custom-maker Hugh Manson in the 1980s. Double-neck guitars usually feature necks parallel to one another, but certain adventurous, ambidextrous artists have had instruments made with necks sprouting from either side of the body.

1997 Gretsch Nashville 6120-6/12

1997 Gretsch Nashville 6120-6/12
This was the first double-neck guitar from Gretsch. It has a non-cutaway body and was only available in orange, which many consider to be the classic color for model 6120.

1975 Rickenbacker 362/12

HOLLOW & SEMI-SOLID ELECTRIC GUITAR

1960 Gibson EDS-1275 Double 12

1988 Rickenbacker catalogue

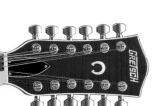

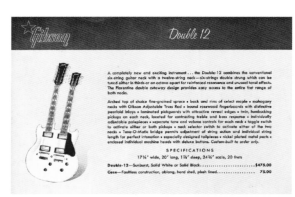

1958 Gibson catalogue

1960 Gibson EDS-1275 Double 12
A rare Gibson from the company's first double-neck line of the late 1950s, this guitar combined six- and twelve-string necks. It was offered alongside the Double Mandolin, which mated six-string and mandolin-style necks. Although production lasted until 1962, these models were built to custom order, and examples are rarely seen.

1975 Rickenbacker 362/12
Double-necks appeared on Rickenbacker pricelists in 1975. This 360-style model, with checkered binding to the body, has one bound "slash" soundhole.

PORTABLE GUITARS
SIX STRINGS ON THE MOVE

The solidbody electric guitar can be a heavy instrument to move about with and needs to be amplified for its intended purpose. These two seemingly obvious factors can sometimes limit the normal instrument's use—on the tour bus, for example. So several manufacturers have made guitars that attempt to offer solutions, some more elegant than others.

First, there are guitars that might be termed "travel minis." Some are effectively entire instruments scaled down in size; others have just the body made smaller. They are designed for convenience, to allow guitarists to practice wherever and whenever they want.

The second kind of go-as-you-please instrument is the "self-contained" guitar, which has a built-in battery-powered amplifier plus loudspeaker. This provides the benefits of all-in portability, plus suitably amplified volume for practice purposes.

The innovative Hoyer Foldaxe from Germany came with a folding neck, remarkably maintaining normal string tension whether folded or unfolded. Hofner's Shorty travel mini came in a self-amplified version that combined the best of both portable worlds.

Another solution was to build an amp and speaker into the guitar case. Such models first appeared in the late 1950s from US companies such as Danelectro. Since then, surprisingly few makers have adopted this idea, although in the early 1980s Peavey issued an Electric Case as an optional extra to its short-scale T-15 and T-30 solidbodies. Despite the advantages of travel minis and self-contained guitars, none has proved successful and few makers produce them in any numbers today.

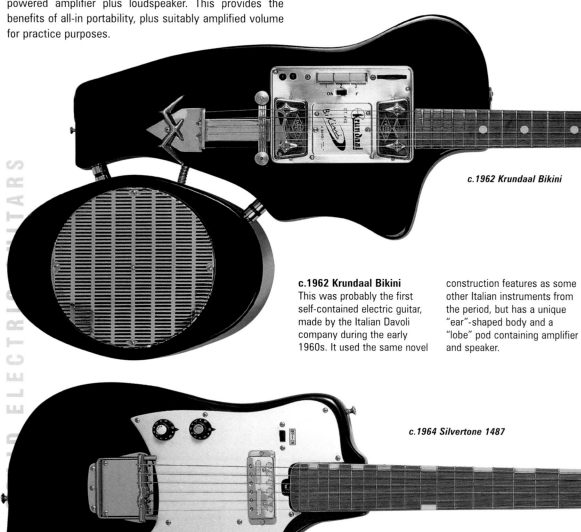

c.1962 Krundaal Bikini

c.1962 Krundaal Bikini
This was probably the first self-contained electric guitar, made by the Italian Davoli company during the early 1960s. It used the same novel construction features as some other Italian instruments from the period, but has a unique "ear"-shaped body and a "lobe" pod containing amplifier and speaker.

c.1964 Silvertone 1487

c.1964 Silvertone 1487
In the USA, the Sears mail-order company used Silvertone as a brand name. It had this particular model made in Japan by Teisco in the mid 1960s. It was similar to the Japanese maker's own version, which Teisco claimed was the world's first self-contained electric.

2003 ad for Johnson acoustic

HOLLOW & SOLID ELECTRIC GUITARS

180

Another acoustic solution: Martin
Backpacker ad from 1994

1964 Silvertone 1457L
A 21-fret rosewood neck, twin lipstick pickups ... and a
five-watt amplifier built into the actual case, with an
eight-inch speaker and tremolo. Silvertone offered this
for just $99 back in the mid 1960s.

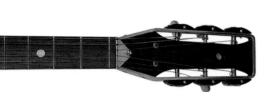

c.1985 Kay K45

c.1985 Yamato

c.1985 Kay K45
This 1980s Korean model was known as the Austin
Hatchet in the USA. It had a laminate through-neck
construction and brass nut, bridge, and inlays. Its
humbuckers were DiMarzio Designed models, and
they were coil-tapped.

c.1985 Yamato
This is a 1980s copy of US maker Mark Erlewine's
Chiquita model. The original was designed with input
from Billy Gibbons.

1986 Kay Busker
The Busker was a low-quality Korean-made model
that offered a lot for little money. The amp section
even included electronic tremolo, an unusual feature
at a budget price.

c.1985 Pangborn Miniature Explorer
A mini-guitar made for ex-Roxy Music guitarist Phil
Manzanera by British maker Ashley Pangborn.

1986 Kay Busker

c.1985 Pangborn Miniature Explorer

181

CHAPTER FOUR

HOLLOW & SEMI-SOLID ELECTRIC GUITARS

The sheer variety of electric guitars with hollow bodies has led to a corresponding range of terms that can confuse the unwary. Generally, a hollowbody electric guitar, as epitomized by many Gretsch models and Gibson "jazz" boxes and their variants, means one that is constructed with a fully hollow body and has on-board electric pickups and controls.

An archtop electric is just that: the top is arched, traditionally by carving, or rather more easily by machine-pressing. Thinline variants evolved from the large and deep-bodied jazz guitars into thinner-bodied instruments.

The term semi-acoustic or semi-solid is probably the one most often misused, and you'll hear it applied to more or less any electric-acoustic instrument. Rickenbacker and a few others use a construction where a solid body is hollowed out to provide control pockets, tone chambers, or both, and then a top or back is added to complete the body. Precisely used, the semi-solid term refers specifically to guitars such as Gibson's pioneering ES-335, which has a block of wood running down the center of a thinline acoustic body. This was devised to retain some of the characteristics of a hollowbody's tone while taking advantage of the feedback-resistant practicality of solidbody electric guitars. It's become a standard, and as such it has been much copied, spawning countless variants.

GIBSON
EARLY ARCHTOPS

In the late 1940s, after some experiments earlier in the decade, Gibson at last began seriously to make production electric guitars. The important new guitars with fitted pickups—the ES-350 (1947), the ES-175 (1949), and the ES-5 (1949)—were aimed at players prepared to commit themselves to fully electric instruments.

At the same time, Gibson began to apply the body cutaway to electrics. There was little point in playing high up the neck on acoustic instruments, as the results were unlikely to be heard. But given a suitably amplified instrument equipped with a pickup, a cutaway offered easier access to the now audible and musically useful upper fingerboard.

The first style of Gibson cutaway appeared on an electric (ES-350) in 1947, and initially guitars with the feature were called Premier and given a P suffix. From 1949, they were called Cutaway types, with a C suffix. The ES-175 of 1949 introduced the new pointed cutaway, but it was not until the 1960s that Gibson applied it to many models that previously had featured the original rounded type.

1956 Gibson ES-175N

1956 Gibson ES-175N
The ES-175 was available in a natural finish (N) and began life in 1949 with one P-90 "dog-ear" pickup, like this example. The two-pickup model, later called the ES-175D, was first introduced in 1951.

2008 Gibson ES-175 Classic

2008 Gibson ES-175 Classic
This guitar has iconic status in the jazz world, and Gibson has kept the model in production. It remains pretty much as it was when originally produced in 1949, with two pickups as an option from 1951 and humbuckers as standard from 1957.

HOLLOW & SEMI-SOLID ELECTRIC GUITARS

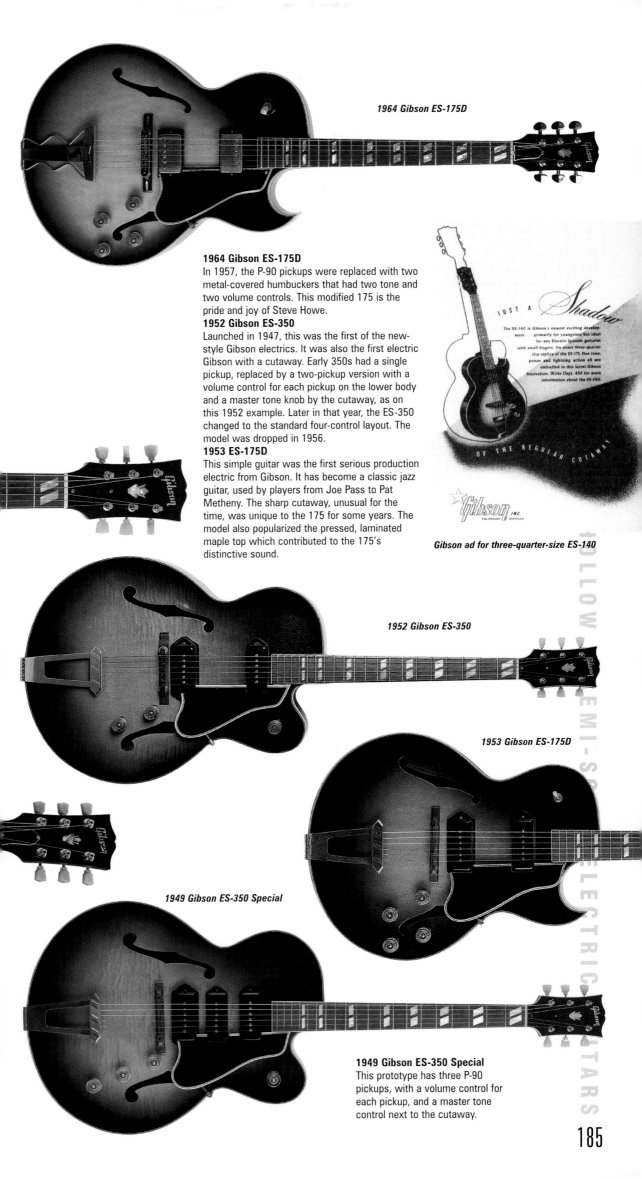

1964 Gibson ES-175D

1964 Gibson ES-175D
In 1957, the P-90 pickups were replaced with two metal-covered humbuckers that had two tone and two volume controls. This modified 175 is the pride and joy of Steve Howe.

1952 Gibson ES-350
Launched in 1947, this was the first of the new-style Gibson electrics. It was also the first electric Gibson with a cutaway. Early 350s had a single pickup, replaced by a two-pickup version with a volume control for each pickup on the lower body and a master tone knob by the cutaway, as on this 1952 example. Later in that year, the ES-350 changed to the standard four-control layout. The model was dropped in 1956.

1953 ES-175D
This simple guitar was the first serious production electric from Gibson. It has become a classic jazz guitar, used by players from Joe Pass to Pat Metheny. The sharp cutaway, unusual for the time, was unique to the 175 for some years. The model also popularized the pressed, laminated maple top which contributed to the 175's distinctive sound.

Gibson ad for three-quarter-size ES-140

1952 Gibson ES-350

1953 Gibson ES-175D

1949 Gibson ES-350 Special

1949 Gibson ES-350 Special
This prototype has three P-90 pickups, with a volume control for each pickup, and a master tone control next to the cutaway.

GIBSON
ARCHTOPS

The ES-5 was part of Gibson's Electric Spanish series of guitars and was originally intended to be an electric version of the popular acoustic jazz model, the L-5. Introduced in 1949, the ES-5 found favor among early rock'n'roll performers like Carl Perkins, and even turned up in Frank Zappa's early career. It is still one of the most elaborate electric guitars that Gibson produced.

It was the first of the ES models to offer three P-90 pickups (Alnico V pickups were at least offered as an option)

and it had a separate volume knob for each pickup and a single master tone control. In 1955, the guitar was renamed the ES-5 Switchmaster, still with P-90 pickups but with separate tone and volume controls for each pickup plus a four-way selector switch mounted on the cutaway bout.

In 1957, Gibson replaced the P-90s with three of its new humbucking pickups, and in 1960 the rounded cutaway was changed to a pointed cutaway. It was reissued in 1996 with a choice of P-90s, Alnicos, or humbuckers.

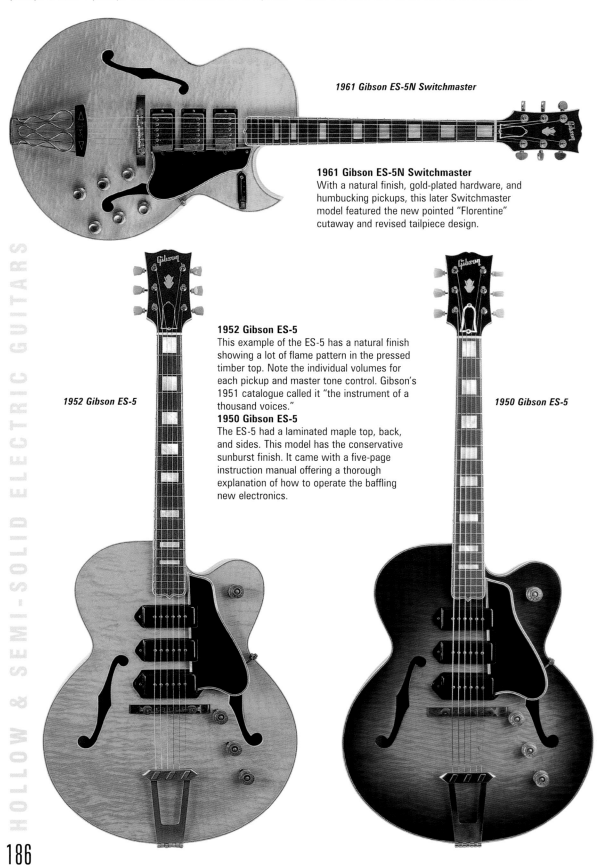

1961 Gibson ES-5N Switchmaster

1961 Gibson ES-5N Switchmaster
With a natural finish, gold-plated hardware, and humbucking pickups, this later Switchmaster model featured the new pointed "Florentine" cutaway and revised tailpiece design.

1952 Gibson ES-5

1952 Gibson ES-5
This example of the ES-5 has a natural finish showing a lot of flame pattern in the pressed timber top. Note the individual volumes for each pickup and master tone control. Gibson's 1951 catalogue called it "the instrument of a thousand voices."

1950 Gibson ES-5
The ES-5 had a laminated maple top, back, and sides. This model has the conservative sunburst finish. It came with a five-page instruction manual offering a thorough explanation of how to operate the baffling new electronics.

1950 Gibson ES-5

HOLLOW & SEMI-SOLID ELECTRIC GUITARS

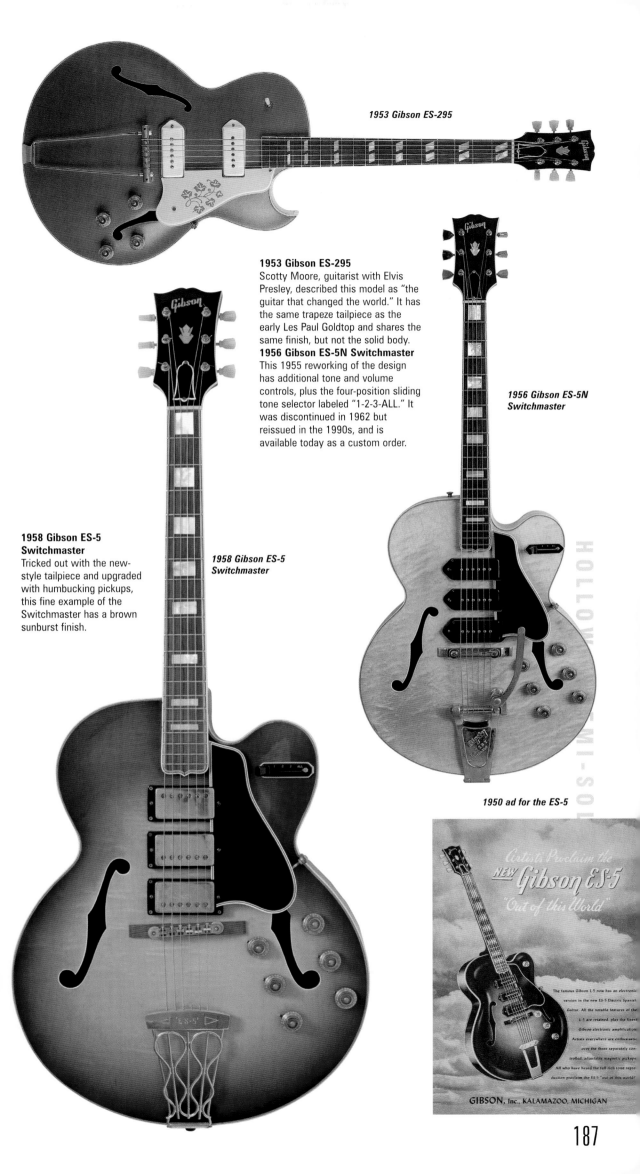

1953 Gibson ES-295

1953 Gibson ES-295
Scotty Moore, guitarist with Elvis Presley, described this model as "the guitar that changed the world." It has the same trapeze tailpiece as the early Les Paul Goldtop and shares the same finish, but not the solid body.

1956 Gibson ES-5N Switchmaster
This 1955 reworking of the design has additional tone and volume controls, plus the four-position sliding tone selector labeled "1-2-3-ALL." It was discontinued in 1962 but reissued in the 1990s, and is available today as a custom order.

1956 Gibson ES-5N Switchmaster

1958 Gibson ES-5 Switchmaster
Tricked out with the new-style tailpiece and upgraded with humbucking pickups, this fine example of the Switchmaster has a brown sunburst finish.

1958 Gibson ES-5 Switchmaster

1950 ad for the ES-5

GIBSON
SUPER 400CES ARCHTOPS

In 1951, two years after the launch of the innovative ES-175 and ES-5 electric guitars, Gibson decided to give the full electric treatment to its two big top-of-the-line acoustic jazz guitars, the L-5 and the Super 400. The results were the CES (initially called SEC) versions of these classic guitars, at last with permanently installed pickups and controls. Both new instruments were issued with a rounded cutaway. Gibson also launched both guitars as two-pickup models. Realizing that players needed a method to switch quickly and effectively between the two pickups, Gibson equipped both the L-5CES and the Super 400CES with a selector near the cutaway to choose both or either of the pickups.

The electric version of the huge acoustic Super 400 guitar appeared, like the L-5CES, in 1951. The two guitars did much to define the archtop electric acoustic guitar

among other makers and, of course, among players. The Super 400CES and the L-5CES have long been seen as guitars for jazz players to aspire to, and over the years some of the great names in music have used these big, impressive models. The Super 4, as it is sometimes known, has always been less popular with guitarists than the L-5CES because of its bulky body—nearly 3½ inches (9cm) deep and 18 inches (about 45cm) wide—and its corresponding awkwardness.

Both the L-5 and the Super 4 have been in continuous production since 1951. Variations on the theme, such as the Wes Montgomery and the Lee Ritenour signature models, kept the L-5 evolving. The guitarist with a jazz leaning and the will to maneuver one of these giants will be rewarded with the distinctive feel and special tone that comes from a real piece of six-string history.

1977 Gibson Super 400CES-WR
Although the Super 400 was usually only available in natural or sunburst finishes, this model has a wine red finish. Gibson

introduced two darker finishes—ebony as well as wine red—to use up stocks of plainer wood that were less suitable for the traditional finishes.

1977 Gibson Super 400CES-WR

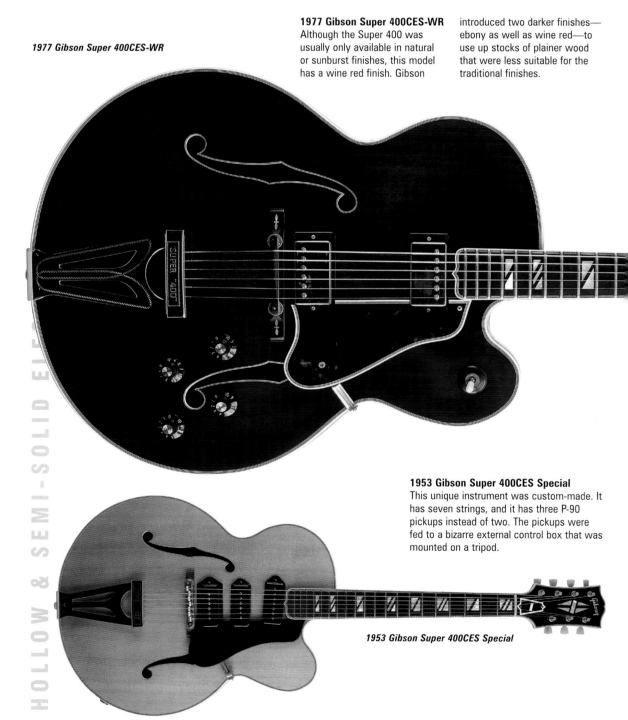

1953 Gibson Super 400CES Special
This unique instrument was custom-made. It has seven strings, and it has three P-90 pickups instead of two. The pickups were fed to a bizarre external control box that was mounted on a tripod.

1953 Gibson Super 400CES Special

1952 Gibson Super 400CESN

1960 Gibson Super 400CES

1952 Gibson Super 400CESN
Early examples were sometimes labelled SEC instead of CES. The N suffix here refers to a natural finish on the carved spruce top.

1962 Gibson Super 400CESN
This later model doesn't differ significantly from the '52 above except for its humbuckers and the pointed cutaway, which was introduced to the model in 1960 until Gibson reverted to the rounded shape in 1969.

1962 Gibson Super 400CESN

1962 Gibson Super 400CESN

1958 ad with Wes Montgomery playing a custom L-5CES

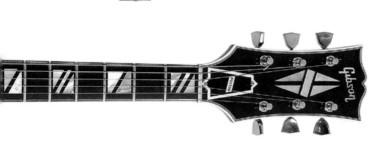

1960 Gibson Super 400CES
Gibson stopped fitting the Super 400 with P-90s in late 1957, and this sunburst-finished model has the new humbucking pickups. Note the high-end headstock inlay and split-block fingerboard inlays, as well as the "marbleized" tortoiseshell pickguard.

1969 Gibson Super 400CES
This guitar has an eyecatching bright-red sunburst finish. The Super 400CES has been used by a variety of famous artists, from Merle Travis to jazz-blues player Robben Ford.

1969 Gibson Super 400CES

GIBSON
L-5CES ARCHTOPS

Lloyd Loar was an experienced musician who started work at Gibson in 1919, at a time when the tenor banjo and mandolin were the dominant instruments in popular music. Between 1922 and 1924, Loar introduced a series of Master Model designs, including the L-5 guitar, which offered significant technical advances over the models of the time (see page 46). Most significantly, Loar would carve and adjust each aspect of body construction, "tuning" each one individually. His design ideas, embodied by the L-5 and to some extent the later CES version, have proved remarkably far-sighted and enduring.

The L-5 model's influence prompted Gibson to return to its elegant lines again and again over the years. Keen to bolster its electric guitar line, in 1951 the L-5 and its bulkier

partner in jazz, the Super 400, were given electric makeovers. Best known of the jazz guitarists to play the L-5CES was Wes Montgomery (1925–1968) who drew a mellow sound from it, thanks in part to his thumb-picking style. Jazz players of the Super 400CES have included Larry Coryell and Kenny Burrell.

In fact, prominent guitarists from virtually every era of electric guitar playing have recorded with the model, notably early adopters such as Eddie Lang and Scotty Moore, and, later, more mainstream superstars like Eric Clapton and John Mayer. The Super 400CES was produced until the 1990s, but Gibson's Custom Shop CES models are still produced today, in the case of the L-5 based on the classic 1958 variant with its two humbuckers and ABR-1 bridge.

2003 Gibson ad for the Japanese market

c.1978 Gibson Super V CES
This variant of the L-5 was made between 1978 and 1993 and has an unusual six-finger tailpiece design. The fingers enabled each string to be individually tensioned.

c.1978 Gibson Super V CES

1997 Gibson Wes Montgomery

1951 Gibson L-5CES

1951 Gibson L-5CES
This is a first-year sunburst version with P-90 pickups. Gibson used rosewood bridges on the first 31 L-5CES models out of the company's Kalamazoo plant in 1951.

1964 Gibson L-5CESN
Here's an L-5CES with a natural finish, humbucking pickups, and the later sharp cutaway. The tailpiece has an art deco "stepped" feel to the design and bears the model's name.

1964 Gibson L-5CESN

1979 Gibson Kalamazoo Award

1979 Gibson Kalamazoo Award
This high-end instrument has gold-plated hardware and a carved top with multiple bindings. Both the wooden pickguard and the headstock have abalone inlays, and the block fingerboard markers are of the same material. It has a single mini-humbucker, and the tone and volume controls are mounted on the pickguard.

1997 Gibson Wes Montgomery
This model is currently in the Gibson Custom Shop line, available in wine red, vintage sunburst, natural, or ebony versions. Montgomery himself ordered a custom version of the L-5CES back in the early 1960s, with a rounded cutaway and single humbucker, and it's that guitar upon which this signature model is based.

GIBSON & OTHERS
ARCHTOP SIGNATURE MODELS

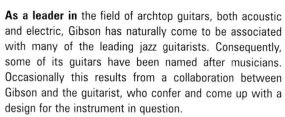

"Gibson Boy"...Tal Farlow

GIBSON, INC., Kalamazoo, Michigan

As a leader in the field of archtop guitars, both acoustic and electric, Gibson has naturally come to be associated with many of the leading jazz guitarists. Consequently, some of its guitars have been named after musicians. Occasionally this results from a collaboration between Gibson and the guitarist, who confer and come up with a design for the instrument in question.

Of course, it is not just Gibson that has gained commercially from the association of famous jazz guitarists with its instruments. Epiphone, a brand name eventually related to Gibson, also gained commercially from the association of famous jazz guitarists with its instruments. Despite the company's popularity with jazz players, however, relatively few "named" instruments were offered. An exception is the thinline Al Caiola model from the

1960s. Guild's Artist Award was originally called the Johnny Smith Award until Smith moved over to Gibson in the early 1960s, and in the late 1950s American maker Kay had issued a line of Barney Kessel jazz models.

Gretsch bravely attempted to market the George Van Eps guitar, a strange, seven-string instrument, around the end of the 1960s. Harmony had the Roy Smeck model (launched 1960), Framus the Attila Zoller model (1960), and Gretsch, again, the Sal Salvador (1958).

It was then the turn of Japanese makers to offer endorsed jazz guitars. These included a trio from Ibanez—the George Benson (1977), Lee Ritenour, and Joe Pass (both 1981)—and two key Aria models, the Herb Ellis (1978) and the Ike Isaacs (1979).

1964 Gibson ad with Tal Farlow

c.1968 Gibson Barney Kessel Regular

c.1968 Gibson Barney Kessel Regular
The Regular model has nickel-plated hardware, as opposed to gold plating on the Custom. The fretboard markers here are the standard double-parallelogram type favoured by Gibson, and the black finish is rare for this model.

1961 Gibson Barney Kessel Custom

HOLLOW & SEMI-SOLID ELECTRIC GUITARS

1962 Gibson Johnny Smith

This guitar, with its cleanly attractive lines, was made by Gibson to "improve" on Smith's own D'Angelico New Yorker Special. The mini-humbucker pickup was designed especially for the Johnny Smith guitars. A two-pickup version, the JSD, joined the model shown, which began production in 1961. In common with other Gibson archtops, fewer of the "blonde" natural-finish type were made, the majority being sunburst.

1962 Gibson Johnny Smith

1961 Gibson ad with Barney Kessel

1964 Gibson Tal Farlow Signature

Only 215 of these were made between 1962 and 1967 (reissues began in the 1990s). The immediately striking feature is the graceful scroll near the cutaway. The guitar would look cluttered if, as usual, the pickup selector switch had also been placed there, so the pickguard was shaped to accommodate the switch's new site. Note also the relatively long 25½-inch (65cm) scale length and the ornate inlays at the fingerboard markers.

1964 Gibson Tal Farlow Signature

1964 Gibson ad with Trini Lopez

1961 Gibson Barney Kessel Custom

The Custom version features gold hardware and "bow-tie" fingerboard markers, reflecting the contemporary jazz player's occasional need for formal stage dress. Note also the headstock decoration and the symmetrical cutaways, rarely seen in a deep-bodied guitar.

GIBSON
THINLINE MODELS

In the years following Gibson's serious introduction of electric archtop jazz guitars such as the ES-175, L-5CES, and the Super 400 CES, the company came to realize that one of the obstacles preventing the wider use of these particular instruments was their deep bodies.

In 1955, Gibson began the launch of a series of guitars in what they termed the new "thinline" style. The Byrdland and ES-350T each possessed a body around two inches (5cm) deep, almost an inch and a half (4cm) shallower than the existing jazz guitars. The 350T was Chuck Berry's axe of choice in the mid to late 1950s when he showed how a rock'n'roll guitar ought to sound.

These two new thinline guitars also featured a shorter scale-length of 23½ inches (60cm) and a shorter, narrower neck, which eased playing. These factors made them less cumbersome than their electric archtop predecessors.

The thinline guitar appealed to players who found the bodies of normal jazz guitars bulky and cumbersome. But these new thinline instruments were, of course, still hollowbodies. So they also found favor with guitarists who

were worried by the heavy weight of the recent solid electric guitars, like Gibson's Les Paul models. There was a third thinline model launched around the same time as the Byrdland and ES-350T, the ES-225T. This had one of Gibson's long and awkward trapeze tailpieces, as on early Les Paul models and the ES-295.

A non-cutaway, single-pickup ES-125T was a further early thinline model in the catalogue, joining the Gibson line in 1956. The following year, a double-pickup version, called the ES-125TD, and a small three-quarter-size variation, the ES-125T ¾, were added to the line.

Around this time, Gibson issued another three-quarter-size thinline model, the ES-140¾T. This was a narrow-body version of the small ES-140¾, and it appeared in 1957.

There have been other thinline versions of standard Gibson models, such as the ES-120T, which was made between 1962 and 1970, and even rare thinline editions of the classic ES-175 and L-5CES. But when Gibson issued the ES-335 in 1958, combining thinline style with solid electric properties, it invented a new guitar: the semi-solid. Thinline guitars would never be the same again.

Byrdland ad from 1955

1957 Gibson Byrdland

1957 Gibson Byrdland
Gibson named this model for two contemporary country guitarists, Billy Byrd and Hank Garland, who may have suggested some of its design features. While clearly based on the L-5CES, the Byrdland had the new thinline body, a shorter neck, and a distinctive looped tailpiece inscribed with its name.

1957 Gibson ES-350T
The ES-350T was introduced as a more affordable alternative to the Byrdland. It had two P-90s, laminated-maple construction, and Gibson's characteristic split-parallelogram inlays, and it was also available in sunburst.

1957 Gibson ES-350T

HOLLOW & SEMI-SOLID ELECTRIC

**2004 Gibson Johnny A.
Signature**

**c.1967 Gibson Byrdland
Special**

2008 Gibson ES-137 Classic

2004 Gibson Johnny A. Signature
Johnny A., the American guitarist and songwriter, enjoyed success in 2001 with 'Oh Yeah'—an unusual achievement for an instrumental single in recent years. His signature guitar has a thinline hollow mahogany body with a carved figured maple top, two 1957 Classic humbuckers, and fancy appointments.
c.1967 Gibson Byrdland Special
This unusual custom model has all the general features of a Byrdland, but with the double-cutaway full-depth body of the Barney Kessel models (see page 192).
2008 Gibson ES-137 Classic
This contemporary version of the thinline combines the ES-137's aesthetic with the sound of a Les Paul Classic. It has a mahogany center block and two humbucking pickups.

1991 Gibson ES-135
This guitar has a laminated maple body with a Chromyte (balsa) center block, two P-100 stacked-coil humbucking pickups, and a Tune-o-matic bridge.
1956 Gibson ES-140T
This three-quarter-scale guitar has a single-bound body with a sharp cutaway. It came with a single P-90 pickup and a plain unbound neck, with dot position markers.

1991 Gibson ES-135

2003 ad for the ES-446S

1956 Gibson ES-140T

GIBSON
THE ES-335

In 1958, Gibson launched the ES-335, a model that effectively combined a hollowbody guitar with a solid. While it appeared to have a thinline hollow body, it actually incorporated a solid block of wood running through the center of the otherwise hollow structure. It also had, for the first time, a pair of symmetrical cutaways.

Guitarists were often plagued by screeching feedback when they tried to play ordinary hollowbody electric guitars at high volume. Feedback is caused by guitar pickups picking up their own sound from the loudspeakers and feeding it back to the system, creating an unpleasant "howlround."

The "semi-solid" 335 offered a depth of tone akin to hollowbody guitars but, thanks to the central body block, was much less prone to feedback at high volume. Many players took to this clever combination, including jazz-rock guitarists such as Larry Carlton and Allan Holdsworth, who found that the 335's fusion of the qualities of hollow jazz guitars and solid rock guitars fell in with their musical aims.

Gibson used descriptive letters added to the ES-335, for example: ES-335TDC. In this case, the suffix indicates a *T*hinline body, *D*ouble pickups, and *C*herry finish, while a TDN was the same but with a *N*atural finish.

In 1969, Gibson introduced the ES-340, which looked much like the 335 but had an unusually-wired pickup selector that provided these three options: out-of-phase; both pickups on; or both pickups off.

1959 Gibson ES-335TD

1959 Gibson ES-335TD
This is an early model 335 that has the single-bound rosewood fingerboard with dot position markers. The very first to be produced came without the binding on the fingerboard.

HOLLOW & SEMI-SOLID ELECTRIC GUITARS

196

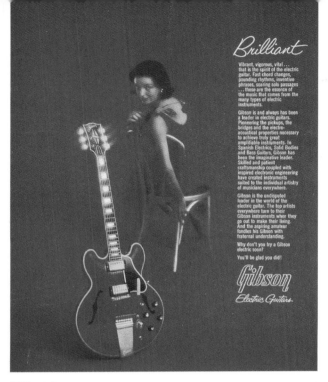

1963 catalogue cover

2008 Gibson ES-335 Dot

2010 Gibson 50th Anniversary 1960 ES-335TDC

2008 Gibson ES-335 Dot
A typical example of a modern variation on the 335's timeless theme, this guitar is in desert-burst finish and has modern-looking control knobs but early-style dot markers.

2010 Gibson 50th Anniversary 1960 ES-335TDC
This anniversary guitar marks the period when the hallowed dot-neck 335 was first offered with a cherry finish and the model reached what many players consider its optimum playability.

1964 Gibson ES-335TDC
This guitar was owned by Eric Clapton, who first used it toward the end of his time with Cream, notably on the group's farewell concerts, and at other moments throughout his career. It has the small-block fingerboard markers that were introduced on the 335 in the early 1960s. Clapton sold the guitar in 2004 for $847,500, to the benefit of his Crossroads charity.

1959 Gibson ES-335TDN

1964 Gibson ES-335TDC

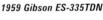

1959 Gibson ES-335TDN
This blonde-finish guitar has the same early dot neck but has a factory-fitted Bigsby tremolo unit. The post holes for the traditional stop tailpiece have mother-of-pearl blanks fitted.

2002 ad for the smaller-body CS-336

GIBSON
THE ES FAMILY

Around the same time as the new ES-335 was launched in the late 1950s, with its effective combination of hollowbody and solidbody electric guitar characteristics, Gibson added two similar guitars to its line, the ES-345 and ES-355. These partners to the ES-335 featured that instrument's new, distinctive symmetrical-cutaway body shape. They also had within their bodies the centrally positioned solid block of wood that gave some of the qualities of a solid-bodied electric guitar to this otherwise light-bodied series of instruments.

Both the 345 and the 355 were offered with stereo wiring and an unusual six-way selector switch called the Vari-tone. This tone-altering circuit was developed by Gibson's pickup expert, Walt Fuller, but proved unpopular

with players. Many 345s and 355s fitted with stereo and Vari-tone capabilities have since been converted to regular wiring. The main visual difference between these two models and the 335 was the double parallelogram fingerboard inlays on the 345 and the large block inlays on the 355, along with the 355's notable split-diamond inlay on the headstock.

Perhaps it was these more regal appointments that attracted blues legend Freddie King to the ES-345 and the King Of The Blues, B.B. King, to the 355, which he settled on in the early 1960s after playing a succession of Gibson hollowbodies and semi-solidbodies. Since 1980, Gibson has provided a signature B.B. King model, some of which feature a fine-tuner tailpiece.

1960 Gibson ES-345TD

1960 Gibson ES-345TD
This guitar has a sunburst finish logged as "Argentine Grey" in Gibson's records, aged over time to a pleasing darker color. George Harrison played a regular sunburst 345 during a 1965 UK tour and for a couple of Beatles promo videos.

1959 Gibson ES-355TDSV
Nearly all 355s came in cherry red, although a small number were made in natural or in cherry sunburst, like this rare example. The guitar also has a non-standard truss-rod cover, personalized with the owner's name.

1983 guitar string ad with a 345 Custom

HOLLOW & SEMI-SOLID ELECTRIC GUITARS

1960 Gibson ES-335TDN Special

2010 Gibson ES-339

2010 Gibson ES-345 VOS Bigsby

LARRY CARLTON
and the GIBSON TP-6

Precision Performers

Ad from 1981 for the TP-6 fine-tuning tailpiece with Larry Carlton

1959 Gibson ES-355TDSV Custom

1960 Gibson ES-335TDN Special
A rare custom order, this 335 has a fingerboard inlaid not with the dots seen on regular examples between 1958 and 1962, but the double parallelogram markers usually associated with its stereo cousin, the 345.

2010 Gibson ES-339
Gibson scaled down the body of the 335 for this recent model. It is fitted with '57 Classic humbuckers and a nifty circuit that stops the high-end EQ dropping off when the volume is turned down.

2010 Gibson ES-345 VOS Bigsby
This is a modern take on the 345 with stunning Alpine White paintwork and gold hardware. Gibson and Epiphone offer various takes on the 335 template, from entry level instruments to painstaking historical recreations.

HOLLOW/SEMI-SOLID ELECTRIC GUITARS

GIBSON
THINLINE VARIATIONS

The double-cutaway body of the ES-335 not only introduced the concept of a semi-hollowbody, it opened the door for new designs in the line of fully hollow thinlines. Prior to the ES-335, all of Gibson's thinlines appeared, from the front view, to be traditional full-depth models with a rounded cutaway (Byrdland, ES-350T), pointed cutaway (ES-225), or with no cutaway (ES-125T), but in 1959, only a year after the ES-335's smashing debut, Gibson introduced a new model with the look of the 335 but without the ES-335's center block.

The model name of this guitar, the ES-330TD, suggests that it was a step down from the ES-335, which it was—but not because of its fully hollow body. In order to offer a less expensive alternative to the 335, Gibson fitted the 330-TD with single-coil P-90 pickups rather than the company's new humbuckers that were standard on all the semi-hollow models (and an even less expensive single-pickup ES-330T was also available). At $210 for sunburst and $225 for natural, the double-pickup ES-330 was about $55 cheaper than the 335.

Due to the ES-330's assigned price point below the ES-335, step-up versions were never introduced. Demand fell off as the 1960s progressed, but Gibson produced the Crest model from 1969 until 1971. The guitar had a deluxe Brazilian rosewood body with multiple binding and was made with either gold-plated hardware (Crest Gold) or silver plating (Crest Silver).

Another strange variant of the ES-335 produced in 1979 was the ES Artist. This guitar shared the semi-hollowbody of the 335 but dropped the f-holes. Gibson asked the engineers at Moog to design a circuit board for the new model offering expansion and compression, but the feature was unpopular with guitarists, and so the model was dropped in 1985.

1970 ad (top) featuring B.B. King with an ES-355TDSV

1976 Gibson Les Paul Signature

HOLLOW AND SEMI-SOLID ELECTRIC GUITARS

1973 ad for the Les Paul Signature

1976 Gibson Les Paul Signature
This was Les Paul's version of the 335, featuring a T-shaped center block and his favored low-impedance pickups. The body has a more pointed lower horn than the 335, and there's a repositioned selector switch, a phase switch, and a three-way output selector dial.

1980 Gibson ES Artist

1980 Gibson ES Artist
The offset dot markers and double pickguards of this model were not typical of Gibson design. This one was owned by Steve Howe, and he used ES Artists on many early Asia recordings and tours.

1960 Gibson ES-330TDN
Gibson used the suffix TDN to indicate a guitar that was Thinline, had a Double-cutaway, and came with Natural finish. This example has the regular black-plastic-covered P-90 pickups.

1960 Gibson ES-330TDN

1960 ad for the Stereo models

1961 Gibson ES-330TDN
The 330 was intended as a cheaper alternative to the 335 and its other companions in the 300 series, but it lacked the feedback-fighting center block and humbuckers that characterized the rest of the line.

1971 Gibson Crest Gold
This short-lived deluxe model has a bound rosewood pickguard and two "floating" mini humbuckers. Note the wood inlay in the tailpiece and also the gold hardware that gives the guitar its Gold distinction.

1961 Gibson ES-330TDN

1971 Gibson Crest Gold

SEMI-SOLID ELECTRIC GUITARS

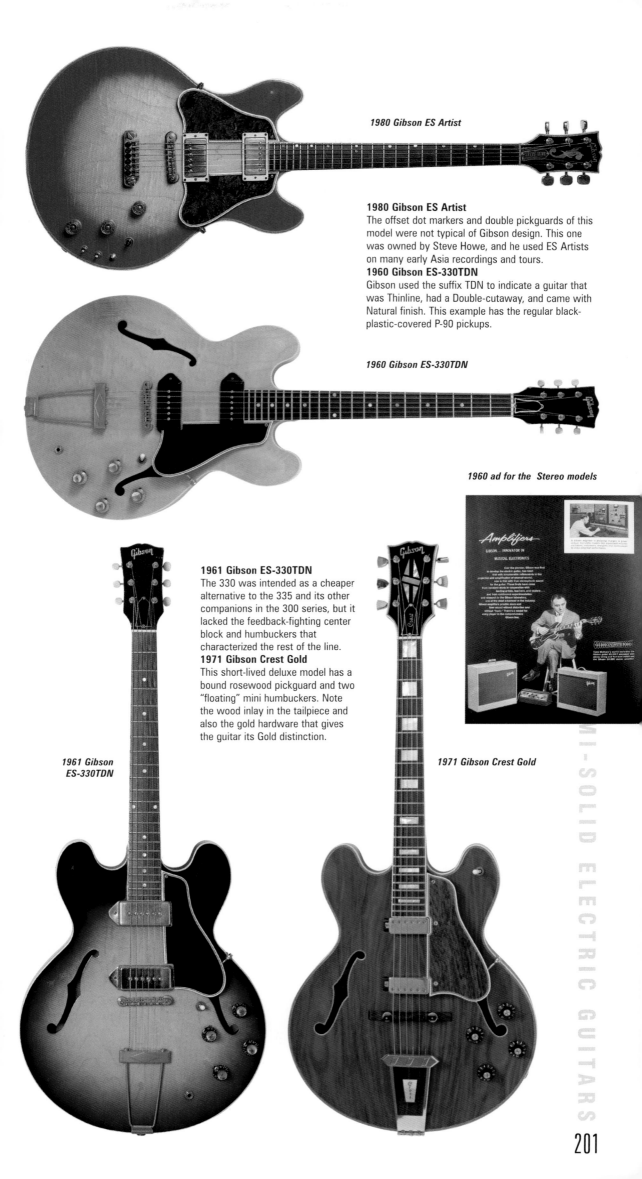

GIBSON
THINLINE SIGNATURE MODELS

Gibson has marketed a number of other semi-solid and thinline hollowbody electric models since it introduced guitarists to the idea of such instruments in the 1950s.

In 1964, Gibson brought out two versions of a model named after Latin pop musician Trini Lopez. The Deluxe version looked much like a Barney Kessel, with its sharp symmetrical cutaways, but both this and the rounded-cutaway Standard model were unusual for Gibson in that they featured a headstock with tuners along one side, in the style of Fender. The Trini Lopez was made until 1970.

Later hollow or semi-solid Gibsons with symmetrical cutaways included the ES-150DC (1969–74), like a deep-bodied 335; the ES-320 (1971–74), with controls on a semi-circular plate; and the ES-325 (1972–78), which was like the 320 but with plain metal rather than black pickups. Gibson absorbed current guitar trends into the existing semi-solid style at various times. For example, the ES-347 followed the late-1970s fad for fine-tuning tailpiece and coil-tapable pickups, which give the choice of single-coil or humbucking effect from one unit. In the 1980s, the ES-369 briefly adopted the vogue for active electronic circuits, giving boosted tonal options.

The ES Artist (1979–85) and the B.B. King (launched 1980) were both without f-holes. The Artist featured an active circuit, while Blues Boy's guitar was an expensive signature model. There were several versions of the B.B. King signature model, including the B.B. King Little Lucille in 1999 and the B.B. King Super Lucille from 2002. Other signature models on the 335 theme followed, with artists such as Eric Clapton, Andy Summers, Tom DeLonge, and Larry Carlton joining the roster. In 2005, Gibson produced a facsimile of Alvin Lee's "Big Red" complete with an extra single-coil Seymour Duncan pickup placed between the humbuckers. The guitar came with the Woodstock-era peace symbol and at first was limited to 50 instruments.

2010 Gibson Trini Lopez

2010 Gibson Trini Lopez
This guitar has signature features like the Firebird-style headstock and slashed- diamond fingerboard inlay, plus the unique diamond-shaped soundholes. The model appeared in 2009.

2008 Gibson B.B. King Super Lucille

2005 Gibson Eric Clapton ES-335TDC

Gibson ES ad with John Lee Hooker from 2001

2008 Gibson B.B. King Super Lucille
Although very similar to the Standard Lucille model, this model only comes in a black finish and has gold-plated hardware and B.B.'s signature on the pickguard.

2005 Gibson Eric Clapton ES-335TDC
This is a copy of the 1964 model ES-335TDC owned and played by Eric Clapton from the final days of Cream until it was auctioned for Clapton's Crossroads Center in 2004, fetching $847,500.

2008 Gibson Lee Ritenour ES-335
This top-quality version of the 335 in cherry red was released in two limited-edition runs of aged and VOS (Vintage Original Spec) versions. It had a thinner, proprietary Lee Ritenour neck shape.

2008 Gibson Lee Ritenour ES-335

2008 ad for the B.B. King Lucille model

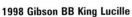

1998 Gibson B.B. King Lucille

1998 Gibson BB King Lucille
B.B. used to stuff the f-holes of his ES-355 to minimize the possibility of feedback. This guitar has no f-holes but is a semi-solid. It has a TP-6 fine-tuning tailpiece and is wired for stereo.

EPIPHONE
ARCHTOPS

Younger guitar players may only know the Epiphone brand as a budget subsidiary of the Gibson company. Yet once upon a time, when the archtop guitar was in the ascendancy, Epiphone was Gibson's arch rival. Building on a distinguished instrument-building history dating back to the 1870s in Greece and Turkey, by the 1930s Epiphone had developed its archtop line, which debuted in 1928 with its Recording models, into a force for Gibson to reckon with (see page 42).

By 1939, Epiphone's electric archtops included the Century, Coronet, and the Zephyr, each fitted with a large, oval-shaped pickup. In 1943, the company's owner, Epi Stathopoulo, died. Control switched to his brothers, Orphie

and Frixo. In 1948, the company debuted its first single-cutaway acoustic archtops based on the Emperor and DeLuxe, and added Tone Spectrum pickups to them a few years later.

Then, in 1951, a strike shut down Epiphone's New York City factory for four months. The company's solution was to relocate production to Philadelphia, Pennsylvania.

In 1957, Frixo Stathopoulo died. This would mark the end of Epiphone's independence, and it was soon bought by Gibson and again relocated, to Gibson's hometown of Kalamazoo, Michigan. Gibson used the Epiphone brand to sell a new line of guitars from 1958.

c.1950 Epiphone Zephyr Emperor Vari Tone
This instrument has a spruce top with maple back and sides. The pickups are the earlier New York type, and the model was renamed the Zephyr Emperor Regent in 1953.

c.1941 Epiphone Zephyr
This non-cutaway body is made from laminated curly maple. Epiphone's Master Pickup of 1937 was designed by Herb Sunshine and was the first to feature screw-adjustable polepieces.

c.1950 Epiphone Zephyr Emperor Vari Tone

c.1941 Epiphone Zephyr

HOLLOW SOLID ELEC

1953 Epiphone Zephyr Emperor Regent

1998 ad with Duke Robillard

1954 Epiphone Zephyr Emperor Regent

1963 Epiphone Electric E112TN

c.1968 Epiphone Sorrento Double

1953 Epiphone Zephyr Emperor Regent
This is a special-option version with DeArmond pickups. The pickup surrounds and control plate for the pushbuttons are gold plated, and the pickguard has the distinctive Greek-E-for-Epiphone logo.

1963 Epiphone Emperor E112TN
A Gibson-made example of the model with three mini humbuckers linked to the more conventional switching system.

1954 Epiphone Zephyr Emperor Regent
This is the renamed Zephyr Emperor Vari Tone with a blonde finish.

c.1968 Epiphone Sorrento Double
This Gibson-made model with two mini-humbuckers and a Tune-o-matic bridge has had an older-style tailpiece fitted, the Frequensator, but trapeze or Bigsby vibrato tailpieces were standard.

EPIPHONE
THINLINES

Epiphone may have been seen as an offshoot of Gibson after the takeover, but the brand kept producing quality instruments that sometimes cost more than their Gibson equivalents. The late 1950s and early 1960s were a golden age for innovative guitar models, especially Gibsons, and the Epiphone line was keeping pace with developments.

The Wilshire solidbody was introduced in 1960, along with the Olympic line. Epiphone's thinline range continued to grow with the single-pointed-cutaway Sorrento in 1960, the double-cutaway Casino in 1961 and Professional in '62, and the Granada and Riviera. The Caiola followed in 1963.

The popularity of Epiphone's thinlines was bolstered when Paul McCartney used a Casino in the studio in the mid 1960s to lay down some memorable guitar solos on 'Ticket To Ride,' 'Drive My Car,' and 'Taxman.' John Lennon and George Harrison used Casinos live in 1966 for the final run of Fab Four concerts.

In 1969, Gibson was purchased by Norlin, and plans were set in motion to move production of Epiphones to Japan. From the 1970s, a succession of Japanese models came and went, including models that evolved into the Strat-style ET-270 and the thinline EA-250. In 1982, there were new Japanese-made reissues of the Emperor, Sheraton, Casino, and Riviera.

Following Gibson's takeover by new owners in 1986, the Epiphone brand was used to sell a multitude of Korean-made models, in all shapes and sizes. From the late 1990s onwards, it has primarily found success with a wealth of Les Paul models, but the vintage draw of the thinlines is still strong, and examples of most of Epiphone's classic hollowbodies and semis are available today, including a healthy line of anniversary and signature models.

1961 Epiphone Sheraton E212T

1961 Epiphone Sheraton E212T

The top thinline electric from the Gibson-made period, the Sheraton had a maple body, and the mahogany neck's rosewood fingerboard featured pearl and abalone inlays in a classic Epi style. Pickups were typical Epiphone mini-humbuckers. The headstock bore Epi's notable vine design, generally reserved for top-of-the-line guitars.

1962 Epiphone Casino Double E230TD

1962 Epiphone Casino Double E230TD

This sunburst-finish example has been strung and set-up for left-handed use by its owner, Paul McCartney. This guitar has a Bigsby vibrato fitted, but Epiphone offered it with an optional Tremotone vibrato.

1995 Epiphone Casino

1995 Epiphone Casino

A reissue with a natural finish, this model is now made in Japan. Recent signature models have included the Inspired By John Lennon model, and the Dwight Yoakam Dwight Trash Elitist model, which had a reverse-Firebird-style headstock.

206

1999 ad with Matthew Sweet

1999 Epiphone Les Paul ES

1999 Epiphone Les Paul ES

A budget-priced copy of the Gibson Les Paul Florentine model, this guitar has a semi-hollow body made of flamed maple and mahogany, and Epiphone humbuckers. The Epiphone brand has been used to market many variations on the Les Paul theme.

1997 Epiphone Supernova

1997 Epiphone Supernova

Oasis guitarist Noel Gallagher played two Epiphone Sheratons in his band's heyday that were finished with Union Jack graphics. Endorsed by Noel, this blue guitar bears his signature on the pickguard.

2010 Epiphone ads featuring Dave Rude of Tesla (opposite, top) and Luther Dickinson of The North Mississippi Allstars (opposite left)

2009 Epiphone Dot

2009 Epiphone Dot

This reissue from Japan has dot markers like the priginal Gibson ES-335—hence its name. A number of Dot guitar models have been released over the past two decades, underlining the 335-style model's popularity.

GUILD
ARCHTOPS & THINLINES

The Guild company was established in New York City in 1952 by Alfred Dronge, who had previously played, taught, and sold guitars. His workers were soon producing archtop and flat-top guitars. By 1956, they had outgrown the New York workshop and moved to New Jersey. During the 1950s, several Epiphone craftsmen joined Dronge, and their influence on Guild can be seen in some of the work, especially the fingerboard inlays.

As well as the electric archtops and thinlines, Guild made a number of other models. Thinlines included the small-bodied Gibson Les Paul-like Aristocrat (also known as the Blues Bird). With its hollow body, light weight, and lower-output pickups, it was in the ballpark of the Gibson model in aesthetics only, and in fact the guitar was more akin to Gretsch's classic Jet series of models.

Duane Eddy, reigning King Of Twang, defected from Gretsch in the 1960s in return for two signature models. British guitarist Bert Weedon was another endorser whose signature appeared on a Guild pickguard.

Guild also offered some less expensive jazz guitars such as the maple-topped Capri CE-100 (its first to feature a sharp cutaway) as well as the higher-end Manhattan X-175 and Mini Manhattan X-170. The various single-cutaway Starfire models, new for 1960, enjoyed success with the beat-group scene, and a double-cut version was released in 1963. Guild was acquired by Fender in 1995.

1978 ad for the Guild X-500

1974 Guild Stuart X-550
The X-550 came in a blonde finish and the X-500 was the sunburst version. Both came with single-coil pickups that were replaced by humbuckers in 1963. The model was discontinued, replaced with the X-700 in 1994 and the Stuart in 2000.

1954 Guild Stratford X-350
This model came with three single-coil pickups that were also replaced by DeArmond pickups in 1962 and by humbuckers in 1963. It shares the elegant harp-shaped tailpiece with its fellow Guild archtops.

1954 Guild Stratford X-350

1974 Guild Stuart X-550

1961 Guild Starfire III
The Starfire I had one single-coil pickup and the II had two pickups, while the model III had two pickups and a Bigsby vibrato. Those three were introduced in 1960, and a double-cut version, the IV, was added to the line in 1963.

HOLLOW & SEMI-SOLID ELECTRI

1963 Guild Bert Weedon

1963 Guild Bert Weedon
Influential British guitarist Weedon died in 2012 and was best known for his Play In A Day tutor book, the starting point for many famous British musicians. The guitar has a similar body shape to the Starfire IV and started life with DeArmond pickups, as seen in this example, whch was owned by Weedon himself. The pickups were changed to humbuckers in late 1963, and the model was dropped in 1967.

1976 Guild Artist Award

1976 Guild Artist Award
This model was introduced in the late 1950s as the Johnny Smith Award. But the guitarist began to endorse Gibson guitars in the early 1960s, so Guild promptly changed the name to Artist Award. High-quality materials are used throughout, including a spruce top, ebony fingerboard, and gold-plated hardware.

1962 Guild Duane Eddy Deluxe DE-500

1997 ad for the Guild Starfire

1962 Guild Duane Eddy Deluxe DE-500
This is, in effect, a single-cutaway version of the Bert Weedon model. This example is owned by Duane himself. A limited-edition DE-500 was introduced in the 1980s to celebrate Duane's 25 years in the recording industry.

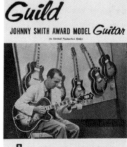

1957 ad with Johnny Smith

1961 Guild Starfire III

GRETSCH
WHITE FALCON

Gretsch is best known for its electric-acoustic guitars made in the 1950s and 1960s. Although many of these classic instruments were designed with strong country-music influences, they can command high prices among pop and rock musicians.

Gretsch began in New York in 1883 when a German immigrant, Friedrich Gretsch, set up a music shop. His son Fred Gretsch founded the Fred Gretsch Manufacturing Co., which started making guitars during the 1930s in the company's Brooklyn factory. Fred Gretsch Jr. presided over the classic Gretsch period, but Baldwin bought the company in 1967, and production ceased in 1981. The operation was back in Gretsch family ownership by 1985, and production of guitars resumed in Japan in 1989.

Gretsch called the original White Falcon "The Guitar Of The Future" when a special prototype was made for exhibition at the NAMM musical instruments trade fair in Chicago in 1954. This show item was designed in part by

musician and Gretsch demonstrator Jimmie Webster, responsible for many of Gretsch's classic instruments and add-on gimmicks during the 1950s and 1960s.

The stunning guitar caused so much interest that Gretsch decided to put this Cadillac of the guitar world into production as the top of its line in 1955. They retained from the unique show guitar the impressive white finish, gold-plated hardware, and—borrowed from the very successful Gretsch drum department—a liberal sprinkling of gold-sparkle plastic.

The original 1955 Falcon had the regular electric guitar's mono output and single rounded cutaway. Stereo output became an option in 1958. Double cutaways became standard in 1962, and the White Falcon was available with single or double cutaways from 1974. After an absence of eight years, the guitar was reissued in 1989 as part of Gretsch's Japan-based comeback, available in single- or double-cutaway body styles.

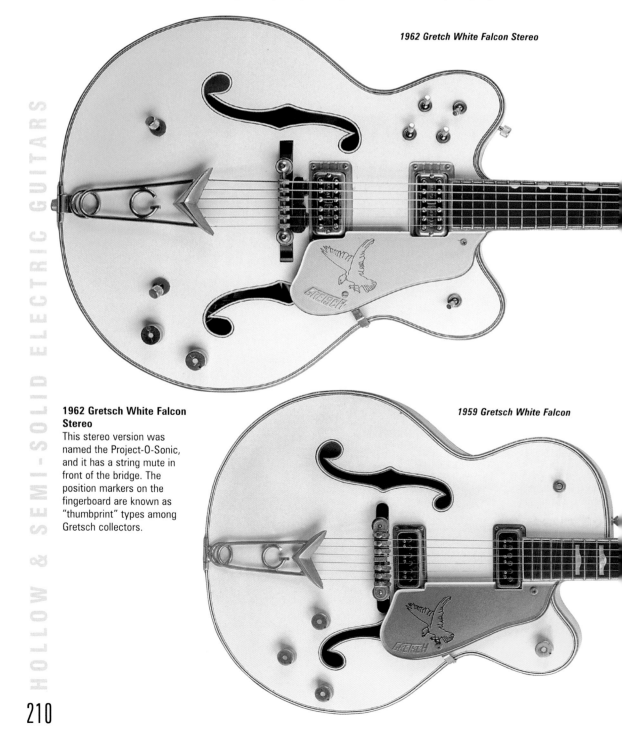

1962 Gretch White Falcon Stereo

1962 Gretsch White Falcon Stereo
This stereo version was named the Project-O-Sonic, and it has a string mute in front of the bridge. The position markers on the fingerboard are known as "thumbprint" types among Gretsch collectors.

1959 Gretsch White Falcon

HOLLOW & SEMI-SOLID ELECTRIC GUITARS

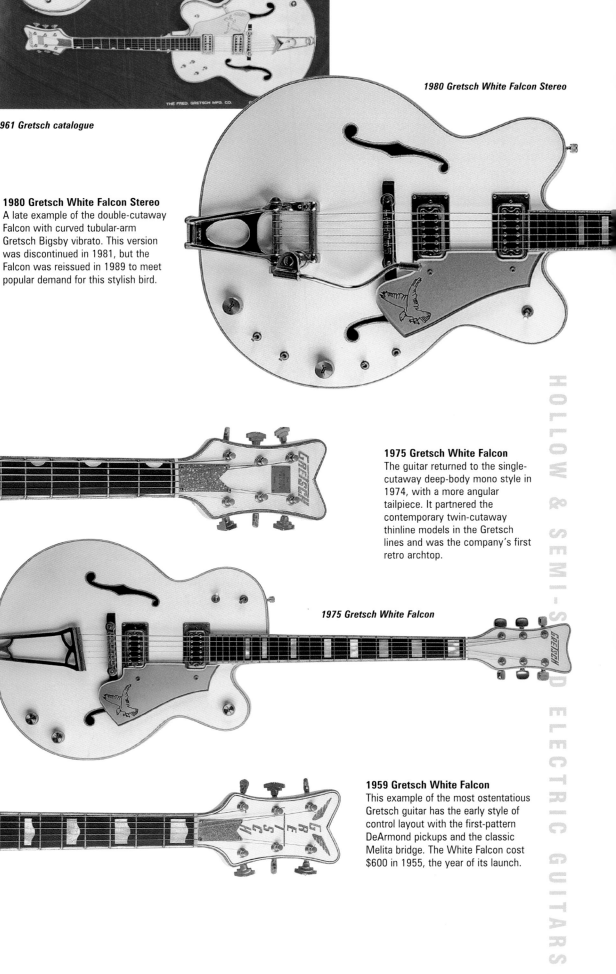

1961 Gretsch catalogue

1980 Gretsch White Falcon Stereo

1980 Gretsch White Falcon Stereo
A late example of the double-cutaway
Falcon with curved tubular-arm
Gretsch Bigsby vibrato. This version
was discontinued in 1981, but the
Falcon was reissued in 1989 to meet
popular demand for this stylish bird.

1975 Gretsch White Falcon
The guitar returned to the single-
cutaway deep-body mono style in
1974, with a more angular
tailpiece. It partnered the
contemporary twin-cutaway
thinline models in the Gretsch
lines and was the company's first
retro archtop.

1975 Gretsch White Falcon

1959 Gretsch White Falcon
This example of the most ostentatious
Gretsch guitar has the early style of
control layout with the first-pattern
DeArmond pickups and the classic
Melita bridge. The White Falcon cost
$600 in 1955, the year of its launch.

GRETSCH
ARCHTOPS

Of the dozen or so hollowbody guitars that Gretsch launched during the 1950s and 1960s, modern musicians have concentrated on seven principal models that might be termed the fashionable Gretsches. These are the Double Anniversary, the Country Club, the Country Gentleman, the Hollow Body (or 6120, or, later, Nashville), the Tennessean, the Viking, and the White Falcon.

Quick identification of these models from a distance can be tricky for the newcomer to Gretsch, as the general impression is of a line of similar big-bodied guitars with one or two cutaways and double pickups, a vibrato arm (usually), and an array of controls.

Anyone who wishes to date a Gretsch guitar should prepare for frustration. Serial numbers exhibit little sequential logic. Hardware and features often tell more about a Gretsch's period, for example the guitar's pickups. The DeArmond Dynasonic pickup, which possessed a single row of centrally-positioned polepieces and nearby adjusting screws, was used originally only in the 1950s, while Gretsch's classic Filter'Tron humbucker (two rows of polepieces) replaced it later in that decade and continued on through to the 1990s in various versions.

Another of Gretsch's fabulously-named creations, the Hi-Lo'Tron pickup, had a one-sided row of screw-top polepieces and was first seen around 1960, while the Super'Tron, without polepieces, appeared about 1963.

2003 ad for 120th Anniversary Model

1957 Gretsch Clipper
With a double-bound top and back, this basic model also had an adjustable ebony bridge. As a cheaper model in the range at the time, it had the typical dot position markers on the fingerboard.

1957 Gretsch Clipper

1958 Gretsch Country Club Stereo 6196
This model was distinguished by its gold-plated hardware and first appeared in 1955. It initially came in sunburst (6192), natural (6193), or this Cadillac Green (6196) finish. Models from the 1970s settled to just sunburst (7575) or natural (7576). A stereo-wired option was also produced at one stage. The original Country Club was first discontinued in 1981.

1958 Gretsch Country Club Stereo 6196

212

1955 Gretsch Chet Atkins 6120
Widely known by its model number, the 6120 was in 1955 the first model of the Chet Atkins series. This one was owned by Chet himself. It moved to a double-cutaway version in 1963, was renamed the Nashville in 1967, and bore model number 7660 from 1971. Early examples have the G-brand logo.

1961 Gretsch Anniversary
This model, unveiled in 1959, had two pickups (there was also a single-pickup version). It came originally as model 6117 in sunburst, or 6118, the beautiful two-tone smoke green shown here. The darker green of the pickguard is matched on the back and sides. The 1970s model was 7560.

1956 Gretsch Chet Atkins 6120

1998 ad for a Duane Eddy signature model

1961 Gretsch Anniversary

1958 Gretsch Tennessean 6119

Keith Scott in an ad from 1999 for the Nashville model, the renamed 6120

1958 Gretsch Tennessean 6119
Starting life with one pickup, the orange 6119 switched to two pickups in 1963. The Tennessean was a popular 1960s guitar, a relatively cheaper model in the Gretsch line. It kept its general appearance when it was given model number 7655 (from 1972 to 1980). This fine early example has real f-holes and one volume control on the cutaway. The single switch affects tone and is sometimes disparagingly known as the mud switch.

GRETSCH
ARCHTOP SIGNATURE MODELS

Chester Burton Atkins (1924–2001), born in Tennessee, was a top country-music session guitarist by the 1940s. He was a pioneer of the solo electric guitar and was voted *Cashbox's* Best Instrumentalist for 14 consecutive years.

As a producer, Chet worked on Elvis Presley's RCA sessions and is credited in part for the creation of the so-called Nashville Sound of the 1960s. He was elected to the Country Music Hall Of Fame in 1973. He recorded many solo albums—standouts for guitar players include his duets with Les Paul, while a few of Chet's earlier cuts became single hits (such as 'Boo Boo Stick Beat' in 1959). Guitarist Jimmie Webster, demonstrator and inventor for

Gretsch, approached Atkins in the early 1950s in an effort to persuade him to switch from his D'Angelico instrument to a Gretsch. After some hesitation from Atkins, Webster suggested he design a guitar from scratch. The first result was the Chet Atkins Hollow Body 6120 in 1955, with the guitarist's suggestions including a metal bridge and nut and also a Bigsby vibrato.

Later models in the Chet Atkins series included the Country Gentleman and the Tennessean. Atkins endorsed Gretsch guitars until the 1980s, when he moved to Gibson, which issued a novel Chet Atkins electric classical model and, in 1986, its own Country Gentleman.

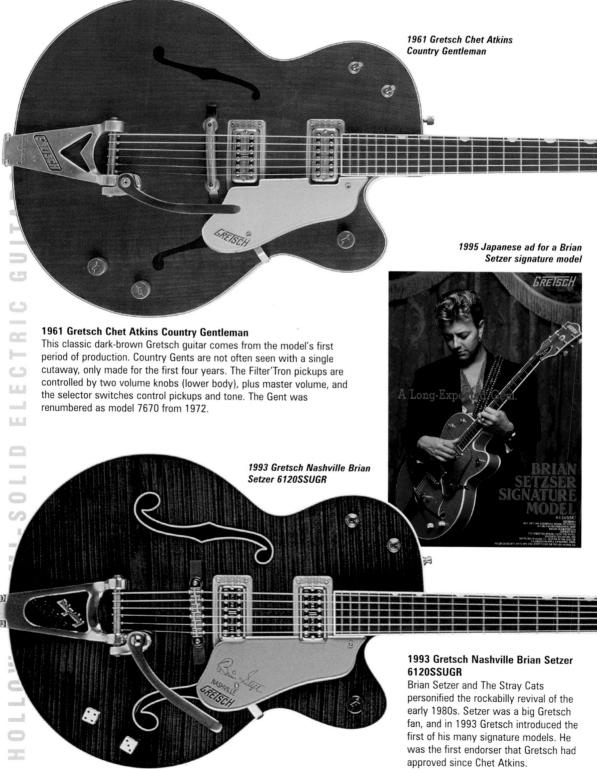

1961 Gretsch Chet Atkins Country Gentleman

1995 Japanese ad for a Brian Setzer signature model

1961 Gretsch Chet Atkins Country Gentleman
This classic dark-brown Gretsch guitar comes from the model's first period of production. Country Gents are not often seen with a single cutaway, only made for the first four years. The Filter'Tron pickups are controlled by two volume knobs (lower body), plus master volume, and the selector switches control pickups and tone. The Gent was renumbered as model 7670 from 1972.

1993 Gretsch Nashville Brian Setzer 6120SSUGR

1993 Gretsch Nashville Brian Setzer 6120SSUGR
Brian Setzer and The Stray Cats personified the rockabilly revival of the early 1980s. Setzer was a big Gretsch fan, and in 1993 Gretsch introduced the first of his many signature models. He was the first endorser that Gretsch had approved since Chet Atkins.

HOLLOW- & SOLID ELECTRIC GUITAR

1967 Gretsch Chet Atkins Country Gentleman Custom Three-Quarters
This three-quarter scale guitar was custom-made for Chet Atkins. Note the double string-mute in front of the bridge.

1993 Gretsch Country Classic II 6122-1962
This is a reissue based on the Country Gentleman with gold-plated hardware and a gold-colored pickguard. The II refers to the double-cutaway body style.

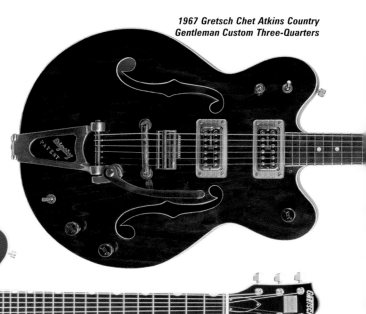

1967 Gretsch Chet Atkins Country Gentleman Custom Three-Quarters

1993 Gretsch Country Classic II 6122-1962

2001 Gretsch Nashville Western 6120W-1957
This was in effect an Eddie Cochran model, but without the guitarist's name attached. It included Cochran's favored P-90 pickup at the neck.

2003 ad for the Round Up

2001 Gretsch Nashville Western 6120W-1957

2003 Gretsch Nashville Classic 6122-1959

2003 Gretsch Nashville Classic 6122-1959
A reissue of the early single-cut Country Gent. The Gretsch-pattern Bigsby tremolo has a tubular arm, and the position markers are classic thumb types.

SEMI-SOLID ELECTRIC GUITARS

215

RICKENBACKER
SEMI-HOLLOW GUITARS

Rickenbacker's role in the grand scheme of guitar design is unfairly overlooked, despite its central importance in the development of early electric designs (see page 79) and its dominance in the electric 12-string guitar market (for more on that subject, see page 174).

While the company's classic electrics are not as prevalent on stages as they once were, back in the 1960s, Rickenbacker rode a cresting wave of popularity thanks to a mix of innovative appointments, attractive aesthetics, and the resulting star endorsements that turned its 300 and 600 Series models into icons.

The sweeping shapes of Rickenbacker's most famous semi-hollow electrics were very different from the lines being drawn by its competitors in the late 1950s. In 1958, the company released a 12-strong line of Capri model guitars. The name was soon dropped, but the numbers would

soon form the backbone of Rickenbacker's catalogue. There were four short-scale guitar models: the 310 (two pickups), 315 (plus vibrato), 320 (three pickups), 325 (plus vibrato); four full-scale models: 330 (two pickups), 335 (plus vibrato), 340 (three pickups), 345 (plus vibrato); and four deluxe full-scale models: 360 (two pickups), 365 (plus vibrato), 370 (three pickups), and 375 (plus vibrato). The 380 series had an impressive carved front and back and a thicker body.

The two-pickup 330 and 360 models are similar, with the 360 distinguishable as the deluxe version by its triangular fingerboard inlays and the addition of binding to the neck (and sometimes to the body). The F-suffix models, however—the F denotes Full Body—had single rounded cutaways and comparatively thick bodies. They were in production from 1959 to around 1980.

1959 Rickenbacker 360F

1959 catalogue (left) and ad (facing page) for early Rickenbacker models.

1968 Rickenbacker 360F
This second version of the model abandoned the traditional two-tier gold plastic pickguard, with tone and volume control mounted on the lower section for a line of control knobs running along the lower edge of the body. Also, the cutaway was flattened.

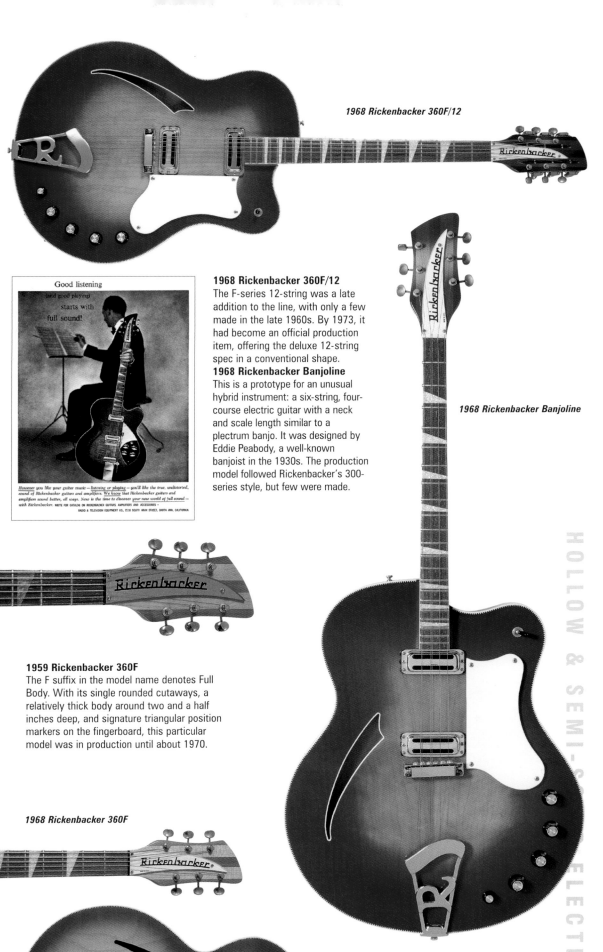

1968 Rickenbacker 360F/12

1968 Rickenbacker Banjoline

1968 Rickenbacker 360F/12
The F-series 12-string was a late addition to the line, with only a few made in the late 1960s. By 1973, it had become an official production item, offering the deluxe 12-string spec in a conventional shape.

1968 Rickenbacker Banjoline
This is a prototype for an unusual hybrid instrument: a six-string, four-course electric guitar with a neck and scale length similar to a plectrum banjo. It was designed by Eddie Peabody, a well-known banjoist in the 1930s. The production model followed Rickenbacker's 300-series style, but few were made.

Good listening
(and good playing)
starts with
full sound!

However you like your guitar music – listening or playing – you'll like the true, undistorted, sound of Rickenbacker guitars and amplifiers. We know that Rickenbacker guitars and amplifiers sound better, all ways. Now is the time to discover your new world of full sound – with Rickenbacker. WRITE FOR CATALOG ON RICKENBACKER GUITARS, AMPLIFIERS AND ACCESSORIES •
RADIO & TELEVISION EQUIPMENT CO., 2118 SOUTH MAIN STREET, SANTA ANA, CALIFORNIA

1959 Rickenbacker 360F
The F suffix in the model name denotes Full Body. With its single rounded cutaways, a relatively thick body around two and a half inches deep, and signature triangular position markers on the fingerboard, this particular model was in production until about 1970.

1968 Rickenbacker 360F

1960 Rickenbacker 375F

1960 Rickenbacker 375F
This three-pickup model had a vibrato unit fitted (without this, it would be a 370F). It has a Germanic feel, a reflection of German luthier and jazz player Roger Rossmeisl, who had a significant involvement in the design of many Rickenbacker models.

RICKENBACKER
SEMI-HOLLOW GUITARS II

Vintage Series

As the promotional literature of the 1960s put it, the Rickenbacker was "the Beatle backer"—and John Lennon's frequent use of a Rickenbacker 325 during the band's rise to fame contributed much to the instrument's popularity, as did George Harrison's subsequent adoption of the 360/12 in 1964. A number of Lennon signature models appeared in 1989.

Another British player who did much for the popularity, if not for the structural integrity, of the Rickenbacker was Pete Townshend, who used and abused various models imported into the UK. Inspired by Townshend's antics, Paul Weller was a prominent later user, and Rickenbacker would enjoy a revival of sorts in the 1980s by association with R.E.M. guitarist Peter Buck.

In its pomp, Rickenbacker was keen to include technological innovations on its models, such as the Rick-O-Sound stereo signal feature of 1960, which split the neck and bridge pickups' output, enabling them to be sent to separate amplifiers with a special cord. The addition of a fifth knob on many models in 1961 introduced the "blend" feature to the Rickenbacker tone circuit, which offered guitarists the ability to blend in signal from the unselected pickup in a pair. Theoretically, at least, it was a clever idea, but it only served to baffle many guitarists for decades to come. Also ignored by the guitar-playing population was the 330SF, a 330 variant with slanting frets, nut, pickups, and bridge. The company explained that these "match precisely the natural angle of the fretting fingers."

Many Rickys have changed little in sound or looks since the company's heyday, and much of their appeal today lies in their embodiment of the past.

1995 catalogue

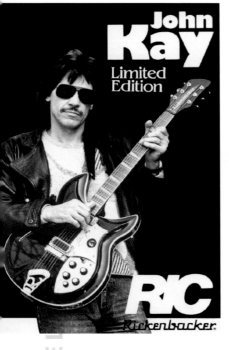

1988 ad with John Kay

1969 Rickenbacker 381
Rickenbacker changed the profile of the body edge for this model, which has a deep carved top that follows the outside line, with a bound edge of checkered black-and-white binding. The body of this guitar is deeper than the other models on this page.

1964 Rickenbacker 325

1964 Rickenbacker 325
This original version of the model has no soundholes, and although it looks like a solidbody guitar, it is in fact a semi-solid. This one belonged to John Lennon and was his favorite guitar in 1964 and '65.

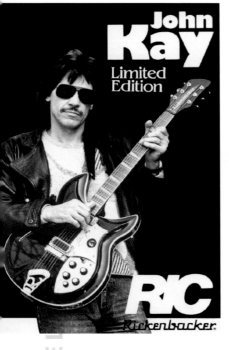

*1965 ad for the 325, known
in the UK as model 1996*

1964 Rickenbacker 325/1996

1964 Rickenbacker 325/1996
This short-scale guitar is the UK "1996"
version of the 325, generally referred to as
the John Lennon after the 325's most
famous player. The guitar has a single
f-hole because the UK agent, Rose-Morris,
requested this feature.

1971 Rickenbacker 360
This is the classic early shape, before the
arrival of the curved-body look of the
example at the bottom of the page. This
guitar is finished in a rare green sunburst.

1969 Rickenbacker 381

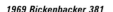

A promo shot for the 365 model of 1959

1971 Rickenbacker 360

1969 Rickenbacker 375

1969 Rickenbacker 375
The three-pickup 375 model has a bound
fingerboard and binding on the back of the
body, and the front of the body now has a
curved "radius." This optional new look for
the deluxe models debuted in 1964.

AMERICAN GALLERY
ARCHTOPS

Makers of electric-acoustic guitars in the USA have been dominated by the major brands, including Gibson, Gretsch, Guild, Rickenbacker, and Epiphone. One major guitar maker, Fender, consistently failed to succeed with electric hollowbody guitars, until it made an Alliance with Gretsch in 2002, while other companies have decided to concentrate solely on solidbody electrics, leaving hollowbody models to specialists.

Mainly during the 1950s and 1960s, some producers such as Harmony and Kay made plenty of models in large numbers for outside clients. These customers were primarily retail-store chains or mail-order organizations, and they did not have guitar-making facilities of their own; instead, they wanted to exploit the big demand for guitars of all kinds by having their own brandnames on a broad line of guitar products. Harmony and Kay also, of course, made and marketed guitars themselves with their own brands.

c.1960 D'Angelico Electric
John D'Angelico's main business was building top-quality acoustic archtops (for which see page 36). His electrics came with plywood bodies, which he bought in from outside suppliers when he was asked to build an electric guitar.

c.1960 D'Angelico Electric

1997 Fender D'Aquisto Deluxe
High-end luthier Jimmy D'Aquisto helped Fender design and produce one of the Master series of guitars that were made by Fender Japan.

1997 Fender D'Aquisto Deluxe

1962 Kay Jazz II K775
This model is similar to one used by a young Eric Clapton in the early 1960s when he played in The Roosters. The Kay brand started life in 1931, and the Chicago-based company also made many cheap guitars for stores and mail-order firms. US production of Kays ended in the late 1960s, but the name was revived in the 1980s.

1962 Kay Jazz II K775

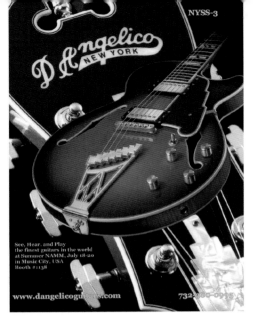

NYSS-3

*2003 ad for revived
D'Angelico brand*

1958 Kay catalogue

2008 PRS SCJ Thinline Ltd

2008 PRS SCJ Thinline Ltd
This limited-eidition PRS model was based on the Archtop and Hollowbody lines, with a maple top and back, mahogany neck, and ebony fingerboard and headstock veneer. PRS's notable bird inlays are in gold here, and this variant of the SCJ is fitted with a Bigsby vibrato for that extra touch of wobble.

c.1965 Harmony Meteor H70

c.1965 Harmony Meteor H70
This was one of Harmony's most popular thinline hollowbody guitars in the 1960s. This is a left-handed sunburst-finish H70, while its twin, the H71, came with a natural finish.

c.1948 Paramount
This was a brandname used in the 1930s and 1940s by a New York City company called Lange, and later also by Gretsch & Brenner. Paramount guitars were made by various suppliers, and this example appears to have been made by Kay. The odd-shaped pickup is a very unusual feature.

c.1948 Paramount

c.1962 Harvey Thomas Custom

c.1962 Harvey Thomas Custom
Hollowbody electrics tend toward traditional designs, dictated largely by conservative players. This rare Harvey Thomas guitar is an exception. Made in Washington in the early 1960s, it is one of the largest of its type ever made. Thomas was not noted for subtlety, even appearing in one of his catalogues dressed in a gorilla suit.

221

AMERICAN GALLERY
ARCHTOPS & SEMI-SOLIDS

In addition to the companies that produced the selected models shown in this section, many other companies made and marketed this kind of electric guitar in the USA. Companies producing archtop electrics in the 1930s were few, but included National and Vega, and also Vivi-Tone, whose rare models were devised by the gifted ex-Gibson designer Lloyd Loar.

However, the rush of electric archtops and thinline models came in the 1950s and 1960s. Semie Moseley's Mosrite brand appeared on a number of f-hole models, while Coral, a line made by the Danelectro company, could be seen on hollowbody versions of its unusual "long horn" body shape and also appeared on more conventional thinlines. Martin, too, produced a limited number of f-hole thinline electrics in the 1970s, as did Ovation.

One major guitar maker, Fender, has consistently failed to succeed with electric hollowbody guitars—for example, the full-body LTD and the Montego models of 1968 and the thinline Coronados of 1966, including the unusual Wildwood series. The bodies of this line were made from timber from beech trees that had colored dyes injected into them during growth, producing distinctive bright hues that ran through the grain of the wood.

Fender also issued the thinline Starcaster, in 1976, and another full-body archtop, the Classic Rocker, in 2000. The thinline concept of the 1970s, which is most closely associated with the Telecaster, has been rekindled in recent years, and 2012's Pawn Shop line features such oddities as the f-hole Offset Special. Fender's smartest move in this area was its alliance with Gretech since 2002.

1968 Fender Coronado II Wildwood

1968 Fender Coronado II Wildwood
Fender's first attempt at a thinline electric, the Coronado was launched in 1966. As well as sunburst or solid colors, it was also offered in gray Antigua or this Wildwood finish, created by injecting dyes into beech trees during growth. This produced unique colored patterns in the timber.

c.1968 Kustom K200C

HOLLOW & SEMI-SOLID ELECTRIC GUITARS

1964 Harmony H77
Chicago-based company Harmony, started in 1892, was at one time the biggest guitar producer in the USA, but American manufacture ceased in 1975. The three-pickup cherry sunburst H77 was the top Harmony hollowbody electric, made from 1964 to 1970.

c.1978 Fender Starcaster
In 1976 Fender tried again to market a thinline electric, but the Starcaster was also unsuccessful, mainly due to Gibson's dominance in the market, and it was dropped in 1979. The model retains a cult following to this day, however.

1964 Harmony H77

c.1978 Fender Starcaster

c.1968 Kustom K200C
These Rickenbacker-influenced guitars were built in Chanute, Kansas, by a company started by Bud Ross, originally producing amplification. These guitars came in three colors—natural as here, blue and wineburst—but few of them were made.

223

AMERICAN GALLERY
SEMI-SOLIDS II

Taking over the old Gibson factory in Kalamazoo, former Gibson employees established the Heritage company in 1985. The more successful models it produced were derived from familiar Gibson designs, and over the years the company has built a reputation for well-crafted instruments at an affordable price.

PRS, known for its high-end solidbody guitars (see page 138) introduced a range of full-body and thinline archtop guitars in 1998, and the range shared the same attention to detail and use of prime-grade timbers. The company later added a number of single- and double-cutaway models, and some of the more recent guitars, such as the SE Custom, are from the PRS budget line of instruments. A 2012 limited-edition version added sparkle finishes and a

Bigsby vibrato, effectively merging the retro-futuristic vibe of classic semi-hollowbodys with some of the more established PRS appointments.

The well-known acoustic guitar makers Taylor and Collings have both introduced electrics to their catalogues, including thinline semi-solid models. Other makers known predominantly for making solidbody guitars have added semi-solid instruments to their lines, including Charvel with the Surfcaster; Hamer's Duo Tone; and Daisy Rock with its semi-solid aimed at the female player.

Dean Zelinsky started the Dean brand in 1976, but he finally cut all ties in 2008 to found a new company, DBZ, which in 2011 introduced the ultra-thin semi-solid Imperial Aliento with distinctive chevron-style soundhole.

serious guitar

2011 Collings ad

1991 Charvel Surfcaster

1991 Charvel Surfcaster
This retro-looking semi-solid came from a company more associated with solidbody superstrats. It has lipstick-style pickups, as found on Danelectros, and triangular fingerboard inlays, reminiscent of Rickenbacker. A more recent and modernized take on the model, the Skatecaster, continues the tradition.

2007 PRS SE Custom Semi-Hollow
Unique to the PRS line, this new-style SE has a semi-hollow construction and features a Rickenbacker-inspired "slash" soundhole.

2007 PRS SE Custom Semi-Hollow

HOLLOW & SEMI-SOLID ELECTRIC GUITARS

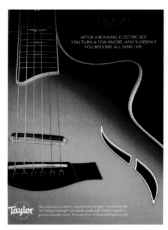

2006 Taylor ad

2004 Daisy Rock ad with Ann & Nancy Wilson

1994 Hamer Duo Tone

2003 Hamer ad featuring Chester Bennington

1994 Hamer Duo Tone

Paul Hamer and Jol Dantzig founded Hamer in Illinois around 1974, making respected Gibson-inspired models. In 1988, Hamer was acquired by Ovation's owners, Kaman. A 1990s introduction by the new firm was the Duo Tone, a hybrid combining electric and acoustic sounds. Hamer was included in the sale of Kaman to Fender in 2007.

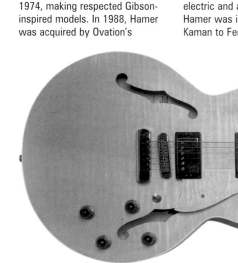

1990 Heritage H-535

1990 Heritage H-535

Heritage set up in the old Gibson building in Kalamazoo in 1985 and achieved success with lines of electric-acoustic and solid models. Some have even been named Parsons Street models after the address in Kalamazoo, and most are based on Gibson lines, such as this ES-335-inspired guitar.

2011 DBZ Imperial Aliento

2011 DBZ Imperial Aliento

Dean Zelinsky left Dean Guitars in 2008 and founded DBZ. This model boasts an ultra-thin hollow body, just half an inch at its thinnest point. Its neck features engraved patterns intended to aid glide and the wicking of moisture.

1994 Washburn ad with Clarence Gatemouth Brown

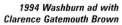

HOLLOW & SEMI-SO...

225

EUROPEAN GALLERY
ARCHTOPS & THINLINES

European makers of hollowbody electrics have for the most part been influenced by guitars from the United States. This is not too surprising, given that most of the invention and innovation among these instruments has originated there.

One factor that sets some European makers apart is their willingness to use the abundant local timbers, often forsaking the American standards of spruce, maple, and so on and opting for, say, Scots pine or sycamore.

The art of the European archtop electric has resided firmly in Germany, principally with Hofner's more expensive instruments. This instrument-making company was founded in 1887 by Karl Hofner in the region that would become East Germany. The firm started to produce guitars in 1925. The Hofner family escaped to West

Germany after World War II, establishing a new factory in Bubenreuth in 1951. The company's first electric archtops appeared in the 1950s, and the firm continues to produce instruments today.

Many other European makers have catered to the demand for hollowbody electrics. In West Germany, Framus, Hoyer, Klira, and Roger have all experimented with these designs.

Hagstrom's Swedish-made Viking was a popular hollow electric, famously used once by Elvis Presley, while in Italy makers included Eko, Galanti, and Welson.

In the UK there have been few makers of hollowbody electrics, although in the 1960s Burns and Wilson did offer a few models. Small makers currently producing such guitars include Chris Eccleshall, Gordon Smith, and Mike Vanden.

c.1961 Hofner Verithin

1967 Vox ad

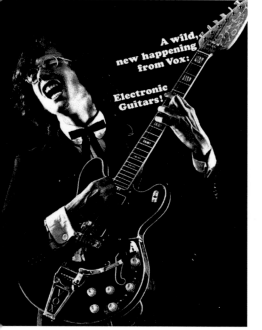

c.1961 Hofner Verithin
During the 1950s, Hofner had kept many European players supplied with decent, affordable guitars when American instruments were hard to get. As US guitars became

more plentiful in the early 1960s, Hofner competed more directly with American instruments. The Verithin, based on Gibson's thinline series, was a staple among up-and-coming pop groups.

1961 Hofner Golden Hofner

1979 Gordon Smith Gypsy "60" SS

1979 Gordon Smith Gypsy "60" SS
Coming from the UK's longest established electric guitar maker, this Gypsy was a thicker-bodied semi-solid Les Paul-shaped instrument with distinctly shaped f-holes, unbound body and neck, and simple dot position-markers.

c.1963 Hopf Saturn 63
The Hopf company of West Germany departed from conventional hollowbody electric styling on this mid-1960s guitar. The Star Club in Hamburg featured it in some of its ads, considering it to be representative of the German beat scene of the time.

c.1956 Hofner Club 50
Launched in the mid 1950s, Hofner's Club models were scaled-down versions of its larger hollow-bodied guitars, but without f-holes. This one has the early-style circular control panel.

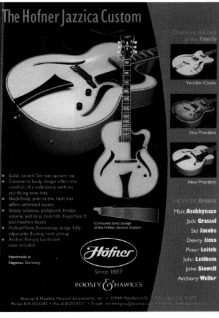

Hofner ads from 2007 and 2001

2006 Framus ad

c.1963 Hopf Saturn 63

c.1956 Hofner Club 50

1961 Hofner Golden Hofner
The top of Hofner's hollowbody electric line, this model was made between 1959 and 1962. It is from an export-only range made by Hofner for Selmer London. Hofner itself described the Golden model as "a masterpiece of guitar perfection."

FAR-EAST GALLERY
ARCHTOPS & THINLINES

The principal Far Eastern guitar-producing country in the late 1960s and early 1970s was Japan. During that period its makers were primarily concerned with copying the guitars made by the best-known American brands. But the Japanese instruments of this period were made for a fraction of the cost of the originals and, inevitably, were generally of much poorer quality.

Later in the 1970s and into the 1980s producers in the Far East—now including makers in Korea and Taiwan as well as Japan—began to manufacture solidbody electrics with more originality and less dependence on US influences. However, when it came to hollowbody electrics, both archtop and thinline types, there was still much reliance on traditional American guidelines. There were two main reasons for this. First, it is hard (and

relatively expensive) for a maker to be original with such guitars. Second, jazz musicians who favor hollowbody guitars are inherently conservative. This combination tends to ensure unadventurously designed guitars.

This type of instrument usually means a bigger investment for the guitar maker when compared to that needed for solidbody electric guitars. This is principally because the production process can be more time-consuming and intense. Far Eastern makers, whose business so often centers on building guitars to a price, have thus traditionally concentrated on solid guitars. Despite this, there is still a reasonable stock of Far Eastern makers of hollowbody electrics, particularly the thinline double-cutaway variety. Among the many Japanese brand names that have appeared on such guitars are Tokai, Teisco, Maya, Fresher, Kimbara, Kasuga, Columbus, Climar, Excetro, and Audition.

c.1968 Teisco Del Rey May Queen

1989 Antoria Rockstar EG-1935

c.1968 Teisco Del Rey May Queen
In 1968, the revamped Teisco began to produce a new line of electric guitars, including this May Queen model that followed the Japanese trend of the time for hollowbody electrics. The eccentric body shape was clearly influenced by Vox's Mando Guitar of 1967, a sort of short-scale 12-string solidbody mandolin.

c.1967 Yamaha SA-15

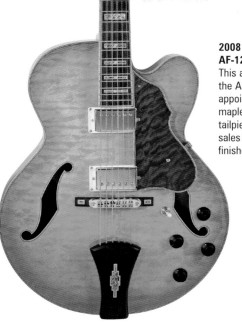

2008 Ibanez Artcore Custom AF-125

This archtop guitar, the flagship of the Artcore range, has luxurious appointments including a quilted maple top with real wooden knobs, tailpiece, and pickguard. Ibanez's sales literature promises hand-finished frets.

2008 Ibanez Artcore Custom AF-125

Ibanez ads from 1991 (right) featuring George Benson and (opposite, from1982) also Joe Pass and Lee Ritenour

1989 Antoria Rockstar EG-1935

Antoria was a UK importer's brand name, used in the 1970s mostly on guitars made in the Fujigen Gakki factory, which also produced Ibanez guitars. However, this later instrument was made in Korea, and it was sold earlier in the 1980s as the Harmony H935. It is clearly influenced by the Gibson ES-335, although Antoria claims it has "double sustain blocks" inside the body.

c.1967 Yamaha SA-15

With its distinctive long lower horn, this guitar has a strong Oriental flavor to the design and is not the usual copy of a US-made instrument. The original take on soundhole shape is a case in point.

1989 Aria Pro II TA-60

TA stands for the Titan Artist series, which appeared in 1981. The influence on this model is clearly from Gibson, despite Aria's inscription on the headstock about an "Original Custom Body." The workmanship is good, and the pink finish of this example is certainly unusual for this style of guitar.

1989 Aria Pro II TA-60

1999 Cort Larry Coryell LCS-1

1990 Yamaha SA-1100

2006 Crafter electric-acoustic ad

1999 Cort Larry Coryell LCS-1

This Korean-built archtop has a pressed solid spruce top with flame-maple sides and back. The pickups are Seymour Duncan-designed humbuckers.

1990 Yamaha SA-1100

This model comes from Yamaha's third generation of the SA ("Semi Acoustic") series, launched in 1977. It is obviously based on Gibson's popular ES-335. The fashion at the time it was issued for so-called blonde hollowbody guitars explains this Yamaha's natural finish.

CHAPTER FIVE
ELECTRIC BASS GUITARS

Simplicity was the key word for the original design of the electric bass guitar. Fender in California invented the instrument, marketing its Precision Bass from late in 1951. The instrument followed the style set by Fender a little earlier with its solidbody Telecaster electric guitar and featured the same straightforward bolt-together construction that turned guitar making into a production-line business.

Most makers now acknowledge that Fender's original designs were remarkably sound, and indeed the Precision and Jazz Bass form the foundation for many of the competing models launched since those early years. The biggest challenge to the Fender style of construction came in the early 1980s when Ned Steinberger in New York City came up with his headless (and almost body-less) bass guitar made from carbon fiber. For a time after that shock to the bass establishment, the influence of Steinberger's design was seen in basses that mixed a headless neck with a conventional body shape.

Bass players have now established a strong identity for their instrument, and the myth of the bass being played by someone not good enough for six-string duties is clearly outdated. Electric bass has its own history of heroes. Witness just two examples among many others, old and new: the rhythmic brilliance of the Motown master James Jamerson, and the virtuosic playing of Jaco Pastorius.

Many instruments compete today for the bassist's attention, some using advanced electronics and combinations of exotic woods and space-age materials. Some music calls for instruments that have more strings to provide access to ever-deeper or more menacing rumblings, and fretless designs maintain their niche in the catalogues of several larger manufacturers, as well as those of boutique bass builders. Fender's innovations live on, in its own and in countless other bass guitars.

FENDER
PRECISION BASS

In 1950, Leo Fender and his colleagues had been the first to market a solidbody electric guitar, but they were not content to stop there. A little later, Fender came up with an exciting new idea, the electric bass guitar.

The Fender Precision was launched in late 1951. Players were used to the acoustic double bass—a bulky, cumbersome, and often barely audible instrument, referred to by Leo Fender as "the doghouse." He reckoned that bass players would welcome a louder, more portable instrument that offered precise pitching of notes. So in 1951, Fender offered for sale the world's first commercially available fretted electric bass guitar, aptly named the Precision Bass, with a 34-inch scale, 20-fret maple neck bolted to a slab ash body featuring two cutaways—a Fender first.

Early Precision players included a number of country & western musicians, who formed a large part of Fender's clientele at the time. There was also the occasional jazz player, such as Monk Montgomery of the Lionel Hampton band. The word spread during the 1950s, and by the early 1960s the bass guitar was established as a new vital component of modern music-making.

1952 Precision ad

1963 Fender Precision Bass

1963 Fender Precision Bass
Around 1959, Fender started fitting rosewood fingerboards to the Precision necks, replacing the one-piece maple neck/fingerboard, but some players said they preferred the smoother feel of the maple board.

1951 Fender Precision Bass

ELECTRIC BASS GUITARS

2010 ad featuring Mike Dirnt

1957 Fender Precision Bass

1957 Precision ad

1957 Fender Precision Bass
Around this time, the Precision changed to the look it kept for more than 30 years. This comprised a wider headstock; controls and jack built into a new pickguard; four bridge saddles rather than two; and a new two-piece pickup in the middle of the body.

1966 Fender Precision Bass
By the early 1960s, Fender had defined its list of automobile-inspired custom colors, and by 1965 the finishes were all metallic. This bass is finished in Firemist Gold.

1955 Fender Precision Bass

1966 Fender Precision Bass

1951 Fender Precision Bass
The Precision appeared in 1951 and was pure simplicity. Its four strings were tuned E-A-D-G, each an octave below the six-string guitar's lowest four strings. The slab body of the original was finished in a natural blonde, and the 20 frets were set directly into the solid maple bolt-on neck.

1955 Fender Precision Bass
From about 1954, the Precision was also offered in two-tone sunburst finish. About the same time, a white pickguard was used. Resembling the curvaceous Strat, its contoured body was less harsh than the form of the slab-sided original.

ELECTRIC BASS G

FENDER
PRECISION VARIATIONS

The early history of the Fender company is littered with examples of innovation. The fact that Fender got so much right when there were no rules concerning electric instruments is remarkable. But it has meant that the company has had little choice but to constantly reissue and repackage its original ideas, prompted partly by the copycat activities of competitors.

Bass is of course no different in this regard, and contemporary trends in guitar-making have sometimes influenced additions to Fender's lines, including the 1980 Precision Bass Special with active circuitry, but such updates have been rare and short-lived. Fender's bass regeneration program began in 1968 when it issued a

version of the original Precision Bass, in the style of the 1952 model, which was named the Telecaster Bass (see following pages). From the early 1980s, Fender has produced many reissues of its essential Precision and Jazz Bass designs, both at its USA and Mexico plants and at offshore factories.

These "new oldies" have proved popular, and Fender has returned to its past frequently over the last decades to provide a retro option at every price point, from Squier's Classic Vibe series to the pro-level American Vintage Series and beyond. Fender's signature Precision models for artists as diverse as Sting, session-player Tony Franklin, and Mike Dirnt have also breathed new life into the lines.

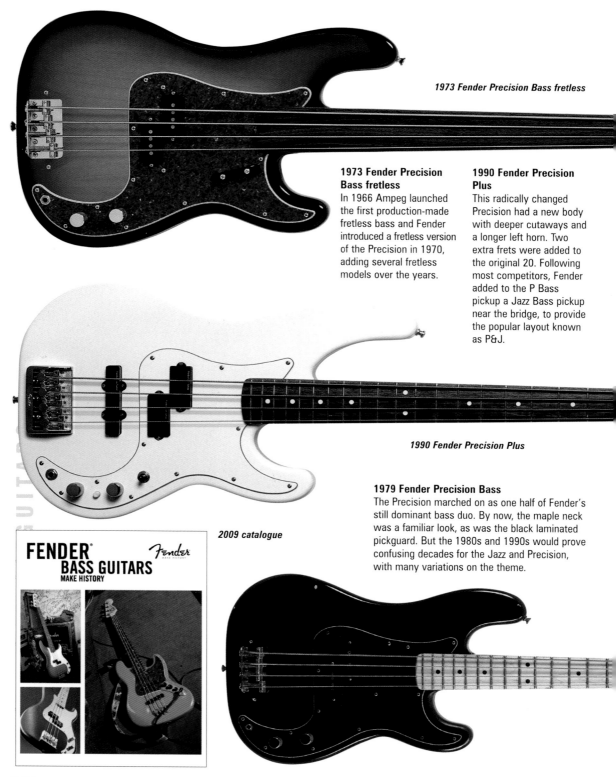

1973 Fender Precision Bass fretless

1973 Fender Precision Bass fretless
In 1966 Ampeg launched the first production-made fretless bass and Fender introduced a fretless version of the Precision in 1970, adding several fretless models over the years.

1990 Fender Precision Plus
This radically changed Precision had a new body with deeper cutaways and a longer left horn. Two extra frets were added to the original 20. Following most competitors, Fender added to the P Bass pickup a Jazz Bass pickup near the bridge, to provide the popular layout known as P&J.

1990 Fender Precision Plus

2009 catalogue

1979 Fender Precision Bass
The Precision marched on as one half of Fender's still dominant bass duo. By now, the maple neck was a familiar look, as was the black laminated pickguard. But the 1980s and 1990s would prove confusing decades for the Jazz and Precision, with many variations on the theme.

FENDER
BASS GUITARS
MAKE HISTORY

1998 Fender American Vintage '62 Precision Bass

1998 Fender American Vintage '62 Precision Bass

By the mid 1980s, Fender had its Japan operation up and running, and the US joined in with the vintage recreations craze. Basses from two classic eras were copied: the 1957-style model, with fretted maple neck; and the '62-style, with rosewood board, like this more recent American Vintage bass.

2006 Fender Classic Series 50s Precision Bass

2006 Fender Classic Series 50s Precision Bass

This Classic Series bass has the look of an oldie that has had its chrome covers removed. Until the early 1980s, Fender basses were supplied with screw-down covers for the bridge and pickup. They were intended as rests for the player's hand. But players often discarded them, finding the bridge cover especially awkward and obstructive. For this reason, bare screw-holes are common on such models.

57 PRECISION·BASS

1982 ad for '57-style Precision reissue

2008 Fender Time Machine '59 Precision Bass

Fender is in a prime spot to benefit from the retro fashion and offers a crowded line of vintage-style models, at the top of which sit the Custom Shop Time Machine replicas, like this N.O.S. ("New Old Stock") P Bass.

2008 Fender Time Machine '59 Precision Bass

1991 Fender Jamerson Tribute Precision Bass

James Jamerson originally played the early Motown sessions on a double bass, switching to an electric Fender Precision Bass in 1961. He eventually settled on a sunburst 1962 model that he played until his untimely death in 1983. Fender introduced this Tribute model in the early 1990s.

1979 Fender Precision Bass

1991 Fender Jamerson Tribute Precision Bass

ELECTRIC BASS GUITARS

FENDER
TELECASTER & JAZZ BASS

Fender's dynamic duo of Precision and Jazz, much like the Tele and Strat, has been consistently popularity with players and influenced the lines of countless companies. Many players rarely venture further than the mainstay Precision or Jazz to satisfy their needs, but Fender has produced a number of other models to meet the perceived demand for something different. Some live on in the company's current catalogue in some refined version or other, and the more outlandish sometimes reappear in the more experimental budget lines, such as the recent Modern Player Jaguar.

The modern Telecaster Bass is in effect a reissue of Fender's first-ever reissue. The original Telecaster Bass was introduced in 1968 as a recreation of the original early-style Precision Bass (which was influenced by the Telecaster guitar design.) The no-frills Telecaster Bass, with its one single-coil pickup, Telecaster-style headstock, and slab body, was modified in 1972 with a humbucker in place of its single-coil, as well as a new pickguard. This version lasted until 1978, when it was discontinued. A Japanese '51 Precision Bass, sharing many of the original Tele Bass's features, appeared in the early 1990s.

Recently, Squier Vintage Modified Precision Bass and Fender Modern Player versions have meant that the Telecaster Bass has remained as an option for beginner and intermediate players.

1968 Fender Telecaster Bass

1968 Fender Telecaster Bass
This early example has had the screw-down covers removed to reveal the single small four-polepiece pickup. Note the Telecaster-style control plate.

1968 Fender Paisley Red Telecaster Bass

1972 Fender Telecaster Bass

236

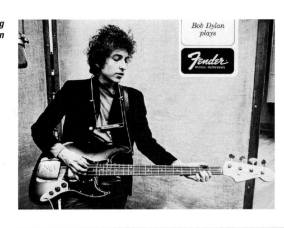

1967 Fender catalogue with four-, five-, and six-string basses

1960 Fender Jazz Bass
This was Fender's second bass model, introduced in 1960. This early model has two stacked control knobs. The offset shape of the Jazz's body is akin to that of Fender's contemporary guitar, the Jazzmaster. It also differed from the earlier Precision Bass, with a neck tapering heavily toward the nut.

1960 Fender Jazz Bass

1968 Fender Paisley Red Telecaster Bass
The Telecaster Bass was first issued by Fender in 1968 and was in effect a reissue of the first type of Precision Bass. In the late 1960s, a few appeared finished in a blue-flower pattern or red paisley, as with this striking instrument.

1960 Fender Jazz Bass
Another early example, this one finished in Olympic White and with the original chrome covers still in place. Unlike the Jazzmaster guitar, the Jazz Bass would indeed find favor among jazz players, and its bright, prominent sound suited a trio format.

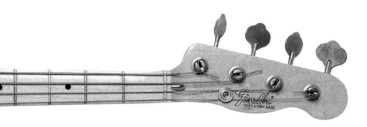

1972 Fender Telecaster Bass
In 1972, a humbucking pickup replaced the single-coils, a change that was happening across the Telecaster six-string line around this time. The restyled pickguard was extended to include the controls. The Tele Bass lasted another seven years.

ELECTRIC BASS GUITARS

FENDER
JAZZ BASS II

1999 ad (opposite) featuring Jaco Pastorius and Jazz Bass

As the Precision took a while to win over musicians who were used to the acoustic double bass, it was not until 1960 that Fender's second guitar-styled bass, the Jazz model, appeared on the market. Playing the role of Stratocaster to the Precision's Telecaster, this refined instrument gave a greater range of sounds and offered a more tightly proportioned neck, not to mention a futuristic offset-waist contoured aesthetic and a different playing experience to that offered by the Precision. As well as this slinkier feel, the single-coil pickups with two polepieces for each string contributed to the instrument's brighter, more treble-oriented tone.

The 1970s saw the Jazz's bridge pickup moved a little closer to the bridge, emphasising this brightness even more—and Fender's recently released '70s Jazz Bass model, with its classic block-marker fingerboard, captures the vibe with distinction.

While the Jazz Bass has gone on enjoy wide and effective use in many different styles of music, it has been particularly successful with the genre of players for whom it was originally intended—and notably with the late and legendary Jaco Pastorius in the 1970s, and Marcus Miller, best known for his work in the 1980s with Miles Davis.

Fender has capitalized on the Jazz's popularity with a range of signature models over the years, encompassing a typically diverse cross-section of artists, and endorsers of Fender basses have ranged all the way from Rush's Geddy Lee to Biffy Clyro's James Johnston.

1998 ad with Marcus Miller

1977 Fender Jazz Bass

1999 Fender Jaco Pastorius Tribute Jazz Bass

1964 Fender Jazz Bass
This pristine example finished in Teal Green has three controls—two volume and one tone—as opposed to the first version of the bass that had two stacked dual-concentric controls.

ELECTRIC BASS

2009 Fender Road Worn 60s Jazz Bass

2005 Fender Jazz Bass 24

2009 Fender Road Worn 60s Jazz Bass

This Road Worn 1960s-style Jazz Bass, finished in distressed Fiesta Red, was made in Fender's plant in Mexico and brought the Time Machine line's aged-finish idea to a more affordable instrument.

2005 Fender Jazz Bass 24

This first 24-fret bass from Fender was manufactured in Korea and has a slightly revised body shape and a 34-inch scale, with two straight eight-polepiece pickups. A five-string version, the 24 V, was released a few years later.

1977 Fender Jazz Bass

This third version of the Jazz Bass can be identified by the "bullet" truss-rod adjuster, at the headstock end of the neck, and block position markers.

1999 Fender Jaco Pastorius Tribute Jazz Bass

Jaco Pastorius released his first solo album in 1976, the same year he joined Weather Report. Bass players were intrigued by Jaco's remarkable skills, deployed on a pair of Jazz Basses, one a fretless, like the Tribute replica pictured here. He popularized the sound of fretless bass, with Weather Report and through his peerless contributions to a series of Joni Mitchell albums in the late 1970s.

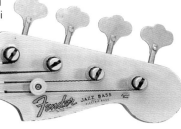

1982 Fender Squier Vintage Series '62 Jazz Bass

1990 Fender Jazz Plus V

1982 Fender Squier Vintage Series '62 Jazz Bass

This Jazz Bass was one of the very first Squier Japanese Vintages off the line, with the small Squier logo on the headstock. Squier became a successful brand in its own right for less expensive Fenders.

1990 Fender Jazz Plus V

Fender's first modern-style five-string bass was a plain and functional instrument without pickup covers or pickguard. It had Lace Sensor pickups and a built-in preamp.

1964 Fender Jazz Bass

FENDER
OTHER BASSES

Beyond the success of its go-to Precision and Jazz templates, Fender has consistently tried to cater to bassists with requirements slightly outside of the classic formula that these basses have defined. Some models have added extra strings, others have taken different body shapes, and others have incorporated tweaks and modifications made by notable artists to create signature models.

The Bass V of 1965 differed from the modern idea of a five-string bass. It had a 15-fret fingerboard and added an extra treble string tuned to C, rather than an extra bass string tuned to B. It never caught on, and faded from Fender's line by 1970. Later, the Jazz Plus V of 1990 marked Fender's first foray into the modern five-string bass realm.

The Mustang Bass, Fender's first short-scale bass, debuted in 1966 and was designed to appeal to guitarists wanting to double on bass. Like Gibson's EB-6 from 1960, the Fender VI (often known as the Bass VI) of 1961 was more or less a six-string guitar tuned an octave lower.

Fender's bass catalogue has included a few surprises among the dependable retro offerings. The Jazz Bass 24 was an affordable Korean-made 24-fret Jazz, while the Deluxe Jaguar Bass is a Japanese-made combination of Jaguar guitar and Jazz Bass.

Signature models, which began with 1993's Stu Hamm Urge Bass, have included Sting's classic early Precision and Geddy Lee's 1970s-styled Jazz model.

1966 Fender Bass V

1962 Fender Bass VI

2011 Fender Jaguar Bass

1966 Fender Bass V
The first five-string bass, the V adds a high C-string to the usual E-A-D-G. It has the full 34-inch scale but a short neck with the fifth string catering for the upper registers. The theory was that it would be easier to play "across" the strings rather than "along" the board. Players disagreed, and the V was shortlived.

2011 Fender Jaguar Bass
Fender has released several Jaguar basses into the wild. A real design hybrid, the affordable 2011 Modern Player version has Modern Player Jazz and P Bass pickups and sports Jazz Bass controls. A newer version, the Deluxe Jaguar model, reinstated the reassuringly confusing Jaguar switch banks.

ELECTRIC BASS GUITARS

1969 Fender Mustang Bass

1969 Fender Mustang Bass
After Fender was taken over by CBS in 1965, the company's marketing strategy changed. The Mustang, offered from 1966, was Fender's first short-scale bass, aimed to be more accessible for the new generation of guitarists now also playing bass. The pictured Mustang is a custom-color Competition striped version.

2008 Classic Vibe ad from Squier

1995 Fender Stu Hamm Urge

1977 Fender Mustang Bass
The Antigua finish was originally devised to cover burn marks on Coronado bodies, which was caused by a binding machine in the factory. Here it is purely decorative.

1995 Fender Stu Hamm Urge
This was the first signature bass from Fender. Hamm, a top-notch US session player, has worked with guitarists Steve Vai, Frank Gambale, and Joe Satriani, as well as releasing a number of solo albums. His signature model had three pickups, a graphite-reinforced neck, and a three-band EQ.

1977 Fender Mustang Bass

1962 Fender VI
The guitar was made for guitarists who wanted a bassier sound. The instrument is essentially a guitar with a longer than usual neck and with its strings tuned an octave lower than a regular guitar. The model was famously used by Jack Bruce in the early days of Cream.

2009 Fender Roscoe Beck IV Bass

2009 Fender Roscoe Beck IV Bass
This Artist Signature series bass was made for the Texas bass veteran and has unusual features including a graphite-reinforced neck and a drop D-tuner for the E string on the four-string model.

ELECTRIC BASS GUITARS

RICKENBACKER
4000-SERIES BASSES

When Rickenbacker launched its first bass guitar in 1957, the instrument had still only been in existence for six years. But the California company's offering to bass players was as idiosyncratic as any of its distinctive six-string electrics. The 4000 model had a long-horned body unlike any other bass guitar before; this and the harmoniously curved headstock set the classic Ricky bass style that the company has followed with only occasional variations ever since.

The simple single-pickup two-control 4000 model lasted until 1984. But by far the most popular version of the Rickenbacker bass is the twin-pickup 4001 model (which first appeared in 1961) and its many descendants, such as the more recent model 4003. Two British players in separate decades—Paul McCartney in the 1960s and Chris Squire in the 1970s—helped to establish Rickenbacker's popularity with bass players. As it had done with its six- and twelve-string electric guitar models, the company made special export versions to cater to the British market.

These days, the classic 4001 model is kept company in the Ricky catalogue by the modernized 4004L Laredo and the eco-conscious 4004Cii Cheyenne.

1957 Rickenbacker 4000

1957 Rickenbacker 4000
A first-year example of Rickenbacker's debut bass guitar. Designed by Roger Rossmeisl, it was the first bass guitar to have through-neck construction, a method some bass builders still favor for the increased sustain it offers.

1964 Rickenbacker 4001S

1964 Rickenbacker 4001S
This model earned Rickenbacker great fame among bass players when it was used by Paul McCartney in the 1960s and later by Chris Squire of Yes in the 1970s. Originally designed as an export-only version of Rickenbacker's 4001 model, it differs in its dot fingerboard markers and the lack of binding.

ELECTRIC BASS GUITARS

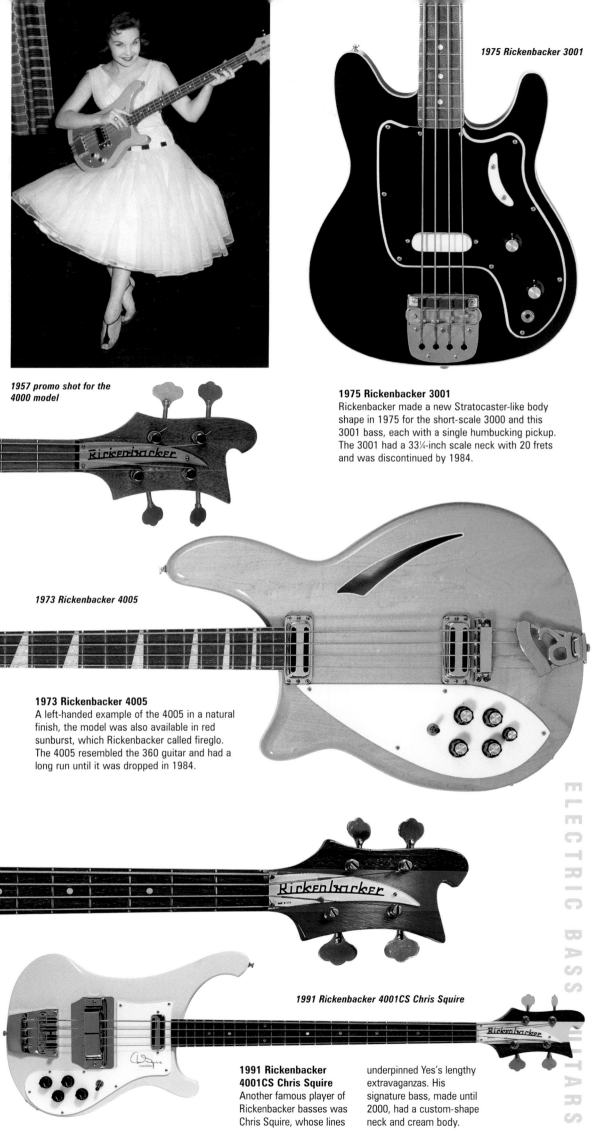

1975 Rickenbacker 3001

1957 promo shot for the 4000 model

1975 Rickenbacker 3001
Rickenbacker made a new Stratocaster-like body shape in 1975 for the short-scale 3000 and this 3001 bass, each with a single humbucking pickup. The 3001 had a 33¼-inch scale neck with 20 frets and was discontinued by 1984.

1973 Rickenbacker 4005

1973 Rickenbacker 4005
A left-handed example of the 4005 in a natural finish, the model was also available in red sunburst, which Rickenbacker called fireglo. The 4005 resembled the 360 guitar and had a long run until it was dropped in 1984.

1991 Rickenbacker 4001CS Chris Squire

1991 Rickenbacker 4001CS Chris Squire
Another famous player of Rickenbacker basses was Chris Squire, whose lines underpinned Yes's lengthy extravaganzas. His signature bass, made until 2000, had a custom-shape neck and cream body.

GIBSON
EB SERIES & OTHER BASSES

Gibson has never been as successful with its bass guitars as with other guitar types. In the 1950s and 1960s, as now, Fender was the undisputed leading maker for basses, and players have regularly marked Gibson's instruments down as "must try harder" basses. Until the mid 1970s, this was usually due to the typical combination of humbucking pickups and short scale-length that Gibson regularly adopted. Some bassists found these features respectively too thick-sounding and too fiddly.

Other musicians made strengths from these apparent weaknesses, notably in the 1960s when Cream's Jack Bruce used the Gibson EB-3's murky sound to great effect

and Andy Fraser of Free provided the solid backdrop for Paul Kossoff's fabled Les Paul stylings. In the modern era, confirmed Gibson bass lover Jared Followill of Kings Of Leon used first an EB-3, then a Thunderbird model. And the short scale-length of many early Gibson bass designs has meant that guitarists who double on bass and guitar usually find them easier to use.

The solid EB-0 and EB-3 are notable for their short scale-length of 30½ inches (about 77.5cm), and although this makes them easier to play, the tone is less defined. Long-scale L-suffix versions of EB basses, at 34½ inches (87.5cm), appeared in the 1970s.

1960 Gibson Bass EB-2

1960 Gibson EB-2
This early version of Gibson's semi-solid bass has a plastic-covered four-polepiece pickup with rear-facing, banjo-style tuning keys. The single pickup EB-2 was withdrawn in 1961, but the model reappeared later in the decade in one- or two-pickup versions.

1960 Gibson Bass EB-2 (below)
It was during 1960 that this model changed from the banjo-stye tuners seen on the example above to this more traditionally-styled headstock with four regular right-angled tuners.

1961 UK catalogue with EB-3 and EB-0

1960 Gibson EB-2

1953 Gibson Electric Bass

ELECTRIC BASS G

244

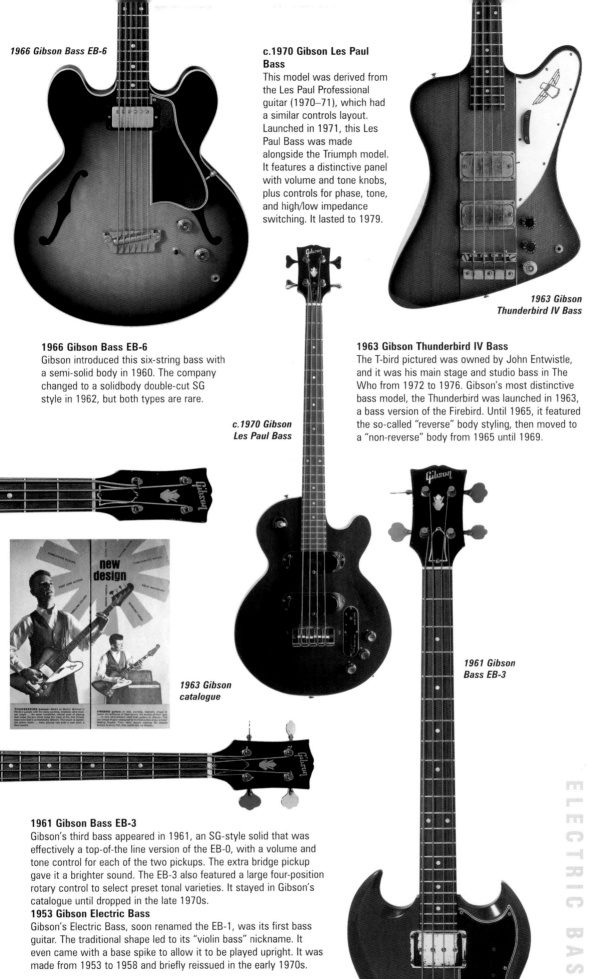

1966 Gibson Bass EB-6

c.1970 Gibson Les Paul Bass

This model was derived from the Les Paul Professional guitar (1970–71), which had a similar controls layout. Launched in 1971, this Les Paul Bass was made alongside the Triumph model. It features a distinctive panel with volume and tone knobs, plus controls for phase, tone, and high/low impedance switching. It lasted to 1979.

1963 Gibson Thunderbird IV Bass

1966 Gibson Bass EB-6

Gibson introduced this six-string bass with a semi-solid body in 1960. The company changed to a solidbody double-cut SG style in 1962, but both types are rare.

c.1970 Gibson Les Paul Bass

1963 Gibson Thunderbird IV Bass

The T-bird pictured was owned by John Entwistle, and it was his main stage and studio bass in The Who from 1972 to 1976. Gibson's most distinctive bass model, the Thunderbird was launched in 1963, a bass version of the Firebird. Until 1965, it featured the so-called "reverse" body styling, then moved to a "non-reverse" body from 1965 until 1969.

1963 Gibson catalogue

1961 Gibson Bass EB-3

1961 Gibson Bass EB-3

Gibson's third bass appeared in 1961, an SG-style solid that was effectively a top-of-the-line version of the EB-0, with a volume and tone control for each of the two pickups. The extra bridge pickup gave it a brighter sound. The EB-3 also featured a large four-position rotary control to select preset tonal varieties. It stayed in Gibson's catalogue until dropped in the late 1970s.

1953 Gibson Electric Bass

Gibson's Electric Bass, soon renamed the EB-1, was its first bass guitar. The traditional shape led to its "violin bass" nickname. It even came with a base spike to allow it to be played upright. It was made from 1953 to 1958 and briefly reissued in the early 1970s.

GIBSON
OTHER BASSES II

Gibson issued some rather more modern designs in the mid 1970s and 1980s. Later in the 1980s, it bought the innovative bass company Steinberger and the smaller Tobias operation. Gibson released in 2009 a high-end Growler five-string model with swamp ash body under the Tobias brandname.

In the 1960s, Gibson issued a short-scale six-string bass, the EB-6 (solid or hollow; see previous page), but many basses were just four-string versions of guitar models, such as the Signature semi of 1973, RD basses of 1977, or Victory Bass of 1981. Originality was reinstated in the 1970s when Gibson brought out a line of new-design basses, the Grabber, Ripper, and G3, and in the late 1980s

with the mini-body 20/20 designed by Ned Steinberger. In the present catalogue, the 1980s connection is upheld thanks to the go-faster stripes and dragster lines of the Kramer D-1 Bass (Gibson has produced guitars and basses using the Kramer brand since the late 1990s.)

The distinctive angular bodies of Gibson's late-1950s "shape" guitars translate well to the bass, and the company offers Thunderbird, Explorer, and V-style basses in both affordable Epiphone and high-end Gibson flavors.

While the majority of Gibson's basses may be derived from its celebrated guitar models, today it's a buoyant line in a market sector that the company has traditionally failed to succeed with.

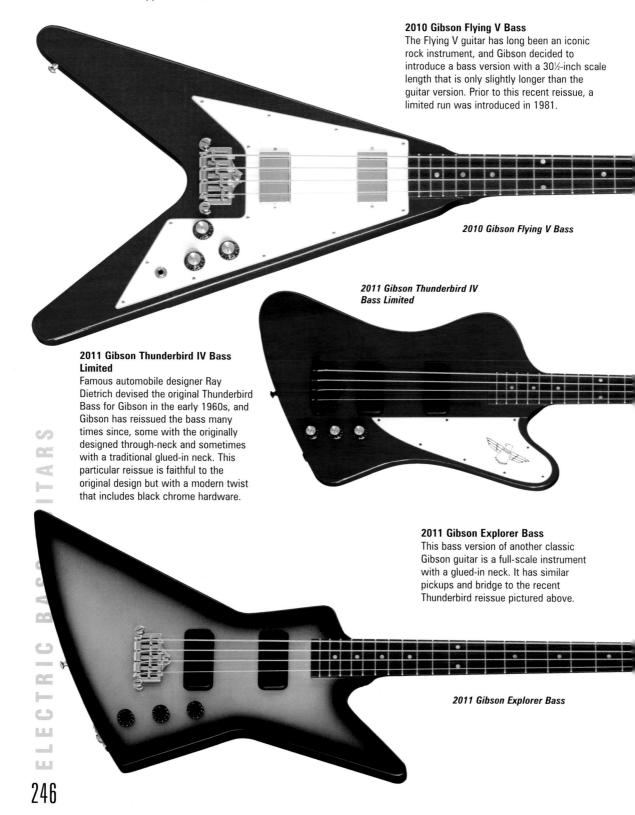

2010 Gibson Flying V Bass
The Flying V guitar has long been an iconic rock instrument, and Gibson decided to introduce a bass version with a 30½-inch scale length that is only slightly longer than the guitar version. Prior to this recent reissue, a limited run was introduced in 1981.

2010 Gibson Flying V Bass

2011 Gibson Thunderbird IV Bass Limited

2011 Gibson Thunderbird IV Bass Limited
Famous automobile designer Ray Dietrich devised the original Thunderbird Bass for Gibson in the early 1960s, and Gibson has reissued the bass many times since, some with the originally designed through-neck and sometimes with a traditional glued-in neck. This particular reissue is faithful to the original design but with a modern twist that includes black chrome hardware.

2011 Gibson Explorer Bass
This bass version of another classic Gibson guitar is a full-scale instrument with a glued-in neck. It has similar pickups and bridge to the recent Thunderbird reissue pictured above.

2011 Gibson Explorer Bass

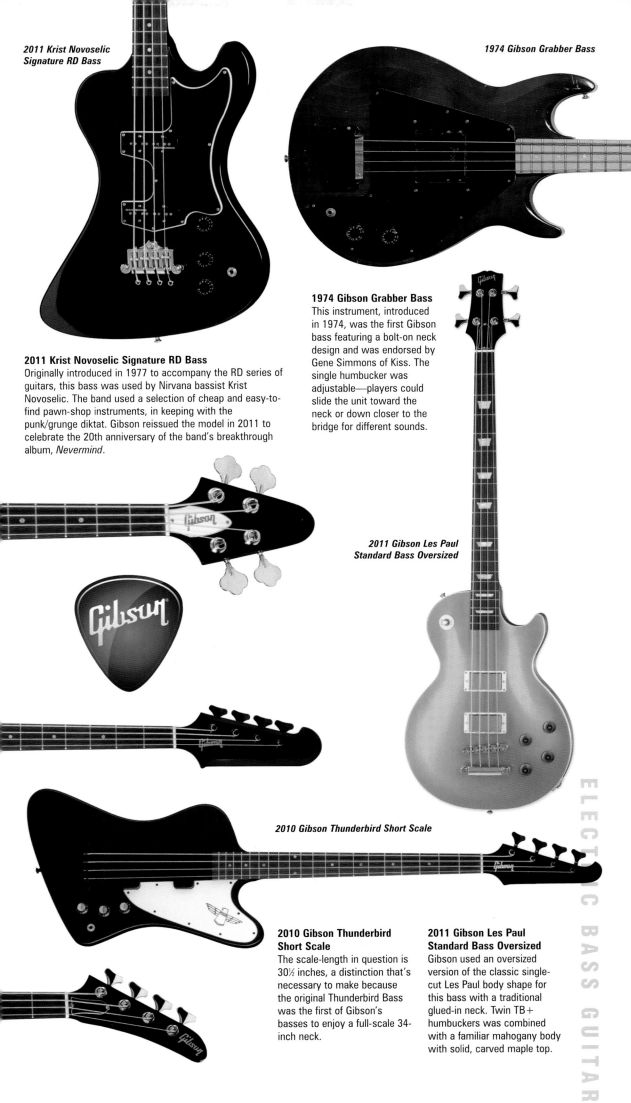

*2011 Krist Novoselic
Signature RD Bass*

1974 Gibson Grabber Bass

1974 Gibson Grabber Bass

This instrument, introduced
in 1974, was the first Gibson
bass featuring a bolt-on neck
design and was endorsed by
Gene Simmons of Kiss. The
single humbucker was
adjustable—players could
slide the unit toward the
neck or down closer to the
bridge for different sounds.

2011 Krist Novoselic Signature RD Bass

Originally introduced in 1977 to accompany the RD series of
guitars, this bass was used by Nirvana bassist Krist
Novoselic. The band used a selection of cheap and easy-to-
find pawn-shop instruments, in keeping with the
punk/grunge diktat. Gibson reissued the model in 2011 to
celebrate the 20th anniversary of the band's breakthrough
album, *Nevermind*.

*2011 Gibson Les Paul
Standard Bass Oversized*

2010 Gibson Thunderbird Short Scale

2010 Gibson Thunderbird Short Scale

The scale-length in question is
30½ inches, a distinction that's
necessary to make because
the original Thunderbird Bass
was the first of Gibson's
basses to enjoy a full-scale 34-
inch neck.

2011 Gibson Les Paul Standard Bass Oversized

Gibson used an oversized
version of the classic single-
cut Les Paul body shape for
this bass with a traditional
glued-in neck. Twin TB+
humbuckers was combined
with a familiar mahogany body
with solid, carved maple top.

EPIPHONE
BASS MODELS

One of the chief reasons Gibson bought its ailing competitor Epiphone in 1957 was because of the rival instrument manufacturer's reputation as a purveyor of quality upright basses—an area Gibson had not pursued in the period immediately following World War II.

Gibson has used the Epiphone brand wisely over the years, and has marketed a fair share of basses with the famous Epi brand on the headstock. The Rivoli, released in 1959, was the first Epiphone electric bass. A companion model to semi-hollowbody archtops such as the ES-335 and the Sheraton, it was more or less identical to Gibson's EB-2. At first it was offered in natural or sunburst, later in cherry, and a two-pickup version was issued in 1970—one of Epiphone's many Rivoli reprises which included 1999's tonally versatile Rivoli II. The Newport in 1961 and Embassy Deluxe in 1963 were a pair of 1960s solidbody bass models. Both were discontinued in 1970.

Leafing through the Epiphone bass catalogue today, you'll notice that it serves the retro crowd with the Viola and Les Paul Special, through to classic rock with the SG-shaped EB range, and on to darker rock with the Goth Thunderbird IV model.

1960 Epiphone Rivoli
This semi-solid twin-cutaway bass was the Epiphone version of the Gibson EB-2. Gibson took over much of the manufacturing and distribution of Epiphone after purchasing the company in 1957.

1960 Epiphone Rivoli

2011 Epi catalogue shot featuring Anthony Arambula with a Rivoli reissue bass

2004 Epiphone The Vinnie Les Paul Standard Bass

2010 Epiphone Zenith Bass

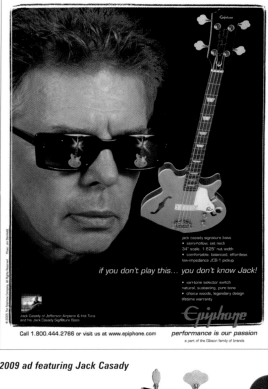

2009 ad featuring Jack Casady

2010 ad featuring Nikki Sixx

2004 Epiphone The Vinnie Les Paul Standard Bass

This signature model for bassist Vinnie Hornsby of alt-metal band Sevendust is derived from Gibson's Les Paul Oversized bass and comes with a fancy flamed-maple body and star-shaped position markers.

2010 Epiphone Nikki Sixx Blackbird Bass

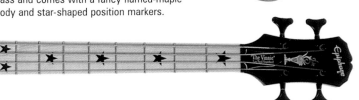

2010 Epiphone Viola Bass

2010 Epiphone Zenith Bass

Today, much of the newer Epiphone line is made in China and Korea. This bass has a semi-hollow chambered body that has a retro-looking "Gypsy"-style cutaway somewhat reminiscent of the Selmer Maccaferri jazz guitars.

2010 Nikki Sixx Blackbird Bass

Mötley Crüe's bassist Nikki Sixx's signature bass is heavily modeled on Gibson's reissued Thunderbird, finished in pitch black with black chrome die-cast hardware and embellished with Iron Cross-style fingerboard inlays and pickguard logo. It also features Epiphone DeepSixx pickups.

2010 Epiphone Viola Bass

A retro-flavored budget version of the famous Hofner "Violin" Bass, complete with a short scale length. The hollow body is made of laminate maple, with a maple top, and it has a maple neck with rosewood fingerboard.

AMERICA
OTHER BASS MAKERS

It is hardly surprising that the bass guitar should flourish so readily in the country where it was invented. Although Leo Fender got so much right with his original Precision Bass in the early 1950s, many later improvements have come from the United States.

Danelectro deserves credit for a noable innovation in the shape of the short-scale (29-inches) six-string bass it added to its U series in 1956. The UB-1 (single-pickup) or UB-2 (double-pickup) models were effectively a guitar tuned an octave lower than usual. This "baritone" sound proved popular with session players wanting to bridge the tone divide between bass frequency and the guitar's tonal register, and the design was a favorite of Duane Eddy.

The big US guitar companies usually offered a line of bass "versions" of six-string guitars. Honorable exceptions include G&L, where Leo Fender, inventor of Fender's seminal bass designs, continued to come up with fresh-looking basses, and the Mississippi-based Peavey company (see page 255), which has been active in attracting bassists to endorse a varied line of new models.

The Ampeg company is best known for its amplifiers, and in particular its tube bass amps. Not so well known are its bass guitars. These began in the early 1960s with an upright electric bass. In the middle of the decade, the New Jersey-based company produced some strange-looking basses, including in 1965 one of the earliest fretless basses, the AUB-1. From 1969 to 1971, Ampeg teamed up with guitar designer and repairer Dan Armstrong to make a range of distinctive so-called "see-through" clear plastic guitars and basses, also known as Lucite models.

1965 Mosrite Ventures Bass
Semie Moseley designed this instrument for Ventures bassist Bob Bogle. He and guitarist Nokie Edwards have signed this example. Their version of 'Surf Rider' was included in Quentin Tarantino's movie *Pulp Fiction*, and it helped to revive their career.

1965 Mosrite Ventures Bass

1963 Harmony H-22
During the 1960s, Harmony of Chicago was the biggest US producer of guitars. Significantly, it did not get around to issuing a bass guitar until 1962, and the result was this bass, typical of the company's varied output. Steve Winwood's bassist brother, Muff, used one in The Spencer Davis Group during the 1960s.

1963 Harmony H-22

c.1958 Danelectro 3412 Short Horn Bass

1963 Gretsch 6070 Bass

1967 Guild Starfire Bass I

1963 Gretsch 6070 Bass
This double-cutaway 34-inch-scale hollowbody bass has painted-on f-holes, in true Gretsch tradition. It was partnered in the catalogue by a 6072 model, which had two pickups.

1967 Guild Starfire Bass I
A popular bass with players in the 1960s, it was used by Jack Casady of Jefferson Airplane and Phil Lesh of The Grateful Dead among others. The model had a hollow body and was equipped with Hagstrom's Bisonic pickup.

1970 Dan Armstrong/Ampeg See-Through Bass

1970 Dan Armstrong/Ampeg See-Through Bass
Dan Armstrong, the designer of this bass and its accompanying six-string electric guitar, used Lucite, or clear plastic, for the bodies of his peculiar instruments in an attempt to improve sustain. Armstrong resurfaced in 1990 with a design for the Westone company and created various amps, effects, and pickup designs. He died in 2004.

1966 Ampeg AEB-1 Bass

1967 Ampeg ad with Joe Long

1958 Danelectro 4623 Long Horn Six-String Bass

c.1958 Danelectro 3412 Short Horn Bass
The first bass that Danelectro produced was manufactured from the same budget materials as the guitar range. The Short Horn bass has 15 frets as opposed to the Long Horn's complement of 24.

1966 Ampeg AEB-1 Bass
Ampeg's unusual bass guitars with large scrolled headstocks first appeared in 1965. Early models had bridge-mounted transducers, but later models (1968–69) had conventional pickups. The AEB-1 shown may have had some modifications.

1958 Danelectro 4623 Long Horn Six-String Bass
Among the innovations Danelectro brought to basses was the six-string bass, in effect a guitar tuned an octave lower than usual. Duane Eddy was its best-known player, and this example belongs to him.

AMERICA
MORE BASS MAKERS II

It was the Alembic company, in the mid 1970s, that finally established the idea of a guitar maker specializing in bass guitars. This was coupled with a realization by players that new sounds and new musical directions could free the bass guitar from its role as a mere backing instrument, and at last it gave the instrument a new and a much more distinctive voice.

The company made several custom instruments for celebrity bass players in the 1970s: it built an eight-string bass for Greg Lake of ELP, and The Who's John Entwistle ordered a classic Explorer-shaped Spider bass complete with spider-web decoration to the body. Some rather more basic developments came from Leo Fender himself. His

Music Man StingRay Bass, which remains a firm favorite among bassmen, did much to persuade the low-note community that active electronics were effective and useful—and building on an Alembic idea.

The essential point of active electronics was to have a small battery-powered pre-amplifier, built into the instrument, which boosts the output and allows a much wider degree of tonal variation. Alembic's earlier offerings of such circuits had been in limited production runs of very expensive instruments.

1971 Alembic Bass

1971 Alembic Bass No.001
Alembic made this first bass for Jefferson Airplane bassist Jack Casady, and it marked the start of a line of instruments that influenced many other bass makers, with exotic woods, active electronics, laminated through-necks, and quality construction.

c.1985 B.C. Rich Bich
Known primarily for making pointy-shape guitars, B.C. Rich built this bass with a through-neck. The model was used by Bernard Edwards of Chic, and a custom-made double-neck with a Bich-like outline was made famous by Derek Smalls of Spinal Tap. This example is owned by former Van Halen bassist Michael Anthony.

1977 Kramer Artist 650B

c.1985 B.C. Rich Bich

1978 Carl Thompson Custom

Dean ads from 2005

1978 Carl Thompson Custom

This impressive left-handed instrument was custom-built for Colin Hodgkinson, a virtuoso bassist best known for his work with 1970s British bass/sax/drums trio Back Door. Carl Thompson is a New York-based builder whose influence on bass history is underrated: he was involved with bassist Anthony Jackson in the development of the modern six-string bass.

1977 Music Man StingRay Bass

1977 Music Man StingRay Bass

Music Man's StingRay Bass did much to popularize active electronics, and furthered Leo Fender's already glowing reputation among bassists. Music Man was acquired by the Ernie Ball company in 1984; the still-popular StingRay Bass continues to head up a thriving bass line.

1977 Kramer Artist 650B

Gary Kramer, previously a partner of Travis Bean, set up his own firm to exploit aluminum necks, producing a wide variety of models from 1976 using necks that combined wood and aluminum. But metal still felt cold and uninviting to some players, and by 1985 the company had rejected the use of aluminum, opting instead for traditional methods.

1985 Spector NS-2

1985 Spector NS-2

A two-pickup version of the first Ned Steinberger-designed bass from 1979, with its distinctive and often-imitated body design. The single-pickup model was the NS-1. The NS models have active pickups and a proprietary tone circuit and are available in a range of modern permutations.

ELECTRIC BASSES

AMERICA
MULTI-STRING BASSES

It was Alembic who made instrument makers aware that bassists were different from guitarists and could be served by companies specializing in bass guitars. Some of these specialists have been absorbed into bigger companies, such as the California-based maker Tobias, begun in 1978 by Mike Tobias. Spector, started in the 1970s by Stuart Spector, was at one stage marketed by Kramer. Tobias and Kramer have been owned by Gibson since the 1990s.

Geoff Gould set up Modulus and built graphite necks for Alembic and other makers, also releasing its own graphite-necked instruments. Ned Steinberger, too, had been seduced by graphite, and realised it eliminated the tonal "dead spots" caused by sympathetic vibrations in some wood necks. At a trade show in 1979, Steinberger debuted its first all-graphite bass, which also featured a headless neck, tuners mounted at the bridge end of the diminutive body, and active pickups provided by EMG.

The headless design appealed to bassists and guitarists alike in the early 1980s. Steinberger was eventually sold to the Gibson Guitar Corp in 1986.

2011 Zon ad

1994 Pedulla Pentabuzz

c.1992 Hamer 12-String Bass

c.1992 Hamer 12-String Bass
The 12 strings are arranged as four groups of three. Each trio consists of the normally tuned E, A, D, or G strings, plus two thinner strings tuned an octave above the norm. The two octave strings are situated "above" the normal strings as the player looks down, so it is quite clearly a bass to play with plectrum downstrokes.

1984 Modulus Graphite Quantum-6

ELECTRIC BASS GUITARS

254

2005 Modulus ad featuring Stefan Lessard

2006 Peavey Cirrus 5

1994 Pedulla Pentabuzz
The current Pedulla company based in Massachusetts was formed in the late 1970s by Michael Vincent Pedulla and his brother, Ted. The company now specializes in basses. The long, sculpted horns and Bartolini pickups are typical, and this Custom has a beautiful flamed-maple body.

2006 Peavey Cirrus 5
This high-end, relatively lightweight five-string bass has a 35-inch scale length and is fitted with active pickups and a three-band EQ system.

*2005 ad for Steinberger five-string
headless bass*

1993 Ken Smith BT Custom V

1993 Ken Smith BT Custom V
Ex-professional bassist turned luthier Ken Smith was among the first group of makers to bring to bassists the multi-string bass with wide string-spacing and the low B-string.

1984 Modulus Graphite Quantum-6
Modulus (originally named Modulus Graphite) was set up to develop the new idea of carbon-graphite necks, which the company produced for Alembic, Music Man, and Zon. The bass shown here has an extra-long 35-inch scale to help the fidelity of the low B-string, and it has tighter string-spacing than most modern sixes.

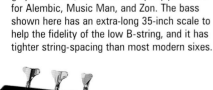

ELECTRIC BASS GUITARS

AMERICA
MULTI-STRINGS & MORE

The roots of multi-string basses lie with Danelectro in the 1950s, when it introduced the world's first six-string bass. But later, players were chasing something that grew from the bass guitar itself, rather than that early idea, which was more of a down-tuned regular guitar.

Players such as Anthony Jackson and Jimmy Johnson led makers to the modern idea of the five- and six-string bass, with a crucial low B-string below the regular E, and, in the case of the six, an extra high-tuned string, too.

By the turn of the millennium, an update of the synth-bass idea came with digital modeling, pioneered by Line 6. However, the Variax modeling basses (the 700 from 2004

and the five-string 705 from 2005), despite having onboard samples of all the classic bass sounds you were ever likely to need, were dropped after a few years. Perhaps this is another indication of many bassists' preference for simple, direct instruments.

G&L was formed at the beginning of the 1980s, and the name stood originally for the forenames of the company's two founders, ex-Fender man George Fullerton, and Leo Fender, with George selling out to Leo in 1986. The G&L basses never achieved the popularity of the Music Man instruments, but not surprisingly they continue to build on typical Fender features and principles.

1999 Lakland 55-94 USA Classic

1999 Lakland 55-94 USA Classic

The Lakland company was founded in Chicago in 1995 and began by making Fender-influenced instruments. The five-string shown here is a fretless version. Lakland has also made signature models for revered sessionmen such as Joe Osborn and Donald "Duck" Dunn.

2000 PRS ad with Jeff Abercrombie

2005 Line 6 Variax 705

1987 G&L L-2000

L-2500

2005 G&L ad with Mike MacIvor

L-2000

MATT WACHTER

2004 G&L ad with Matt Wachter

1989 Fodera Jackson Contrabass

1989 Fodera Jackson Contrabass

The origins of the modern low-B six-string bass are complex, to say the least. Top session bassist Anthony Jackson helped Vinnie Fodera develop the concept with this instrument.

2005 Line 6 Variax 705

An update of the synthesizer-bass idea came with digital modelling, pioneered by Line 6. Despite the benefits of modeling, this five-string Variax modeling bass, with onboard samples of classic basses of yesteryear, was discontinued in 2007.

2000 PRS Electric Bass Maple Top

2000 PRS Electric Bass Maple Top

This well-established guitar maker has also delved into the bass realm. This early example has passive electrics, but later models were active, incorporating an onboard preamp to boost the tone at the lower end of the sound spectrum.

1987 G&L L-2000

This G&L design, reminiscent of the P Bass, has an ash body and bolt-on maple neck, which is glued back together after having been sawn in half, in a bid to prevent warping. The pickups are Leo Fender's own G&L Magnetic Field Design models, with eight adjustable polepieces.

EUROPE
BRITISH BASS MAKERS

Some European companies and workshops have followed the lead of the US Alembic set-up in establishing the idea that makers can specialize in building bass guitars. These makers nearly always treat the bass guitar as an individual instrument, not merely a four-string version of the six-string electric guitar.

For instance, bass-maker Wal, working in southern England, designed its Custom bass with little reference to the six-string guitar. Co-designers Ian Waller and Pete Stevens decided to develop a bass as a bass and, as they once described it, not to do as most manufactures do: make a six-stringed instrument, and then put a long neck on it and call it a bass. This attitude reflects that of the inventor of the bass guitar, Leo Fender, who chose to design the bass guitar as a new instrument in its own right. Of course, the electric bass leans on general six-string guitar design, but in detail the two are quite separate. The finest bass-makers worldwide know this well.

Britain's bass-makers have been successful. In the 1970s, Haymen made popular semi-pro basses, its 4040 model evolving into the Shergold Marathon bass, and John Diggins' high-quality Jaydee basses were chosen by the likes of Mark King of Level 42. In the 1980s, good small makers like Overwater, Nightingale, and Goodfellow appeared, while in 1990, Status, known for its headless basses, issued its first bass with a headstock, the Matrix model.

1989 Status Series II
Rob Green helped popularize the headless concept by combining it with the carbon graphite through-neck style with added body wings. This provided a more familiar style that a number of bassists, especially those in Europe, found more appealing than Steinberger's mini-bodied headless bass.

1989 Status Series II

1967 Vox Stinger IV

2004 Rotosound ad with Andy Bell and a Burns Bison

'I beef up my bison with rotosound'

1967 Vox Stinger IV
This Italian-made Vox succeeded the original British-built Wyman Bass. There was also an active version, called the Constellation IV. Note the very narrow neck and the huge headstock.

1989 Wal MB4 MIDI Bass

Australian bass player and electrical engineer Steve Chick put together a bass synthesizer as a hobby, and his design ideas were put into practise in a shot-lived collaboration between makers Wal in the UK and Valley Arts in the USA.

1989 Wal MB4 MIDI Bass

2003 Status Buzzard Bass

2003 Status Buzzard Bass

The Who's bassist John Entwistle commissioned Status to design and build a bass from graphite. It features active tone controls and has fancy colored LEDs in the fingerboard. The classic basket-weave texture associated with graphite can be seen on the body.

1990 Wal Custom Mk I Bass

1963 Burns Bison Bass

1990 Wal Custom Mk 1 Bass

London repairer Ian Waller teamed up with Pete Stevens in the mid 1970s to design the Wal bass, at first with a leather pickguard. The company became Electric Wood in 1978, with the Custom model appearing a few years years later. The example shown is a "lined fretless" version.

1963 Burns Bison Bass

The huge Bison (1962–64) was the finest bass from UK company Burns. It had a sycamore body, low-impedance circuitry and, unusually for a bass, three pickups. Black was the standard finish.

1988 Overwater C Bass

While other makers offer five-string basses to provide additional low notes, UK maker Chris May and bassist Andrew Bodnar designed this model with a long 36-inch scale, allowing the possibility to tune two tones below standard (C-F-Bb-Eb).

1989 Jaydee Mark King

Built by UK maker John Diggins, this model was named for Level 42 bassist Mark King, who was an early Jaydee user. Note the wooden pickup covers as well as the additional three-pin jack, for studio use.

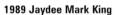

1989 Jaydee Mark King

1988 Overwater C Bass

EUROPE
MORE BASS MAKERS

Sir Paul McCartney's long-standing association with Hofner's hollowbody bass has ensured that it has remained in production since its birth in 1956. The Beatles' bassist bought his first Hofner "Violin Bass" in Hamburg, probably at the end of 1960. It had a long Hofner logo going down the headstock, and the two pickups were close together. It was used on many of the Beatles' live performances.

The second Hofner bass, which Paul has used throughout his career, was presented to him by Hofner at the Beatles' Royal Variety Show performance in London in November 1963. This Hofner was also used extensively in

the studio, where it later competed with Paul's Rickenbacker 4001 bass. However, McCartney can be seen using it during the Beatles' 1969 rooftop concert in the film *Let It Be,* and Paul has regularly put it into service again on his subsequent tours.

Rolling Stone bassist Bill Wyman was another busy endorser of basses in the 1960s. He lent his name to the German Framus company's Star Bass, and he also endorsed the Vox Wyman Bass from the UK.

Framus was founded by Fred Wilfer in 1946, and in 1982 Fred's son Hans-Peter Wilfer started the Warwick

1967 Hagstrom H-8
Among the first production eight-string basses, the H-8 was built by the Swedish company Hagstrom. The strings are arranged in four pairs, the second of each pitched an octave above the regular string. Use of the big sound that results is limited to specialist situations; Jimi Hendrix featured one on *Spanish Castle Magic*.

1967 Hagstrom H-8

c.1960 Goya Deluxe

c.1960 Goya Deluxe
This bass was made by the Swedish company Hagstrom and was branded for sale in the US as a Goya. The instruments developed a reputation for being almost indestructible, although the wonderful glitter-plastic finishes did have a tendency to crack.

2008 Warwick Corvette Double Buck Five-String

2008 Warwick Corvette Double Buck Five-String
Warwick's growing reputation for quality construction, distinctive design, and the use of exotic woods is exemplified in the Corvette line of basses. Passive MEC humbuckers and a preamp combined with several coil-tapping options expands its tonal range.

company in Erlangen, near Nuremburg, Germany. Helped by distinctive instruments and strong endorsers such as Jack Bruce and John Entwistle, it's now recognized as one of the premier international bass brands. Early models from Warwick included the Streamer (1983), the Thumb (1984), the Buzzard (1986), and Dolphin (1989). The more radical 1995 Corvette model consolidated the company's success.

Outside of the UK and Germany, other European manufacturers have made their mark. Swedish maker Hagstrom came up with one of the first eight-string bass guitar designs in 1967. The H-8 used the principles behind the 12-string guitar to pair courses of strings where one string is an octave higher than the other. You can hear the resulting resonance on 1967's *Spanish Castle Magic* by The Jimi Hendrix Experience.

France's Vigier, a leading exponent of carbon-fiber technology, has a full line of forward-looking bass designs, including fretless options and a signature Roger Glover Custom version of the Excess model.

1956 Hofner 500/1

1956 Hofner 500/1

This German-made bass appeared in 1956 and is still made today, although its popularity peaked in the 1960s with the Beatles link. Hofner has taken the opportunity to produce high-end reissues of authentic vintage-spec versions, such as 2007's 500/1-62, with equally high-end price tags.

1984 Vigier Nautilus Arpege

Frenchman Patrice Vigier has produced a number of unusual basses, and offers more construction options than many makers. This instrument is equipped with an electronic system that stores and recalls settings.

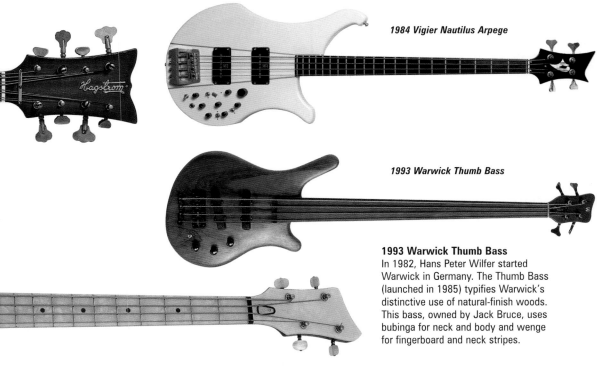

1984 Vigier Nautilus Arpege

1993 Warwick Thumb Bass

1993 Warwick Thumb Bass

In 1982, Hans Peter Wilfer started Warwick in Germany. The Thumb Bass (launched in 1985) typifies Warwick's distinctive use of natural-finish woods. This bass, owned by Jack Bruce, uses bubinga for neck and body and wenge for fingerboard and neck stripes.

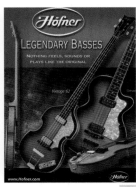

1957 Hofner Model 333 Bass

This large-bodied bass is the same model purchased by the original Beatles bassist, Stuart Sutcliffe, in Germany in 1960. Lennon and Harrison also used Hofner guitars during the band's early career.

1957 Hofner Model 333 Bass

THE FAR EAST
BASS MAKERS

It was around the turn of the 1960s and the early 1970s that various Japanese manufacturers established themselves as producers of copies of American guitars, basses included. The earliest examples were poor, and the expression "Japanese copy" quickly became derogatory. Most of these early Japanese copyists chose the obviously successful American models. Fender's Precision and Jazz models were by far the most common target.

Gradually, the Japanese began to get better and better at copying, and slowly their reputation improved. By the middle of the 1970s, some Japanese makers had begun to produce their own designs, rather than strict copies, although the influence was still coming from American basses. A good example is the way in which Japanese makers such as Aria popularized the through-neck design feature in the late 1970s, which had been introduced by specialist US bass makers like Alembic.

The 1980s saw many Japanese and American companies shifting their production bases into other Eastern countries, in common with the manufacturing of regular six-string guitars, as ever guided principally by the lure of cheaper labor costs.

2007 ad for the Ibanez Giger Series Bass

1980 Aria Pro II SB-1000

1980 Aria Pro II SB-1000
The SB-1000 has been a long-standing and successful bass for Aria and is the company's most popular model. The lighter wood of the through-neck visible on the body is testament to its late-1970s design. A new five-string model has recently been made available.

1980 Ibanez Musician Limited Edition

1980 Ibanez Musician Limited Edition
This special-edition version in Ibanez's Musician line was a short-lived addition to the bass range in the early 1980s. It came with the regular three-band EQ, a fashionable hi-fi appointment of the time.

1979 Ibanez Musician MC924
This fretless bass belonged to Sting, who used it for a good deal of his Police work. Ibanez, along with Aria, redefined the image of Japanese basses in this era as well-made and fine sounding instruments, bringing many features of more expensive custom-makers such as Alembic to a more affordable line of basses.

1979 Ibanez Musician MC924

2005 Fernandes ad featuring Robert Trujillo

2008 Ibanez ad featuring Paul Gray

**2008 Ibanez
SR300**

1985 Roland G77

1985 Roland G77
Synthesizer giant Roland's second short-lived bass synth was launched in 1985, looking like the 707 guitar version. A separate synth control unit completed the set-up. Roland has persevered with synths for guitar players, however, and recent developments in the area offer good usability.

2008 Ibanez BTB475
The deep cutaways allow easy access to the big five-piece maple and bubinga through-neck. This affordable boutique-style model comes with specially designed Bartolini pickups.

2008 Ibanez SR300
The heavily sculptured body, bright metallic finish, and ebony fingerboard are signs of quality on this bass from Ibanez's recent lines.

2008 Ibanez BTB475

1985 Westone Rail
This odd Japanese headless bass had a sliding pickup. The central block housing the pickup could be moved on the chrome "rails" after the securing screw on the side was loosened. Despite its modern appearance, the Rail Bass was made of wood, with the neck bolted to the body.

1985 Westone Rail

ELECTRIC BASS GUITARS

THE FAR EAST
BASS MAKERS II

Guitars made in the East sometimes ended up with a variety of names on the headstocks of otherwise identical instruments. This is because some manufacturers there often produced guitars and basses for a number of different customers throughout the world.

Korea used to be the main base for Oriental instrument manufacture—and brands used on the basses pouring from its factories at various times including Washburn (since the late 1980s), Squier (since 1987), Epiphone (since 1986), Hohner, Charvette, Cort, Starforce, Marlin, Hondo, Columbus, Tanglewood, Fenix, and more.

Today, the rise of China's various OEM facilities (it means Original Equipment Manufacturing) has made it the most prolific maker of guitars and basses in this part of the world. Budget and mid-priced basses principally from China and the other traditionally strong Eastern manufacturing centers now dominate the lower tiers of the market, and, in the case of Japanese giants such as Ibanez and Yamaha, offer a long-established presence toward the high-end as well.

c.1991 Tune Bass Maniac Standard

ESP ad from 2007 featuring Slayer, Children Of Bodom, Dragon Force and Cradle Of Filth

c.1991 Tune Bass Maniac Standard
Tune's founder Fugitani Hatzukazu set up his own operation in order to produce original designs. The 25-fret Bass Maniac, introduced in 1983, was notable for the access it gave players to the upper frets, made possible by an extended neck with a heel-less joint. The overall style and ergonomics of the Tune instruments were widely copied in the 1980s.

1990 Yamaha TRB5P
Compare this to other five-string basses and the changes made to the design of such basses becomes apparent. The neck is less narrow, meaning wider string spacing. Note also the chamfered horns, fashionable at this time.

1989 Tune TWB-6
This Japanese model represents the modern-era six-string bass. It is tuned like a bass guitar with an extra low and an extra high string, and the strings are as widely spaced as on a four-string bass.

1987 Yamaha BB5000

2011 Yamaha ad with Chris Glithero

2004 Cort ad with T.M. Stevens

1990 Yamaha TRB5P

1990 Yamaha TRB6P

1987 Yamaha BB5000

This bass is from the Taiwan-made BB series of the mid and late 1980s. The 5000 did much to popularize the use of five-string basses, and like the Music Man it places the fifth machine head on the opposite side of the headstock to the normal four.

1990 Yamaha TRB6P

The six-string version of this instrument has a wide neck, and all TRB models have individual "bimorphous" piezo elements for each string, built into a bridge machined from solid brass.

1989 Tune TWB-6

ELECTRIC BASS

265

CHAPTER SIX
BEYOND GUITARS

A few brave makers added built-in special effects like tone-boosts and distortion to guitars in the 1960s, producing some gimmicky sounds. The instruments were sometimes expensive, often rather heavy, and pretty unsuccessful. But they can be considered as the forerunners of the guitar synthesizer.

Roland, a leading Japanese synthesizer-maker, led the charge in the late 1970s and early 1980s but never achieved great success, as the early guitar synths were expensive and complex. The introduction of MIDI (Musical Instrument Digital Interface) subsequently brought the musical potential of synthesized sound to more players at affordable prices. But it seems that, as a general rule, guitarists are more comfortable with simple instruments and have remained reluctant to adopt every technological advance thrown at them.

A guitar that has the ability to produce a variety of classic sounds at the flick of a switch was the next major advancement. In 2003, Line 6 launched the Variax guitar, and this successful "modeling" guitar has been improved over the years. At the time of writing, it includes instantaneous tonal imitations of dozens of classic guitar models and access to different tunings during live performance.

Fender introduced its version of the "modeling" guitar, the VG Stratocaster, in 2007, collaborating with Roland to link guitar and synthesizer, resulting in an instrument where everything happened inside the guitar. Gibson added an automatic tuning system to this new breed of instrument, dubbed the Robot guitar. The company has produced Robot-enabled versions of many of its classic models, and more recently added the hi-tech Firebird X model to its line. It remains to be seen if the modern player is any more interested in bells and whistles than his predecessors.

SPECIAL EFFECTS
BUILT-IN SOUNDS

It was in the 1960s that special effects and gimmicky sounds for the electric guitar became popular. They were offered as separate foot-operated pedals that could provide tone-boost, volume control, distortion, and wah-wah.

Some makers chose to build effects into the guitar itself, and the more comprehensively equipped versions of these instruments can be considered the forerunners of the guitar synthesizer. Unfortunately, the amount of wood removed from the bodies of these guitars to make way for the extra electronics adversely affected their natural sustain and tone. Also, while the additional circuitry certainly made the fashionably funny noises, it was invariably at the expense of decent, normal guitar sounds. The instruments shown here must have seemed like good ideas at the time, but they were all short-lived and provided strong arguments that electronic effects were best kept separate from the guitar.

During the psychedelic era of the late 1960s, Indian music had a heavy influence on rock musicians. Guitarists liked the sound of the sitar but most found it impossible to play. One enterprising American company, Danelectro, came up with instruments that played like guitars, but gave a sitar sound. This effect came from a special bridge, designed by leading US session guitarist Vinnie Bell.

c.1982 Kay LP Synth

c.1982 Kay LP Synth
Made in Korea in the early 1980s, this cheap guitar was loosely based on the Gibson Les Paul Recording model. However, unlike the Gibson, it had four built-in battery-powered effects: tremolo, distortion, repeat, and "whirlwind."

1966 Vox Guitar Organ

1976 Godwin Guitar Organ

1976 Godwin Guitar Organ
For years, makers had been trying to produce a guitar that sounded like an organ. This Italian attempt from 1976 used the Vox method, in which the frets are wired to a set of organ tone-generators. A string touching a fret completes a circuit and produces the relevant organ note. The Godwin had a huge array of knobs and switches giving organ pipe sounds and electronic effects.

BEYOND

1967 Coral Sitar

1968 Danelectro ad

1969 Danelectro Electric Sitar

1967 Coral Sitar
The electric sitar brought the sound of the original, rather complicated acoustic instrument to many guitar players. The key to imitating the sound was the flat plastic bridge that gave it a "buzzy" edge. However, the instrument proved extremely difficult to keep in tune, thus restricting its use.

1966 Vox Guitar Organ
The UK company Vox pioneered the guitar organ, producing the first commercial instrument in 1966. In effect it combined a Vox Continental organ with a normal Vox Phantom solidbody guitar. Like the later Godwin, it was short-lived.

1969 Danelectro Electric Sitar
This version of the electric sitar has a solid poplar body, compared to the Coral's semi-solid construction. Danelectro made both versions.

c.1973 Guyatone Rhythm Guitar

c.1968 Hofner 459/VTZ

c.1973 Guyatone Rhythm Guitar
This Fender-influenced Japanese guitar came complete with an onboard drum machine offering five preset rhythms via a rotary selector and "start" switch. The black knobs controlled drum volume and tempo.

c.1968 Hofner 459/VTZ
The German company's better-known 500/1 "Violin Bass" inspired a guitar equivalent in the 1960s. The active version pictured here incorporates a series of controls for treble and distortion boosts, plus an overall selector switch.

269

GUITAR SYNTHESIZER
EARLY ATTEMPTS

As keyboard synthesizers evolved in the 1970s, certain manufacturers of these instruments saw the possibility of applying the technology to the guitar. Put simply, this was a development of the guitar organ idea: to produce keyboard sounds from a guitar. But early guitar organs were unreliable. They were also very heavy, because makers put all the bulky circuitry into the guitar. Synthesizer electronics, however, were becoming increasingly small and generally reliable.

Roland, a leading Japanese synthesizer-maker, was established in 1974. The company soon began experiments with guitar synthesizers and developed the concept of a two-piece outfit consisting of a guitar (called a "controller") and a separate synthesizer box. A series of such models appeared between 1977 and 1985: all the guitars were made for Roland by Fujigen Gakki, best known for its Ibanez and Greco instruments. Roland must have believed very strongly in the idea. For eight years the company developed the concept and tried to create a market, while no other makers seemed confident enough to provide any real competition.

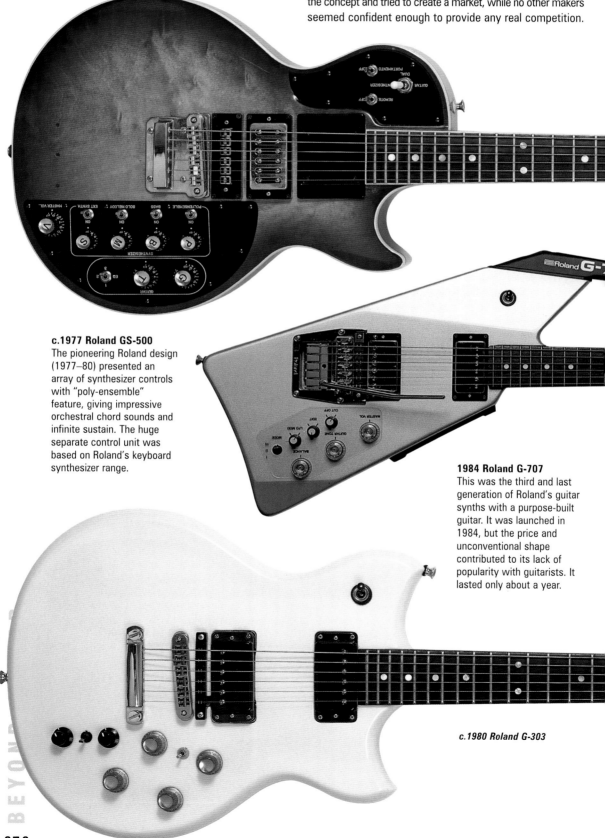

c.1977 Roland GS-500
The pioneering Roland design (1977–80) presented an array of synthesizer controls with "poly-ensemble" feature, giving impressive orchestral chord sounds and infinite sustain. The huge separate control unit was based on Roland's keyboard synthesizer range.

1984 Roland G-707
This was the third and last generation of Roland's guitar synths with a purpose-built guitar. It was launched in 1984, but the price and unconventional shape contributed to its lack of popularity with guitarists. It lasted only about a year.

c.1980 Roland G-303

Roland's guitar synths never achieved the success that the company clearly believed they deserved. Potential sales were hindered by various factors, not least of which was that, with Roland's system, guitarists had no choice but to use the supplied guitar. They also had to modify their playing style to accommodate the idiosyncrasies of the instrument. The outfits were expensive, too. Some players thought that having to buy an extra guitar just to obtain the new synth sounds was an expensive luxury.

Roland's insistence on synthesizer terminology seemed to imply that guitarists could become synth experts overnight. In reality, most guitarists like things simple and direct, and were often baffled by these seemingly complex instruments. The Roland guitars were of high quality, but this wasn't enough to tempt many players away from their beloved Fenders and Gibsons. The peculiar styling didn't help popularity, giving the impression that Roland wanted to create a market rather than sell to the existing one.

1987 Casio DG-20 Digital Guitar
Casio's DG-20 and the DG-10 were 1987 budget attempts at guitar synthesis. The 20 had plastic "strings" triggering onboard synth sounds, an internal speaker, built-in rhythm unit, drum pads, and MIDI output.

1987 Casio DG-20 Digital Guitar

c.1977 Roland GS-500

1984 Roland G-707

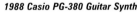
1988 Casio PG-380 Guitar Synth

1988 Casio PG-380 Guitar Synth
Tokyo-based Casio entered the keyboard market in 1980. It launched this self-contained guitar synth in 1988, the first to combine a quality electric guitar with an on-board synthesizer. It could also control external synthesizers from its MIDI jack.

c.1980 Roland G-303
The second Roland guitar synth system (1980–85) came with a range of different guitars. The 202 and 505 were Fender-styled; the 303 and 808 were more Gibson-influenced. Controls were the same as on the later 707, but this 303 also has a coil-tap switch.

GUITAR SYNTHESIZER
EARLY ATTEMPTS II

In the mid 1980s, several British and Japanese companies decided there was enough interest in the guitar synthesizer to warrant their involvement. Roland, virtual creators of the genre, decided to abandon guitar systems, opting instead for a rack-unit driven by a hex pickup suitable for any electric guitar. Ironically, most of the competition chose Roland's original idea and offered purpose-built guitars, and some refined this still further by offering completely self-contained guitar synths with all sound-generation circuitry built into the guitar.

The introduction of MIDI—the Musical Instrument Digital Interface—in 1983 broadened the potential sounds available to the synth guitarist. MIDI is a communication system agreed by all the major makers that enables synthesizers to be linked and to control one another. MIDI-equipped guitar "controllers" could therefore use the sounds from suitable synthesizers when connected to them. In theory, any brand of MIDI guitar could be used with any brand of MIDI synthesizer.

Despite the great advances made in sound synthesis at the time, guitarists were slow to embrace the new technology. This was due in part to hi-tech manufacturers failing to grasp what guitar players really wanted. Applying keyboard technology directly to the guitar has failed to work completely successfully, and only a minority of guitarists were willing to accept the inherent compromises of this method. Most guitarists want and are content to use simple instruments, while makers have occasional outbursts of over-complication.

These ultimately doomed attempts to combine the guitar and the synthesizer may seem quaint and archaic to the modern guitarist, but experiments such as these paved the way for many of the tremendous advances in digital modeling technology that players take for granted today.

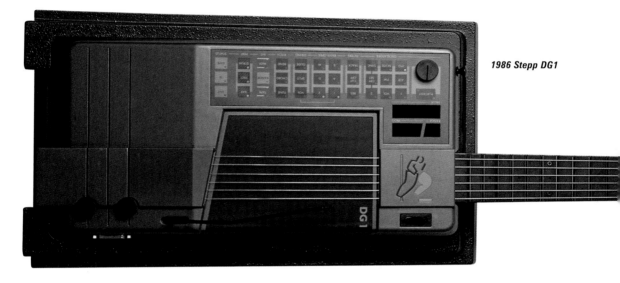

1986 Stepp DG1

1986 Stepp DG1
This British invention was the first self-controlled guitar synth (1986–88). Its own sounds were synthesized, but it also had limited control over external MIDI synths. The later DGX did not have the built-in synth, but did possess wider MIDI control.

1984 Synthaxe

1986 ad for Ibanez synth guitar and rackmount box

*1985 Ibanez
IMG2010*

1985 Ibanez IMG2010
The revolutionary X-ING guitar synthesizer had on-controller pitch stability and high sound quality. Although popular, fewer than 500 were built.

*1987 Casio MG500
MIDI Guitar*

1987 Synthaxe ad for $9,990 system

1987 Casio MG500 MIDI Guitar
This, along with the Fender-style 510, came out in 1987. It was an electric guitar with facilities for controlling external synths via MIDI. This model was made for Casio by Fujigen Gakki.

1984 Synthaxe
A British attempt from the 1980s to change the way guitarists played, this model had equally-spaced frets and separate "trigger" and fretting strings. The appearance and sizeable cost deterred most players from buying this unusual MIDI controller.

GUITAR MODELING
LINE 6 VARIAX

Sound modeling was a new technology applied to guitar playing as musicians entered the 21st century. This now much more widespread idea is based on the provision of digital recreations of classic guitar and amp sounds. The California-based Line 6 brand was born out of the company Fast Forward Designs started by Marcus Ryle and Michel Doidic, who were both former designers for Oberheim, the makers of electronic effects devices and early synthesizers. Line 6 quickly became innovators in this field,

amassing a large collection of vintage amps and effects units and setting about creating software models to reproduce the "classic" sounds. Using this sonic database, it developed a new breed of modeling amps, initially with the AxSys 212 and then with the Vetta range. Soon, the POD effects unit showed the world what could be done.

In 2003, the company launched a modeling guitar called the Variax. The early versions looked rather stark and plain, mainly due to the lack of magnetic pickups sitting

2008 Line 6 Variax 600

2011 James Tyler Variax US Custom Shop JTV-59US

2003 Line 6 Variax ad

2005 Line 6 Variax 300

2005 Line 6 Variax 300
This early budget model manufactured in Indonesia had the electronics mounted under the pickguard, instead of the method used in later models where they were mounted in a cavity accessed from the rear of the body.

BEYOND GUITAR

atop the plain pickguards (although there was a wealth of onboard technology under the skin). Recently, the Variax has been redesigned with much input from noted LA luthier James Tyler, with a line of new models with the Tyler logo on the headstocks. The Custom Shop models are produced in the US, and the budget line of instruments comes from Korea and Indonesia.

Further improvements were made to the sonic qualities of the guitars' piezo systems due to the collaboration with specialists L.R. Baggs, who cured the infamous piezo "clang" that was noticeable at higher volume levels. The guitars have preset alternative tuning options: the instruments stay tuned to standard pitch while the electronic system shifts the pitch and outputs a new tuning. The brand has many enthusiastic endorsees, from Radiohead's Ed O'Brien to The Edge and Johnny Marr.

2005 Line 6 ad for the Variax 300

2010 Line 6 Variax Bass 705

2008 Line 6 Variax 600
This companion to the 300 had a better-quality finish, a vibrato, and 28 digital models. It was fully compatible with the Variax Workbench system of downloadable patches, enabling players to customize settings to their own preferences.

2010 Line 6 Variax Bass 705
The five-string version of the Variax bass model mirrored the guitar versions, with a wide range of sound options available including "classic" four-string and "vintage" eight-string sounds.

2008 Line 6 Variax Acoustic 700
This thinline style single cutaway in fact has a cedar top over a chambered solid body and comes with recreations of the sounds of a dozen "classic" acoustics. Part of the Variax's success is the ease of switching between sounds.

2011 James Tyler Variax US Custom Shop JTV-59US
This James Tyler-designed evolution of the Variax comes with 11 alternative tuning options, over 20 classic guitar models (plus a sitar and a banjo), and is constructed in the USA using hand-selected tonewoods. The JTV-69 adds a vibrato to the mix, and the metal-focused JTV-89 offers more down-tuning options.

2008 Line 6 Variax Acoustic 700

GUITAR MODELING
FENDER

Fender entered the world of multiple amp sounds in 2001 with the Cyber Twin amp, and at that time ex-Steely Dan guitarist Jeff Baxter was working closely with Roland, the Japanese music-technology pioneer. In 2003 Baxter went to Ikutaro Kakehashi, founder and chairman of Roland, and suggested a Fender-Roland modeling guitar. His proposal eventually turned into the American VG Stratocaster, which was launched in 2007.

Two separate versions of Fender-Roland Stratocasters had previously appeared in the late nineties—the Standard Roland GR-Ready and the Roland Ready Stratocaster—but both guitars required an external synth to get new sounds, often utilizing the Roland VG-88.

However, with the new American VG Stratocaster everything happened inside the guitar and was simple and functional, unlike some of its major competitors. The only connection the guitarist needed was a regular jack to a regular amp. The instrument already had a standard Strat sound and, with the use of two extra knobs and a Roland GK bridge pickup, a whole new range of sounds became available. The Mode Control knob provided normal Strat, modeled Strat and Telecaster, Humbucker, and Acoustic, and there was an additional five-way selector that gave variations within each setting, in addition to a simulated 12-string sound.

Despite all this innovation, the original VG only lasted around two years in the Fender catalogue. It was apparently another victim of the way players reject most ideas they perceive as extreme. However, not to be diverted from producing a successful modeling guitar, Fender, in collaboration again with Roland, issued a new version in 2012, the G-5 VG Stratocaster.

The VG was not the only modeling guitar that Fender released. The Acoustasonic Tele is essentially a Telecaster with a chambered body and a unique solid rosewood bridge housing a Fishman acoustic pickup; the guitar also comes with a Twisted Tele single coil pickup in the neck position. The sound is created with Fishman's Aura Image Casting Technology and controlled through a relatively simple panel on the side of the guitar's body.

2007 Fender American VG Stratocaster

2007 Fender American VG Stratocaster
The guitar has a solid alder body with a traditional three-color sunburst finish. The onboard digital modeling provides flick-of-a-switch access to a range of altered tunings, and different guitar models.

2012 Fender G-5 VG Stratocaster

2012 Fender G-5 VG Stratocaster
The revised model has slightly modified switching and is available with a maple fingerboard. It claimed to offer "ideal-performance" pickup models for yet more control over tone and response.

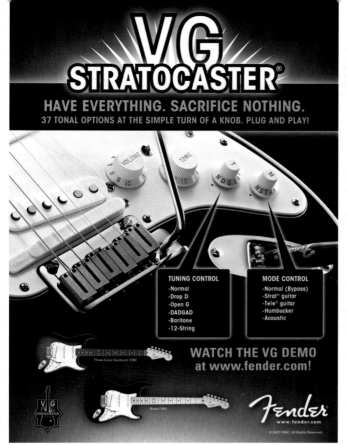

NEW!
VG Stratocaster® Guitar
See pages 10-13

Fender FRONTLINE IN HOME
THE SPIRIT OF ROCK-N-ROLL

2011 Fender ad with Roland-Ready Strat and black G-5 version of VG (above).

2009 Fender catalogue cover featuring original VG (above right).

2012 Fender catalogue portrait of Roland-Ready and G-5 VG (right)

2012 Fender catalogue shot of Roland pickup next to bridge (below).

2010 Fender Acoustasonic

2010 Fender Acoustasonic With a chambered ash body and a Tele-shaped rosewood bridge, this acoustic/electric hybrid offers modeling sounds through its Fishman system plus traditional Telecaster tones.

277

GUITAR MODELING
GIBSON

In 2006, Gibson began shipping its long-promised digital guitar, the HD.6X-Pro. This was essentially a Les Paul with an extra "hex" pickup that allowed the player to feed various combinations of strings through a computer for use with recording software or similar programs. The next major development came in 2007, with the introduction of a series of so-called Robot guitars that were regular Gibson models, starting with the Les Paul, with a clever self-tuning system using powered tuning pegs linked to an onboard database, with standard tuning plus six programmable tuning options.

The first Les Paul Robot, in Blue Silverburst nitrocellulose, was a limited-edition release in selected stores, with only ten instruments allocated for each store. Gibson vowed that particular finish would never again appear on one of its guitars. Gibson's ads claimed it was the world's first self-tuning guitar, although Transperformance had developed a system earlier. Used by Jimmy Page and Graham Nash, it requires heavy modification of the instrument, including some routing work.

In 2008, Gibson introduced the Dark Fire, again based on the Les Paul but with an improved Robot tuning system

2007 Gibson Les Paul Robot Ltd

2007 Gibson Les Paul Robot Ltd
The modified Tune-o-matic bridge measures the individual tuning of each string, and a control unit sends a signal for any adjustments through the tailpiece and the strings to the motorized tuning pegs.

2008 Gibson SG Les Paul Robot

2008 Gibson SG Les Paul Robot
A new Robot-equipped SG with twin humbuckers. The current Robot product line numbers five different guitar models: Les Paul Studio, SG, Explorer, Les Paul Junior, and Flying V.

with longer battery life. Gibson further extended the digital guitar's features and potential with a large library of downloadable effects patches. These hi-tech Dark Fires have yet to catch on in a big way with players, who generally tend to have a conservative and skeptical outlook on seemingly complex new technology. Meanwhile, Gibson extended the Robot tuning system to other models including SGs, Les Paul Juniors, Explorers, and Flying Vs, and introduced the all-new ultra-light Firebird X in 2011.

The Firebird X is based on the original Firebirds from 1963, but it has larger-radius curves and is ultra-light due to a chambered body made from swamp ash, already a lightweight timber. It has three mini-humbuckers and a bridge piezo pickup coupled with all the technology found in the Dark Fire, plus the Robot self-tuning system.

2011 Gibson Firebird X
This variant of the Firebird is very light, with a chambered body made from swamp ash. It comes with three mini-humbuckers, a Hexaphonic piezo bridge pickup, and a wealth of built-in effects, but the guitar carries a rather hefty price tag.

2011 Gibson ad

2011 Gibson Firebird X

2010 Gibson Dusk Tiger Les Paul

2010 Gibson Dusk Tiger Les Paul
With highly figured exotic wood top and metal top plates, the guitar has Robot tuning combined with ten preset tones. There's also a blending switch for controlling the two humbuckers with the piezo pickup unit mounted in the bridge.

2010 Gibson Flying V Robot

2008 Gibson Dark Fire
Gibson up-rated the lithium rechargeable battery system that powers the Robot tuning system for the Gibson Dark Fire and added to a catalogue of downloadable effects for the new-for-2008 model.

2010 Gibson Flying V Robot
The Flying V Robot model has a new Tune Control Bridge. This replaces the traditional Tune-o-matic tailpiece with a unit that includes special saddles, which each send tuning info to the guitar's tuners via CPUs.

2008 Gibson Dark Fire

GLOSSARY

Alternative terms are shown (in brackets) following the key word.

acoustic
General term for any hollowbody acoustic guitar. An acoustic musical instrument is one that generates sound without electrical amplification. Also, a term related to sound or hearing.

action
Often used to describe just the height of the strings above the tops of the frets; thus "high action," "low action," "buzz-free action" etc. In fact, action refers to the entire playing feel of a given instrument; thus "good action," "easy action" etc.

active (active electronics, active circuit)
Circuit in some guitars that boosts signal and/or widens tonal range with necessary additional (usually battery) powering. Refers to a pickup or circuit that incorporates a pre-amp. See *pre-amp*.

Alnico
Magnet material used for pickups: an alloy of aluminum, nickel, and cobalt. Nickname for Gibson pickup with flat-sided polepieces.

amplifier
Electrical circuit designed to increase a signal; usually, an audio system for boosting sound before transmission to a loudspeaker.

analog
A system which reproduces a signal by copying its original amplitude waveform. Examples include the groove of an old vinyl recording, the electrical signal on a magnetic tape recording, or the voltage levels of an analog synthesizer. As opposed to digital, where the signal is recorded as a series of numbers.

anodized
Finish given to metal by electrolysis. Often refers to Fender's gold-tinted aluminum pickguards of the 1950s.

archtop
Guitar with arched body top formed by carving or pressing. Usually refers to hollowbody or semi-acoustic instruments; thus "archtop jazz guitar."

backline
Amplifiers and speakers used for on-stage sound.

backplate
Panel fitted over cavity in rear of guitar body, allowing access to pots and wiring or vibrato springs.

Bakelite
The first plastic (invented 1909) and used for some guitars from the 1930s to the 1950s.

ball-end
Metal retainer wound on to the end of a guitar string and used to secure it to the anchor point at the bridge.

Bigsby
Almost generic term for a simple, single-spring, non-recessed vibrato system. Developed by Paul Bigsby.

binding
Protective and decorative strip(s) added to edges of the body and/or fingerboard and/or headstock of some guitars.

blade pickup (bar pickup)
Pickup (humbucker or single-coil) that uses a long single blade-polepiece per coil, rather than individual polepieces per string.

block markers
Square-shape or rectangular-shape fingerboard position markers.

blond (blonde)
Natural finish, usually enhancing plain wood color; or (on some Fenders) slightly yellowed finish.

bobbin
Frame around which pickup coils are wound.

body
The main portion of the guitar, on to which are (usually) mounted the bridge, pickups, controls etc. Can be solid, hollow, or a combination of the two.

bolt-on-neck
Neck-to-body joint popularized by Fender – and actually most often secured by screws.

bookmatched
Wood split into two thin sheets and joined to give symmetrically matching grain patterns.

bound
See *binding*.

bout
Looking at a guitar standing upright, the bouts are the outward curves of the body above (upper bout) and below (lower bout) the instrument's waist.

bracing
Series of wooden struts inside hollowbody guitar providing strength and affecting tone.

bridge
Unit on guitar body that holds the saddle(s). Sometimes also incorporates the anchor point for the strings.

bridge pickup
Pickup placed nearest the bridge.

bridgeplate
Baseplate on to which bridge components are mounted.

bullet
Describes appearance of truss-rod adjustment nut at headstock on some Fender-style guitars.

capo (capo tasto, capo dastro)
Movable device which can be fitted over the fingerboard behind any given fret, shortening the string length and therefore raising the strings' pitches.

cavity
Hollowed-out area in solidbody guitar for controls and switches: thus "control cavity."

center block
Solid wooden block running through the inside of a true semi-acoustic guitar's body.

chamfer
Bevel or slope to body edges.

coil(s)
Insulated wire wound around bobbin(s) in a pickup.

coil-split
Usually describes a method to cut out one coil of a humbucking pickup giving a slightly lower output and a cleaner, more single-coil-like sound. Also known, incorrectly, as *coil-tap*.

coil-tap (tapped pickup)
Pickup coil which has two or more live leads exiting at different percentages of the total wind in order to provide multiple output levels and tones. Not to be confused with *coil-split*.

combo
Combination amplifier/speaker system in one unit.

contoured body
Gentle curving of solid guitar body, aiding player comfort.

control cavity
Hollowed-out area in solidbody guitar's body for controls, pickups and so on.

control(s)
Knobs and switch levers on outside of guitar activating the function of electric components that are usually mounted behind the pickguard or in a body cavity.

course
Usually means a pair of strings running together but tuned apart, usually in unison or an octave apart, as on a 12-string guitar. Technically, can also refer to a single string (or, rarely, a group of three strings).

custom color
A selected color finish for a guitar, as opposed to natural or sunburst. Term originated by Fender in the late 1950s, now widely used.

GLOSSARY

cutaway
Curve into body near neck joint, aiding player's access to high frets. A guitar can have two ("double," "equal," "offset") cutaways or one ("single") cutaway. Sharp (Gibson's "florentine") or round (Gibson's "venetian") describe the shape of the horn formed by the cutaway.

digital
A system which stores and processes analog information by converting it into a series of numbers.

dings
Small knocks, dents or other signs of normal wear in a guitar's surface. A true indicator of aged beauty if you're selling; a cause for mirth and money-saving if you're buying.

distortion
Signal degradation caused by the overloading of audio systems. Often used deliberately to create a harsher, grittier sound.

dive-bomb
See *down-bend*.

dog-ear
Nickname for some P-90 pickups, derived from the shape of the mounting lugs on cover. See also *soap-bar*.

dot markers
Dot-shape position markers on fingerboard.

dot-neck
Fingerboard with dot-shape position markers; nickname for Gibson ES-335 of 1958-62 with such markers.

double-locking vibrato
See *locking vibrato*.

double-neck
Large guitar specially made with two necks, usually combining six-string and 12-string, or six-string and bass.

down-bend
Downward shift in the strings' pitch using a vibrato. In extreme cases this is known as "dive-bombing."

droopy headstock (pointy headstock)
Long, down-pointing headstock popularized on 1980s superstrats.

effects
Generic term for audio processing devices such as distortions, delays, reverbs, flangers, phasers, harmonizers and so on.

electric
A term simply applied to any electric guitar (in other words one used in conjunction with an amplifier).

electro-acoustic (electro)
Acoustic guitar with built-in pickup, usually of piezo-electric type. The guitar usually has a built-in pre-amp including volume and tone controls. For the purposes of this book, such a guitar is not considered to be an electric guitar. (To qualify, it must have at least one magnetic pickup.)

equalization (EQ)
Active tone control that works by emphasizing or de-emphasizing specific frequency bands.

feedback
Howling noise produced by leakage of the output of an amplification system back into its input, typically a guitar's pickup(s).

f-hole
Soundhole of approximately "f" shape on some hollowbody and semi-acoustic guitars.

figure
Pattern on surface of wood; thus "figured maple" and so on.

fine-tuners
Set of tuners that tune strings to very fine degrees, usually as fitted to a locking vibrato or bridge.

fingerboard (fretboard, board)
Playing surface of the guitar that holds the frets. It can be simply the front of the neck itself, or a separate thin board glued to the neck.

finish
Protective and decorative covering, often paint, on wood parts, typically the guitar's body, back of neck, and headstock.

fixed bridge
Non-vibrato bridge.

fixed neck
See *set-neck*.

flame
Dramatic figure, usually on maple.

flat-top
Acoustic with flat top (in other words, not arched) and usually with a round soundhole.

floating bridge
Bridge not fixed permanently to the guitar's top, but held in place by string tension (usually on older or old-style hollowbody guitars).

floating pickup
Pickup not fixed permanently to the guitar's top, but mounted on a separate pickguard or to the end of the fingerboard (on some hollowbody electric guitars).

floating vibrato
Vibrato unit (such as the Floyd Rose or Wilkinson type) that "floats" above the surface of the body.

frequency
The number of cycles of a carrier wave per second; the perceived pitch of a sound.

fretboard
See *fingerboard*.

fretless
Guitar fingerboard without frets; usually bass, but sometimes (very rarely) guitar.

frets
Metal strips positioned on the fingerboard of a guitar (or sometimes directly into the face of the solid neck) to enable the player to stop the strings and produce specific notes.

fretwire
Wire from which individual frets are cut.

glued neck
See *set-neck*.

hang-tag
Small cards and other documents hung on to a guitar in the showroom.

hardtail
Guitar (originally Fender Strat-style) with non-vibrato bridge.

hardware
Any separate components (non-electrical) fitted to the guitar: bridge, tuners, strap buttons and so on.

headless
Design with no headstock, popularized by Ned Steinberger in the early 1980s.

headstock
Portion at the end of the neck where the strings attach to the tuners. "Six-tuners-in-line" type (Fender-style) has all six tuners on one side of the headstock. "Three-tuners-a-side" type (Gibson-style) has three tuners on one side and three the other.

heel
Curved deepening of the neck for strength near body joint.

hex pickup
Provides suitable signal for synthesizer.

high-end (up-market, upscale)
High- or higher-cost instrument, usually aimed at those seeking the best quality, materials and workmanship.

horn
Pointed body shape formed by cutaway: thus left horn, right horn. See also *cutaway*.

humbucker
Noise-canceling twin-coil pickup.

Typically the two coils have opposite magnetic polarity and are wired together electrically out-of-phase to produce a sound that we call in-phase.

hybrid
Technically, any instrument that combines two systems of any kind, but now used to indicate a guitar that combines original-style magnetic "electric" pickups with "acoustic"-sounding piezo pickups.

inlay
Decorative material cut and fitted into body, fingerboard, headstock etc.

intonation
State of a guitar so that it is as in-tune with itself as physically possible. This is usually dependent on setting the string's speaking length by adjusting the point at which the strings cross the bridge saddle, known as intonation adjustment. Some bridges allow more adjustment, and therefore greater possibilities for accurate intonation, than others.

jack (jack socket)
Mono or stereo connecting socket used to feed guitar's output signal to amplification.

jackplate
Mounting plate for output jack (jack socket), usually screwed on to body.

laminated
Joined together in layers; usually wood (bodies, necks) or plastic (pickguards).

locking nut
Unit that locks strings in place at the nut, usually with three locking bolts.

locking trem
See *locking vibrato*.

locking tuner
Special tuner that locks the string to the string-post and thus aids string-loading.

locking vibrato
Type of vibrato system that locks strings at nut and saddles (hence also called "double-locking") to stabilize tuning.

logo
A brandname or trademark, usually on headstock.

low-end (bargain, down-market)
Low- or lower-cost instrument, often aimed at beginners or other players on a budget.

lower bout
See *bout*.

luthier
Fancy name for guitar maker.

machine head
See *tuner*.

magnetic pickup
Transducer using coils of wire wound around a magnet. It converts string vibrations into electrical signals.

master volume/tone
Control that affects all pickups equally.

MIDI
Musical Instrument Digital Interface. The industry-standard control system for electronic instruments. Data for notes, performance effects, patch changes, voice and sample data, tempo and other information can be transmitted and received.

mod
Short for modification; any change made to a guitar.

mother-of-pearl (pearl)
Lustrous internal shell of some molluscs, eg abalone, used for inlay. Synthetic "pearloid" versions exist.

mounting ring
Usually plastic unit within which Gibson-style pickups are fitted to the guitar body.

neck
Part of the guitar supporting the fingerboard and strings; glued or bolted to the body, or on "though-neck" types forming a support spine on to which "wings" are usually glued to form the body.

neck pitch
Angle of a guitar's neck relative to the body face.

neckplate
Single metal plate through which screws pass to achieve bolt-on neck (Fender-style).

neck pickup
Pickup placed nearest the neck.

neck-tilt
Device on some Fender (and other) neck-to-body joints allowing easier adjustment of neck pitch.

noise
Any undesirable sound, such as mains hum or interference.

noise-canceling
Type of pickup with two coils wired together to cancel noise, often called humbucking. Any arrangement of pickups or pickup coils that achieves this.

nut
Bone, metal or (now usually) synthetic slotted guide bar over which the strings pass to reach the tuners and which determines string height and spacing at the headstock end of neck.

nut lock
See *locking nut*.

offshore
Made overseas; more specifically and often used to mean outside the US.

PAF
Gibson pickup with Patent Applied For decal on base.

passive
Normal, unboosted circuit.

pearl
See *mother-of-pearl*.

pearloid
Fake pearl, made of plastic and pearl dust.

pickguard (scratchplate)
Protective panel fitted flush on to body, or raised above body.

pickup
See *transducer*.

pickup switch (pickup selector)
Selector switch that specifically selects pickups individually or in combination.

piezo pickup (piezo-electric pickup)
Transducer with piezo-electric crystals that generate electricity under mechanical strain – in a guitar, it senses string and body movement. "Piezo-loaded saddles" are bridge saddles with an integral piezo element.

pitch
The perceived "lowness" or "highness" of a sound, determined by its frequency.

plectrum (flat pick)
Small piece of (usually) plastic or metal used to pluck or strum a guitar's strings.

P-90
Early Gibson single-coil pickup.

pointy
A type of body design prevalent in the 1980s and since with a jagged, pointed, angular outline.

pointy headstock
See *droopy headstock*.

polepieces
Non-magnetic (but magnetically conductive) polepieces are used to control, concentrate and/or shape the pickup's magnetic field. Can be either adjustable (screw) or non-adjustable (slug), as in an original Gibson humbucker. Magnetic polepieces are those where the magnet itself is aimed directly at the strings, as in an original Stratocaster single-coil.

position markers (fingerboard markers)
Fingerboard inlays of various designs used as a guide for fret positions.

pot (potentiometer)
Variable electrical resistor that alters voltage by a spindle turning on an electrically resistive track. Used for volume and tone controls, and so on.

pre-amp (pre-amplifier)
Guitar circuit, usually powered by a battery, that converts the pickup's output from high to low impedance (pre-amp/buffer) and can increase the output signal and boost or cut specific frequencies for tonal effect.

pre-CBS
Fender guitars made before CBS takeover in 1965.

pressed top
Arched top (usually laminated) of hollowbody guitar made by machine-pressing rather than hand-carving.

purfling
Usually synonymous with binding, but more accurately refers to the decorative inlays around the perimeter of a guitar *alongside* the binding.

quilted
Undulating figure, usually on maple.

radius
Slight curve, or camber, of a fingerboard surface, the strings, or the bridge saddles.

refinished (refin)
New finish added, replacing or over the original.

resonator
Generic term for guitar with metal resonator in body to increase volume.

retro
A past style reintroduced, often with some changes, as a "new" design, usually with deliberate references. Thus retro guitars use flavors of mainly 1950s and 1960s designs to inform new designs.

retrofit
Any component (pickup, vibrato, tuner and so on) added to a guitar after it leaves the place where it was made that fits directly on to the intended guitar with no alteration to the instrument.

reverb (reverberation)
Ambience effect combining many short echoes; can be imitated electronically.

rout
Hole or cavity cut into a guitar, usually into the body. Such cavities are said to be routed into the body.

saddle(s)
Part(s) of a bridge where the strings make contact; the start of the speaking

length of the string, effectively the opposite of the nut.

scale length (string length)
Theoretical length of the vibrating string from nut to saddle; actually twice the distance from nut to 12th fret. The actual scale length (the distance from the nut to saddle after intonation adjustment) is slightly longer. See *intonation*.

selector
Control that selects from options, usually of pickups.

semi
See *semi-acoustic*.

semi-acoustic (semi-solid, semi)
Electric guitar with wholly or partly hollow body. Originally used specifically to refer to an electric guitar with a solid wooden block running down the center of a thinline body, such as Gibson's ES-335.

semi-solid
See *semi-acoustic*.

serial number
Added by maker for own purposes; sometimes useful for determining construction and/or shipping date.

set-neck (glued neck, glued-in neck, fixed neck)
Type of neck/body joint popularized by Gibson which permanently "sets" the two main components together, usually by gluing.

shielding (screening)
Barrier to any outside electrical interference. Special paint or conductive foil in control/pickup cavity to reduce electrical interference.

signal
Transmitted electrical information, for example between control circuits, or guitar and amplifier, etc, usually by means of a connecting wire or cord.

single-coil
Original pickup type with a single coil of wire wrapped around (a) magnet(s).

slab board (slab fingerboard)
Fender type (1959-62) in which the joint between the top of the neck and the base of the fingerboard is flat. Later this joint was curved.

"slash" soundhole
Scimitar-shaped soundhole, used primarily by Rickenbacker

soap-bar
Nickname for P-90-style pickup with a cover that has no mounting "ears." See *dog-ear*.

solid
General term for any solidbody guitar.

soundhole
Aperture in the top of a hollowbody or semi-acoustic guitar's body. It may increase sound projection, or simply be for decoration.

spaghetti logo
Early Fender logo with thin, stringy letters resembling spaghetti.

stock
State, irrelevant of condition, of a guitar where everything is exactly as supplied new. Individual items on a guitar exactly as supplied new ("stock pickup").

stop tailpiece
See *stud tailpiece*.

strap button
Fixing points on body to attach a guitar-strap; usually two, on sides (or side and back) of guitar body.

string length
Sounding length of string, measured from nut to bridge saddle (see also *scale length*).

string-retainer bar
Metal bar typically placed behind locking nut to seat strings over curved surface of locking nut prior to locking. Also occasionally used like a string tree to increase behind-the-nut string angle on guitars without nut locks.

string tree (string guide)
Small unit fitted to headstock that maintains downward string-tension at nut.

stud tailpiece (stop tailpiece)
Type of tailpiece fixed to solid or semi-acoustic guitar top, either as a single combined bridge/tailpiece unit, or as a unit separate from the bridge.

sunburst
Decorative finish: pale-colored center graduates to darker edges.

superstrat
Updated Fender Stratocaster-inspired design popularized in the 1980s: it had more frets, deeper cutaways, changed pickups, and a high-performance (locking) vibrato.

sustain
Length of time a string vibrates. Purposeful elongation of a musical sound, either by playing technique or electronic processing.

synth access
A guitar that has a built-in pickup to enable connection to an outside synthesizer unit.

synthesizer
An electronic instrument for sound creation, using analog techniques

(oscillators, filters, amplifiers) or digital techniques (FM or harmonic synthesis, sample-plus-synthesis etc). Preset synthesizers offer a selection of pre-programmed sounds which cannot be varied; programmable types allow the user to vary and store new sounds. Guitar synthesizers at first attempted to build much of the required circuitry into the guitar itself, but the trend now is to synth-access systems.

system vibrato
See *vibrato system*.

tab (tablature)
System of musical notation indicating the position of the fingers on frets and strings.

tag
See *hang-tag*.

tailpiece
Unit on body separate from the bridge that anchors strings. (See also *trapeze tailpiece*, *stud tailpiece*.)

thinline
Hollow-body electric guitar with especially narrow body depth; term coined originally by Gibson for its mid-1950s Byrdland model.

through-neck (neck-through-body)
Neck that travels the complete length of a guitar, usually with "wings" added to complete the body shape.

toggle switch
Type of selector switch that "toggles" between a small number of options. Sometimes called a leaf switch.

tone wood
Fancy name for wood used in making musical instruments.

top nut
See *nut*.

transducer
Unit that converts one form of energy to another; the term is sometimes used generically for piezo-electric pickups, but applies to any type of pickup or, for example, loudspeaker. See *magnetic pickup*, *piezo pickup*.

trapeze tailpiece
Simple tailpiece of trapezoidal shape.

tremolo (tremolo arm, tremolo system, trem)
Erroneous but much-used term for vibrato system. The musical definition of tremolo is a rapid repetition of a note or notes. This is presumably where Fender got the name for their amplifier effect, which is a regular variation in the sound's volume.

truss-rod
Metal rod fitted inside the neck, almost always adjustable and which can be used to control a neck's relief.

truss-rod cover
Decorative plate covering truss rod's access hole, usually on headstock.

Tune-o-matic
Gibson-originated bridge, adjustable for overall string height and individual string intonation.

tuner
Device usually fitted to the headstock that alters a string's tension and pitch. Also called machine head or (archaically) tuning peg.

tuner button
The knob that the player moves to raise or lower a tuner's pitch.

up-bend
Upward shift in the strings' pitch made by using a vibrato.

upper bout
See *bout*.

vibrato (vibrato bridge, vibrato system, tremolo, tremolo arm, trem, wang bar, whammy)
Bridge and/or tailpiece which alters the pitch of the strings when the attached arm is moved. Vibrato is the correct term because it means a regular variation in pitch.

vibrato system
System comprising locking vibrato bridge unit, friction-reducing nut and locking tuners.

waist
In-curved shape near the middle of the guitar body, usually its narrowest point.

wang bar
See *vibrato*.

whammy
See *vibrato*.

wrapover bridge
Unit where strings are secured by wrapping them around a curved bar.

zero fret
Extra fret placed in front of the nut. It provides the start of the string's speaking length and creates the string height at the headstock end of the fingerboard. In this instance the nut is simply used to determine string spacing. Used by some manufacturers to equalize the tone between the open string and the fretted string.

INDEX

PICTURE KEY

OWNERS KEY

The guitars we photographed came from the collections of the following individuals and organisations, and we are grateful for their help. The owners are listed here in the alphabetical order of the code used to identify their instruments in the Instruments Key below.
AA Aria UK; **AC** The Acoustic Centre; **AE** Adrian Lovegrove; **AG** Arbiter Group; **AI** Adrian Ingram; **AJ** Anthony Jackson; **AK** Alan Hardtke; **AL** Andrew Large; **AM** Andy Manson; **AN** Adrian Ashton; **AO** Albert Molinaro; **AR** Alan Rogan; **AS** Ashmolean Museum; **AT** Arthur Ramm; **AU** Allan Russell; **BA** The Bass Centre; **BB** Boz Burrell estate; **BC** Brian Cohen; **BD** Bob Daisley; **BF** Brian Fischer; **BG** Barrie Glendenning; **BM** Bill Marsh; **BP** Bill Puplett; **BR** Bryant's Music; **BU** Buzz Music; **BW** Bert Weedon; **CA** Chet Atkins; **CB** Clive Brown; **CD** Chris Dair; **CG** Collings Guitars; **CH** Colin Hodgkinson; **CK** Clive Kay; **CL** Chappell of Bond Street; **CN** Carl Nielsen; **CO** Country Music Hall Of Fame; **CP** Chris DiPinto; **CS** Carlos Santana; **DB** Dave Brewis; **DC** Don Clayton; **DE** Duane Eddy; **DG** David Gilmour; **DH** Dave Hunter; **DL** Dave Merlane; **DM** David Musselwhite; **DN** David Noble; **DQ** Danny Quatrochi; **DU** Dave Burrluck; **DZ** DBZ Guitars; **EC** Eric Clapton; **ES** Ervin Somogyi; **FA** Frank Allen; **FE** Fender Musical Instruments Corp.; **FF** Fausto Fabi; **GB** *Guitar & Bass*; **GE** Giddy-Up-Einstein; **GF** Guitar Factory; **GG** Gruhn Guitars; **GI** Gibson Guitar Corp.; **GL** Guitar Gallery; **GM** Garry Malone; **GO** Geoff Gould; **GR** Gretsch Guitars; **GT** Graeme Matheson; **GU** *Guitarist*; **GW** Gary Winterflood; **HG** House Of Guitars; **IA** Ian Anderson; **IB** Ibanez; **JA** James Tyler Guitars; **JB** Jack Bruce; **JD** Jerry Donahue; **JE** John Entwistle; **JH** John Sheridan; **JI** James Sims; **JJ** Jim Roberts; **JM** Juan Martin; **JO** John Hornby Skewes & Co Ltd; **JR** John Reynolds; **JS** John Smith; **JT** Juan Teijeiro; **LP** Les Paul; **LS** Line 6; **LW** Larry Wassgren; **MA** C.F. Martin & Co; **MB** Mandolin Brothers; **MF** Mo Foster; **MI** Michael Anthony; **MJ** Mike Jopp; **ML** Malcolm Weller; **MN** Mansons Guitar Shop; **MP** Maurice Preece; **MS** Mike Slubowski; **MT** Mick Watts; **MU** Music Ground; **MW** Michael Wright; **NC** Neville Crozier; **NR** Nick Rowlands; **OC** Ollie Crooke; **PA** Paul McCartney; **PC** anonymous private collector; **PD** Paul Day; **PE** Peavey Electronics Corp.; **PM** Paul Midgley; **PQ** Pat Quilter; **PR** Paul Reed Smith Guitars; **PU** Paul Unkert; **PZ** Phil Manzanera; **RB** Robin Baird; **RC** Russell Cleveland; **RE** Reflections Marketing; **RF** Rock Fatory; **RG** Robin Guthrie; **RH** Richard Chapman; **RI** Rickenbacker International Corporation; **RR** Ron Brown; **RS** Robert Spencer; **RT** Randy Hope-Taylor; **RU** Ray Ursell; **SA** Scot Arch; **SB** Steve Boyer; **SC** Scott Chinery; **SH** Steve Howe; **SI** Simon Carlton; **SJ** Scott Jennings; **SL** Steve Lewis; **SM** Sharon Malone; **SN** Sam Benjamin; **SO** Steve Ostromogilsky; **SR** Stuart Ross; **SS** Steve Soest; **ST** Sotheby's; **SU** Suhr Guitars; **TA** Taylor Guitars; **TB** Tony Bacon; **TE** Teuffel Guitars; **TF** Tim Fleming; **TH** Tony Hicks; **TO** Tom Anderson Guitarworks; **TP** Tim Philips; **VH** Vince Hockey; **VS** Vince Smith; **WA** Washburn Guitars; **WS** William Warren Smith; **WW** Warwick GmbH & Co; **YA** Yamaha-Kemble Music UK; **YO** Yoko Ono; **YS** Yoshi Serizawa; **ZZ** Zeke Zirngiebel.

INSTRUMENTS KEY

This key identifies who owned which guitars at the time they were photographed. After the relevant **bold-type** page number(s) there is a model identifier followed by the owner's initials (see the alphabetical list in the Owners Key above).

Considering each spread, the key first lists guitars on the left-hand page only, then guitars that go across both pages, and then guitars on the right-hand page only. So you might see listings for 12 (the left-hand page), 12–13 (across the spread), and then 13 (the right-hand page). If there are several guitars above one another, they are listed from top to bottom, indicated by the abbreviation t-b. Occasionally, t on its own means top, b means bottom. If there are several guitars next to one another, they are listed from left to right, indicated by the abbreviation l-r. Again, occasionally you'll see l on its own, for left, and r for right.

12–13 t-b RS; RS; SH. **13** RS. **14** SH. **14–15** t-b AS; SC. **15** SC. **18–19** t-b RU; ML. **19** t-b BC; ML. **20** RC. **20–21** t-b YS; RC. **21** t-b RC; RC. **22** RC. **22–23** t-b RC; RC. **23** t-b RC; RU; l-r MW; MW. **24** t-b RC. **24–25** RC. **25** l-r ML; JT; t-b JM; RC. **26** l-r SC; SC. **27** l-r MA; SC. **28** MA. **28–29** t-b AK; MA. **29** t-b SC; MW; IA. **30** IA. **30–31** GL; MB. **31** t-b MA; IA; VH; MB; DM; SC. **32** t-b MA; SC. **32-33** CO. **33** t-b MA; MA. **34** AC. **34–35** tb GG; AC. **35** t-b AC; GG; AC. **36–37** all SC. **38–39** t-b SC; BM. **39** both SC. **40–41** all SC. **42–43** t-b BM; SC. **43** t-b SC; SC; SC; MU. **44–45** both SC. **45** t SC; l-r RH; BM. **46–47** all SC. **48** both SC. **49** t-b RI; RI; l-r MW; SC.

50–51 both SC. **51** t-b GB; SC. **52–53** t-b LW; RH. **53** l-r BP; SC; b SC. **54** CO. **54–55** PC. **55** t-b GB; HG; SC. **56** l-r GI; GI. **56–57** DG. **57** l-r HG; GB; b YO. **58–59** t-b MW; SC; MW. **59** t-b SC; SC; SC; MW. **60–61** HG; HG. **61** t-b GB; HG; GB. **62** TA. **62–63** t-b GB; SC. **63** t-b SC; GB; ES. **64–65** t-b AM; VS; HG. **65** t-b GB; MU; SC. **66** IB. **66–67** GB. **67** t-b GB; MW; MW. **68–69** t-b WA; YA. **69** t-b DG; MW; TF. **70–71** t-b BR; PD. **71** t-b WA; GI; GI. **72–73** t-b CB; SC. **73** t-b DH; PD; PC. **74** t-b PQ; DG. **74–75** t-b both SH. **75** l-r PC; SH; b PC. **78–79** both RI. **79** RI. **80–81** AI. **81** SC. **82–83** t-b SC; CO. **83** LP/CO. **84–85** t-b CO; SC. **86–87** t-b DG; GG. **87** SC. **90** t-b BF; SC. **90–91** DG. **91** BF. **92** l-r PM; SO; BF. **92–93** PM. **93** t-b BF; PD; JD; PM. **94–95** t-b AG; FE; FE. **95** all FE. **96–97** both DG. **97** MB. **98–99** t-b RC; SA. **99** all SA.

100 SA. **100–101** t-b SL; PM. **101** t-b SI; PM; SI; PM. **102** FE. **102–103** both FE. **103** l-r MS; FE; t-b FE; AG. **104** PM. **104–105** t-b RG; RB. **105** t-b RB; SC; GG. **106** both AG. **106–107** FE. **107** l-r FE; AG. **108–109** all FE. **110–111** t-b BU; PM; GB. **111** t-b PD; GB; GU; GB. **112** MS. **112–113** t-b MS; PA. **113** l-r GG; SC. **114–115** both MS. **115** t-b DN; SC; JS. **116-117** t-b AR; PA; SC. **117** t-b MJ; AT. **118** GU. **118–119** t-b MS. **119** l-r GI; MS; t-b DN; MS; MS; SC. **120–121** t-b MS; DN. **121** l-r GI; GI; t-b GI; PU; SI. **122** t-b MS; GI. **122–123** GM. **123** l-r GI; GI; t-b GI; DN. **124–125** t-b SC; PZ; GI. **125** l-r GL; NC; SO; b AR. **126** PD. **126–127** CB. **127** l-r PD; GI; t-b CD; GB; GB. **128** GI. **128–129** t-b AR; MW. **129** t-b RI; PD; RI; AR; GR. **130–131** AL. **131** l-r GB; PC; t-b MW; CK. **132–133** t-b PD; GB. **133** l-r GB; MW. **134** t-b MW; PE. **134–135** GB. **135** t-b GB; WA; GB; GB. **136–137** t-b GB; JO. **137** t-b FE; GU; GU. **138–139** t-b CS; PR. **139** t-b PR; WS; SM; TH; PR; PR. **140–141** t-b CG; TA. **141** t-b JA; SU; TO. **142** l-r both PD. **142–143** PM. **143** all PD. **144–145** t-b GB; GU; GU. **145** l-r PD; MW; MW; b PD. **146–147** t-b GU; PC. **147** all PD. **148** MW. **148–149** both PD. **149** t-b all PD.

150 PD. **150–151** t-b both PD. **151** t-b PD; PD; MW; TE. **152–153** all PD. **153** t-b PD; PD; PD; CN. **154** PD. **154–155** t-b PD; LW. **155** l-r GB; MW; t-b PD; PD. **156** l-r MW; PD; GB. **157** t-b PD; MW; MW; PD; PD; l PD. **158–159** t-b PD; PD; MW. **159** t-b PD; MW; GB. **160–161** all MW. **161** t-b PD; PD; GB; MW. **162–163** t-b PD; MW; GU. **163** l-r MW; IB; b GB. **164** IB. **164–165** t-b IB; GU. **165** t-b GB; GB; IB; GU. **166** GB. **166–167** PD; YA. **167** t-b GB; YA. **168–169** t-b PD; MW. **169** t-b JO; GB; GB. **170** t-b MW; DG. **170–171** MU. **171** l-r PD; SC; t-b PD; GB; DC. **172** PD. **172–173** t-b MW; PD. **173** t-b RG; PR; AG. **174** PD. **174–175** t-b RI; ZZ. **175** t-b JH; DB; RB; l FA. **176** FE. **176–177** t-b SC; PD. **177** l-r BA; SH; PD; t-b PR; WA. **178–179** GR; RI. **179** SC. **180–181** t-b PD; MW. **181** l-r MW; PD; PD; t-b PD; PZ. **184–185** SC; GI. **185** t-b SH; BG; GG; SC. **186** l-r SC; SC; t SA. **187** l-r MS; SA; t GG. **188–189** all SC. **190–191** t-b SR; GI. **191** l-r BM; SA; b BM. **192–193** t-b SC; DB. **193** t-b both GL. **194–195** t-b both SA. **195** t-b SC; GI; GB; MS; l MS. **196–197** t-b GW; SC. **197** t-b GI; GI; EC. **198** MS. **198–199** SC. **199** l-r SC; GI; GI.

200 GM. **201** t-b SH; MS; l-r GW; MS. **202–203** both GI. **203** l-r GI; MS; b GI. **204–205** AE; SC. **205** t-b SC; SC; SC; CB. **206** GI. **206–207** t-b PA; SC. **207** t-b GB; GB; GI. **208** l-r AI; GG. **209** t-b BW; AL; DE; BW. **210–211** t-b JR; GG. **211** t-b GG; MB. **212** JR. **212–213** JR. **213** t-b CA; GG; PC. **214–215** t-b GG; GR. **215** t-b CA; GR; GR; GR. **216–217** all RI. **218–219** t-b RI; YO. **219** t-b NR; SJ; SB. **220** t-b both SC. **220–221** t-b CP; FE. **221** t-b PR; AL; PD. **222–223** t-b GT; MW. **223** t-b PD; TP. **224–225** t-b GB; PR. **225** t-b GU; CL; DZ. **226–227** t-b BW; BP. **227** t-b DU; TB; RR. **228–229** t-b MW; MU; MW. **229** t-b GU; AA; MW; YA. **232–233** t-b BD; JE; JE. **233** t-b BD; BA. **234–235** t-b BA; BA; JI. **235** t-b FE; MN; FE; FE. **236–237** t-b RG; BA; TB. **237** t-b AR; AU. **238–239** t-b MU; FE; JE. **239** t-b FE; FE; RT; SN. **240–241** t-b DL; JE; FE. **241** l-r AG; BA; t-b BA; FE. **242–243** t-b MI; RI; PD. **243** t-b both RI. **244–245** t-b AR; AR; JE. **245** l-r DB; JE; t-b RF; DB. **246–247** all GI. **247** l-r GI; PC; t-b GI; GI. **248–249** t-b BD; GI; GI. **249** both GI.

250 MP. **250–251** t-b PC; PC. **251** t-b JJ; SC; FF; DE; l BA. **252–253** t-b GE; MF; MI. **253** t-b CH; AN; AO. **254–255** t-b BA; BA; GO. **255** t-b PE; BA. **256–257** BB; BA; GF. **257** t-b AJ; PR. **258–259** t-b BA; CN; BA. **259** t-b OC; BA; JE. **260–261** t-b BA; PC; WW. **261** t-b BA; BA; JB; ST. **262** DQ. **262–263** t-b BA; PC; PD. **263** l-r MI; IB; b IB. **264–265** t-b BA; YA; BA. **265** t-b MU; BA. **268** PD. **268–269** t-b both PD. **269** l-r DG; PD; t-b both PD. **270–271** t-b PD; DG; PD. **271** t-b both PD. **272–273** t-b both RE. **273** l-r MW; PD. **274–275** t-b LS; JA; LS. **275** t-b both LS. **276–277** all FE. **278–279** t-b MS; GI; GI. **279** all GI.

Guitar ads, catalogues, etc came from the Balafon Image Bank.

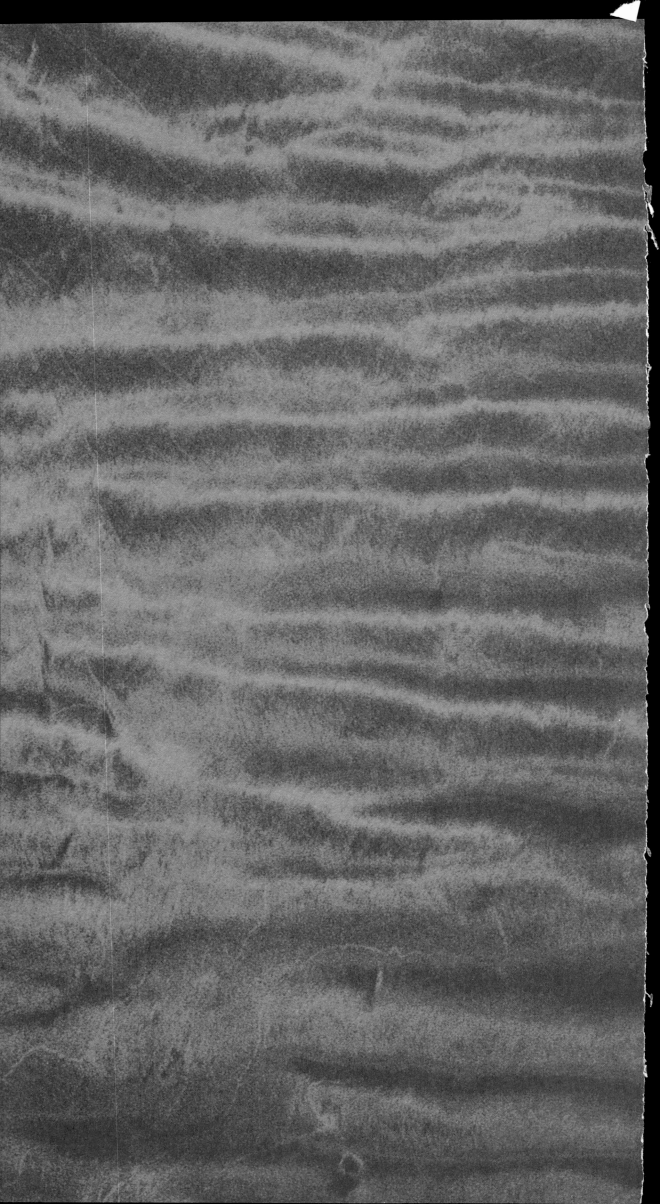